Eighth edition
Copyright © October 2006
Alastair Sawday Publishing Co. Ltd

Published in 2006
Alastair Sawday Publishing,
The Old Farmyard,
Yanley Lane, Long Ashton
Bristol BS41 9LR
Tel: +44 (0)1275 395430
Fax: +44 (0)1275 393388
Email: info@specialplacestostay.com
Web: www.specialplacestostay.com

The Globe Pequot Press
P. O. Box 480, Guilford,
Connecticut 06437, USA
Tel: +1 203 458 4500
Fax: +1 203 458 4601
Email: info@globepequot.com
Web: www.globepequot.com

Design:
Caroline King

Maps & Mapping:
Maidenhead Cartographic Services Ltd

Printing:
Butler & Tanner, Frome, UK

UK Distribution:
Penguin UK, 80 Strand, London, UK

ISBN-10: 1-901970-75-2
ISBN-13: 978-1-901970-75-3

Paper and Printing: We have sought the
lowest possible ecological 'footprint' from
the production of this book, using super-
efficient machinery, vegetable inks and
high environmental standards. Our printer is
ISO 14001-registered.

The publishers have made every effort to
ensure the accuracy of the information
in this book at the time of going to
press. However, they cannot accept
any responsibility for any loss, injury
or inconvenience resulting from the
use of information contained therein.

ALASTAIR SAWDAY'S
SPECIAL PLACES TO STAY

BRITISH
HOTELS, INNS
& OTHER PLACES

Contents

Alastair Sawday Publishing

Our main aim is to publish beautiful guidebooks but, for us, the question of who we are is also important. For who we are shapes the books, the books shape your holidays, and thus are shaped the lives of people who own these 'special places'. So we are trying to be a little more than 'just a publishing company'.

New eco offices

In January 2006 we moved into our new eco offices. With super-insulation, underfloor heating, a wood-pellet boiler, solar panels and a rainwater tank, we have a working environment benign to ourselves and to the environment. Lighting is low-energy, dark corners are lit by sun-pipes and one building is of green oak. Carpet tiles are from Herdwick sheep in the Lake District.

Environmental & ethical policies

We make many other gestures: company cars run on gas or recycled cooking oil; kitchen waste is composted and other waste recycled; cycling and car-sharing are encouraged; the company only buys organic or local food; we don't accept web links with companies we consider unethical; we bank with the ethical Triodos Bank.

We have used recycled paper for some books but have settled on selecting paper and printing for their low energy use. Our printer is British and ISO14001-certified and together we will work to reduce our environmental impact.

In 2005 we won a Business Commitment to the Environment Award and in April 2006 we won a Queen's Award for Enterprise in the Sustainable Development category. All this has boosted our resolve to promote our green policies. Our flagship gesture, however, is carbon offsetting; we calculate our carbon emissions and plant trees to compensate. In future we will support projects overseas that plant trees or reduce carbon use.

Carbon offset

SCAD in South India, supports the poorest of the poor. The money we send to offset our carbon emissions will be used to encourage village tree planting and, eventually, low-carbon technologies. Why India? Because the money goes a long way and admin costs are very low.
www.salt-of-the-earth.org.uk

Ethics

But why, you may ask, take these things so seriously? You are just a little publishing company, for heaven's sake! Well, is there any good argument for not taking them seriously? The world, by the admission of the vast majority of scientists, is in trouble. If we do not change our ways urgently we will

Who are we?

doom the planet and all its creatures – whether innocent or not – to a variety of possible catastrophes. To maintain the status quo is unacceptable. Business does much of the damage and should undo it, and provide new models.

Pressure on companies to produce Corporate Social Responsibility policies is mounting. We are trying to keep ahead of it all, yet still to be as informal and human as possible – the antithesis of 'corporate'.

The books – and a dilemma
So, we have created fine books that do good work. They promote authenticity, individuality and good local and organic food – a far cry from corporate culture. Rural economies, pubs, small farms, villages and hamlets all benefit. However, people use fossil fuel to get there. Should we aim to get our readers to offset their own carbon emissions, and the B&B and hotel owners too?

We are gradually introducing green ideas into the books: the Fine Breakfast scheme that highlights British and Irish B&B owners who use local and organic food; celebrating those who make an extra environmental effort; gently encouraging the use of public transport, cycling and walking. This year we are publishing a *Green Places to Stay* focusing on responsible travel and eco-properties around the globe.

Our Fragile Earth series
The 'hard' side of our environmental publishing is the Fragile Earth series: *One Planet Living, The Little Food Book* and *The Little Money Book.* They consist of bite-sized essays, polemical, hard-hitting and well researched. They are a 'must have' for anyone who seeks clarity about some of the key issues of our time.

Lastly – what is special?
The notion of 'special' is at the heart of what we do, and highly subjective. We discuss this in the introduction. We take huge pleasure from finding people and places that do their own thing – brilliantly; places that are unusual and follow no trends; places of peace and beauty; people who are kind and interesting – and genuine.

We seem to have touched a nerve with thousands of readers; they obviously want to stay in special places rather than the dull corporate monstrosities that have disfigured so many of our cities and towns. Life is too short to be wasted in the wrong places. A night in a special place can be a transforming experience.

Alastair Sawday

Acknowledgements

If you enjoy this book, spare a thought for the man who put it together. Tom had to navigate perilous waters, for the hotel industry is renowned for its fissures and controversies. Every hotel owner is an emperor in his own land, doing things better than all others and defying anyone to regulate him – let alone move him. So Tom, in pursuit of his – and our – idea of 'special', was bound to bump up against 'things'. His utter commitment to getting the book right, to rejecting those who didn't fit, has made this another very special edition.

Eleven thousand (carbon-offset and largely gas-powered) miles were driven by this lone enthusiast. He invaded the outer Hebrides and the Home Counties. He did all the inspecting, all the writing, and – with our support – all the selecting. So this is very much his book and I offer him my very real thanks.

Thanks, too, to David Hancock for generously sharing his encyclopedic knowledge of Britain's inns; and to Rebecca Stevens, Maria Serrano, Christine Buxton and Tom Germain back here in the office, partners in the compilation of this book.

Alastair Sawday

Series Editor
Alastair Sawday

Editor
Tom Bell

Editorial Director
Annie Shillito

Writing
Tom Bell

Inspections
Tom Bell

Accounts
Bridget Bishop,
Jessica Britton, Christine Buxton, Sandra Hasell, Sally Ranahan

Editorial
Jackie King, Jo Boissevain, Florence Oldfield, Maria Serrano, Rebecca Stevens, Danielle Williams

Production
Julia Richardson,
Rachel Coe, Tom Germain, Rebecca Thomas, Allys Williams

Sales & Marketing & PR
Siobhán Flynn,
Andreea Petre Goncalves, Sarah Bolton

Web & IT **Russell Wilkinson,**
Chris Banks, Joe Green, Brian Kimberling

Previous Editors
Nicola Crosse, Stephen Tate

A word from Alastair Sawday

The wise men and women of the hotel and tourist 'industries' – perish the word – have got together to devise a new ratings system for hotels. And they have succeeded. Those who have argued for a unified system have won the day, and perhaps they were right. But I would like to put another point of view.

Every decent hotel is a creative endeavour. Every hotel owner worthy of the name is a mad inventor, social entrepreneur and risk-taking business person all at once. The very best of them are precious, indefinable and slightly bonkers – no more amenable to objective judgment than artists. What they provide us with is far, far more than mere 'facilities', comforts, things. They give us a part of themselves, an insight into their imaginations, a share of their way of being in the world. They are, for heaven's sake, human beings. Would we objectify humanity in the same way? I know we try, but it doesn't really work – and it shouldn't.

I have just returned from one of my favourite hotels, where things often go wrong. The cleaning is temperamental, the owner given to changing moods, and perfection is elusive. But things go right nearly all the time. It is fun, unpredictable, comfortable where it matters, and profoundly human. Above all, it is an experience – rooted in generosity of

Photo Tom Germain

spirit and a zest for life. I defy any bureaucrat to rate it, and so does the owner.

The 'industry' needs fewer bureaucrats and more entrepreneurs of the imagination. We need more humanity and fewer ticked boxes. I do understand that in this day and age boxes make sense for the computers who analyse them; but subjective judgements – as offered in this book – make sense to the human beings who read them.

My advice to readers is to ignore the official ratings given to any hotel. Better to read between the lines of a good guide book. The rating may tell you if you can get a drink at four in the morning, but it won't tell you if the owner is a booze-stricken tyrant.

Alastair Sawday

Introduction

THIS BOOK IS CRAMMED WITH WONDERFUL NEW EXPERIENCES. I URGE YOU TO FOLLOW YOUR NOSE AND SEEK THEM OUT.

Some years ago the *Good Hotel Guide* awarded The Inn at Whitewell in Lancashire one of its much-prized Cesar awards. A journalist on *The Times* read its glowing entry and concluded that the guide had got it wrong, that no hotel could be worth such praise. Moved by a strong desire to set the record straight, the journalist sacrificed his weekend and took flight for the country, selflessly putting the inn to the test. In his subsequent article he assured his readers that he had been right all along, that the guide had got it wrong: the inn, he confessed, was far better than they had let on.

Richard Bowman, who died last year, bought the inn back in the 1970s. He was advised not to touch it with a bargepole, but ignored the advice completely and subsequently established one of the loveliest hotels in the land, part country house, part village inn. He stuffed it with vintage luggage, fishing rods, four-poster beds, claw-foot baths. Its success derived not merely from the comforts on offer, but from a kind and cheerful laissez-faire spirit with which he infused the place. Richard was not a man to get overly ruffled; when his kitchen fell into

the river below, he simply remarked that he could now indulge his two great passions – fishing and eating – at the same time.

Richard had time for everyone, even editors of hotel guides. He wore half-moon glasses, a constant smile and, occasionally, an MCC tie. He told tales, spilled beans and made us laugh. Tens of thousands of people passed though his inn and emerged all the better for it. He was a great hotelier, one who brought happiness to many, but if there is a final word to add, it is this: he was also a lovely human being. We salute him.

Richard Bowman,
the Inn at Whitewell (1933–2005)

Photo Mr Underhill's, entry 174

Introduction

He would, no doubt, have been on the side of the breakfast cook who I encountered in the course of compiling this book, and whose robust singing could be heard above his sizzling sausages. His tunes – I use the word generously – escaped from the kitchen and toured the dining room, entertaining most of us waiting for our bacon and eggs, though one woman closed her eyes and shook her head, as if catastrophe had struck. Her reaction begged the question: was his singing worthy of a complaint or a round of applause? For what it's worth, I'm on the side of the chef.

Complaints in hotels are common: frazzled owners snap, tired rooms aren't worth the money, expensive food is badly cooked. This guide is lucky to have an army of readers who report regularly; this year their feedback led to 17 hotels being dropped. When standards fall, when owners cease to care, when guests are used as cash points, we have no qualms about removing a hotel from the guide. This book exists to solve problems, not to cause them. When the grapevine suggests otherwise, we act.

Some complaints are less clear-cut than others. The most difficult to deal with are those that involve a clash of personalities. Both guest and owner can feel hard done by. Small hotels are at their happiest when a mutual respect exists between staff and guests. This tranquillity can be disturbed by a stubborn owner who refuses to indulge a simple request, or by a guest who believes that because he is paying, he can treat staff however he likes. Both misunderstand a crucial point: service is reciprocal, given in order to be received. Those who fail to give it can hardly be surprised if their victims revolt; those who fail to accept it neuter the best efforts of the staff. Both are hard to take.

As for sublime service, there is little to beat it in a hotel. Its ingredients are uniquely human: dedication, kindness, awareness and generosity of spirit. It is the instinct to put others first and to do so with a smile. We are lucky to receive it when it comes our way and our most special stays are often marked by the extraordinary thoughtfulness of staff and owners. But is it a commodity we should factor into the bill, one we have a right to demand? Chain hotels think so and mould their staff into corporate models of patience and politeness. They are dressed in uniforms, taught how to smile and programmed with sterile language. A little of their naturalness is taken from them, and although it works to some extent, there is a falseness in it. I, for one, do not want the people who serve me to be subject to such methods. I prefer to run the risk of the odd human firework display than to be met by robotic acquiescence.

Bad service in good hotels is actually quite rare – it is what differentiates them from the rest. More often than not you fall into the care of staff and owners who are happy to go the extra mile. They whisk you in, pamper you rotten, share their local knowledge and enjoy your company. It is a tough job to do – long hours, low pay – and the vast majority do it with consideration and kindness.

It is a truism of travel that we are more likely to criticise and complain when closer to home. At home we are less forgiving. The intricacies of language, culture and social etiquette are at our fingertips; we understand the lay of the land and feel better equipped to fight our battles. Abroad, we fall into unfamiliar worlds full of different conventions; generally, we are more accepting as a result. The further we travel, the wider our eyes stretch. There is a freedom to be found in sweeping across savannahs new. This book is crammed with wonderful new experiences. I urge you to follow your nose and seek them out. The inns and hotels featured within are scattered across Britain's four corners. Lose yourself in the soft hills of the south, plunge

into the lush valleys of Wales, wind up through the glorious dales to the fells of the north, then tramp across the wild glens of mighty Scotland or cross by ferry to the Outer Hebrides.

If I can pass on a single tip to eager travellers, it is this: if you travel out of season, you will avoid the crowds and often pay less for it. Staff will not be rushed, sofas will not be taken, the table by the window will be yours. Often you will be upgraded to better rooms. If you have the chance to travel in April and May or September and October the weather can be good, too. I cannot emphasis enough how wonderful Britain can be at these times. These are the months in which we like to inspect so not to encroach upon hotels in busy periods. We wouldn't have it any other way.

Photo The Pear Tree Inn, entry 212

Introduction

In these pages you will find swish hotels, cosy inns, restaurants with rooms and other places that defy obvious labels. Hotels can vary from huge, humming and slick to those with only a few rooms that are run by owners at their own pace. In some you may not get room service or have your bags carried in and out. If these things are important to you, then do check when you book: a simple question or two can avoid regrettable misunderstandings.

In some smaller hotels there may be a fixed menu for dinner with very little choice, so if you have dishes that leave you cold, it's important to say so when you book for dinner. If you decide to stay at an inn, remember that they can be noisy, especially at weekends, and in some remote corners 'time' can be called late. All these places are special in one way or another. All have been visited and then written about honestly so that you can take what you like and leave the rest. Those of you who swear by Sawday books trust our write-ups precisely because we don't have a blanket standard; we include places simply because we like them. But we all have different priorities; do read and choose carefully.

Quick reference indices
At the back of the book you'll find a number of quick-reference indices showing those places that offer a particular service, perhaps a room for under £90 a night, or a property with a swimming pool. They are worth flicking through if you are looking for something specific, like deep peace, a pet-friendly hotel or somewhere to get married.

Maps
Each property is flagged with its entry number on the maps at the front. Please don't use these maps as anything other than a general guide or a good starting point for planning your trip. Use a decent road map for real navigation. Most places will send you detailed instructions once you have booked your stay.

Driving in Britain
I drove 10,000 miles in four months compiling this book, most of it fuelled by LPG gas (45p a litre). The days of traffic-free roads are almost

Photo right Angel Inn, entry 226
Photo left The Cotswold House Hotel, entry 104

over, with roads clogged across the country. If you want to avoid the traffic either get up early or head north. Once you're passed York the number of cars decreases noticeably, though the A1 north of Newcastle can still be a pain. The Highlands of Scotland are the only area left in Britain where you'll find an empty road. Once you're past Fort William on the west or Pitlochry in the middle, you'll be on your own. Across the country speed cameras sprout up daily by the dozen. You may like to know that the AA now plots each one on its road atlas.

Bedrooms

Bedrooms are described as double, twin, single or suite. A double may contain a bed which is anything from 135cm wide to 180cm wide. A twin will contain two single beds

Photo Hambleton Hall, entry 171

(usually 90cm wide). Some suites will have separate sitting rooms, but the trend at the moment is for one big room, not two small ones. Family rooms can vary in size, as can the number of beds they hold, so do ask.

Bathrooms

All bedrooms have their own bathrooms unless we say that they don't. If you have your own bathroom but you have to leave the room to get to it we describe it as 'separate'. There are very few places in the book that have shared bathrooms and they are usually reserved for members of the same party. Again, we state this clearly.

Prices

We quote the lowest price for two people in low season to the highest price in high season. All prices include a full breakfast unless stated. Only a few places have designated single rooms; if no single rooms are listed, the price we quote refers to single occupancy of a double room. In many places prices rise when local events bring people flooding to the area, a point worth remembering when heading to Edinburgh for the festival or Glyndebourne for the opera.

Half-board

The price quoted is per person per night and includes dinner, usually three courses. Mostly you're offered a table d'hôte menu. Occasionally you eat à la carte and find some dishes carry a small supplement. There are often great deals to be had, mostly mid-week in low season.

Weekend bookings

Most small hotels do not accept one-night bookings at weekends. Small country hotels are rarely full during the week and the weekend trade keeps them going. If you ring in March for a Saturday night in July, you won't get it. If you ring at the last moment and they have a room, you will.

Meals

Breakfast is included in the room price unless otherwise stated. If only a continental breakfast is offered, we let you know. If we were to give awards for the best breakfasts in this book one would certainly go to Bark House in Devon (entry 83) everything is brought to your table, there's not a carton in sight, though Victorian sugar shakers do make an appearance. Often you will feast on local sausage and bacon, eggs from resident hens, homemade breads and jams. In some you may have organic yogurts and beautifully presented fruit compotes. If you want the best porridge and kippers, head north to Scotland. It was noticeable this year that an increasing number of places have stopped serving freshly-squeezed orange juice at breakfast,

Photo Gilpin Lodge, entry 51

a policy most would like to see reversed. A few places serve lunch, most do Sunday lunch (often very well-priced), the vast majority offer dinner. In some places you can content yourself with bar meals, in others you can feast on five courses. Most offer a three-course, fixed-price menu, for about £30 without wine. In many restaurants you can also eat à la carte. Very occasionally you eat communally - if you loathe making small talk with strangers eschew these places. Some large hotels (and some posh private houses) will bring dinner to your room if you prefer, or let you eat in the garden by candlelight. Always ask for what you want and sometimes, magically, it happens.

Closed

When given in months this means the whole of the month stated.

Symbols
See inside back cover for the full list.

Children
Our symbol shows places which are happy to accept children of all ages. This does not mean that they will necessarily have cots, high chairs etc. Having said that, there are several places in this book that are ideal for families with young children. Many have huge swathes of lawn for running and tumbling, a swimming pool for fun and plenty of games and other things to do. Plenty of other children around means you won't be quite so embarrassed when your child has the loudest tantrum of its life in the dining room, and a newly-found friend for your little dear can sometimes leave you time to read at least the first page of your novel.

Photo above Simpsons, entry 8
Photo right Combe House, entry 86

If you want to get out and about in the evenings, check when you book whether there are any babysitting services. Even very small places can sometimes organise this for you.

Pets
Our symbol shows places which are happy to accept pets. It means they can sleep in the bedroom with you, but not on the bed. It's really important to get this one right before you arrive as many places make you keep dogs in the car. Check carefully: Spot's emotional wellbeing may depend on it.

Owners who have pets of their own are given a cat symbol. If you are allergic to, or simply don't like animals, beware. Sometimes there are geese, swans, peacocks, ducks, horses.

Payment
Those places that do not accept credit or debit cards are marked with a cash/cheque symbol.

Smoking
Anti-smoking legislation is sweeping across the country. In Scotland it is now illegal to smoke in public places. In July 2007 the same will be true of the rest of Britain. There is some uncertainty as to how this will effect hotels; it is possible that if a hotel permits it, you'll be able to smoke in bedrooms; but the vast majority of hotels do not allow smoking in

bedrooms. Bars, restaurants and sitting rooms will become smoke-free. Smokers will have to make do with the garden. Ireland has already proved that you can run a pub or restaurant without a single whiff of smoke and people still come. In fact, a number of pubs in this book have already banned smoking completely. They feared it would be a problem but far from it. People now telephone to ask if they really are smoke-free and then come for that reason. The days of smoky bars are disappearing fast.

Wheelchair access
All the hotels that have the wheelchair symbol have been called anonymously and asked a series of questions about ease of movement,

Photo Jolyon's Boutique Hotel, entry 276

width of doors, the need for ramps, gravelled paths, accessibility of bathrooms and type (most are wet rooms). Forty-one properties had the symbol before the call; 14 have it now. It is still only a guide and not perfect at that – if a hotel scored four out of five I awarded the symbol. I urge you to ring and make sure you will get what you need. In a couple of the hotels wheelchairs may have to take different routes to the dining room or gardens, in a couple there may be a need for a ramp or a single shallow step to navigate, in one there is a lift, in another there is a bath. In short, there may be the odd hindrance, but you can also have much greater confidence in this sign than before. Thanks to readers for their feedback, please keep it coming.

Limited mobility
The limited mobility symbol shows those places where at least one bedroom and bathroom is accessible without using stairs. The symbol is designed to satisfy those who walk slowly, with difficulty, or with the aid of a stick. A wheelchair may be able to navigate some areas, but in our opinion these places are not fully wheelchair friendly. If you use a chair for longer distances, but are not too bad over shorter distances, you'll probably be OK; again, please ring and ask. There may be a step or two, a bath or a shower with a tray in a cubicle, a good distance between the

car park and your room, slippery flagstones or a tight turn.

Booking and cancellation

Most places ask for a deposit at the time of booking, either by cheque or credit/debit card. If you cancel – depending on how much notice you give – you can lose all or part of this deposit unless your room is re-let. It is reasonable for hotels to take a deposit to secure a booking; they have learnt that if they don't, the commitment of the guest wanes and they may fail to turn up. Some cancellation policies are more stringent than others. It is also worth noting that some owners will take this deposit directly from your credit/debit card without contacting you to discuss it. So ask the hotel to explain their cancellation policy clearly before booking so you understand exactly where you stand; it may well avoid a nasty surprise.

Parking

Parking can be tricky or expensive in towns; call owners for advice when you book.

Arrivals and departures

Housekeeping is usually done by 2pm, and your room will usually be available by mid-afternoon. Normally you will have to wave goodbye to it between 10am and 11am. Sometimes one can pay to linger.

Photo No.1 Sallyport, entry 157

Special green entries

For the second time we have chosen, very subjectively, four places which are making a particular effort to be eco-friendly and have given them a double-page spread and extra photos to illustrate what they're up to.

This does not mean there are no other places in the guide taking green initiatives – there are many – but we have highlighted just a few examples. The four places that had a green page in the last edition have been given a new green leaf symbol 🍃.

Subscriptions

Owners pay to appear in this guide. Their fee goes towards the high costs of inspecting and producing an all-colour book and maintaining a sophisticated web site. We only include places that we like and find

Introduction

special for one reason or another, so it is not possible to buy your way onto these pages. Nor is it possible for the owner to write their own description. We will say if the bedrooms are small, or if a main road is near. We do our best to avoid misleading people.

Regulations

We do not check such things as fire alarms, swimming pool security or any other regulation with which owners of properties receiving paying guests should comply. This is the responsibility of the owners.

Feedback

We cannot be everywhere at once and things can be mercurial in the world of hotels and inns. So do tell us if your stay has been a joy or not, if the atmosphere was great or stuffy, whether the owners or staff were cheery or bored. The accuracy of the book depends on what you, and our inspectors, tell us. Please do not tell us if your starter was cold, or the bedside light was broken, or the shower head was scummy. Tell the owner, immediately, and get them to do something about it. Most owners, or staff, are more than happy to correct problems and will bend over backwards to help. Far better than bottling it up and then writing to us a week later! A lot of the new entries in each edition are recommended by our readers, so do

keep telling us about new places you've discovered too.

Disclaimer

We make no claims to pure objectivity in choosing these places. They are here simply because we like them. We try our utmost to get our facts right but we apologise unreservedly if any errors have sneaked in.

Internet

www.specialplacestostay.com has online pages for all the special places featured here and from all our other lovely books – around 5,000 places to stay in total. There's a searchable database, a snippet of the write-up and colour photos. If you're looking for somewhere to stay for a holiday, check out our dedicated British holiday home web site, www.special-escapes.com

Finally

We hope you enjoy these places. They all have something special to offer, whether it be fine views and great antiques, a fire in your bedroom (or bathroom!), food that is fresh as the day or a dazzling garden. The owners of these properties often go beyond the call of duty and strive to provide the best that they can.

Tom Bell

Photo Lower Brook House, entry 101

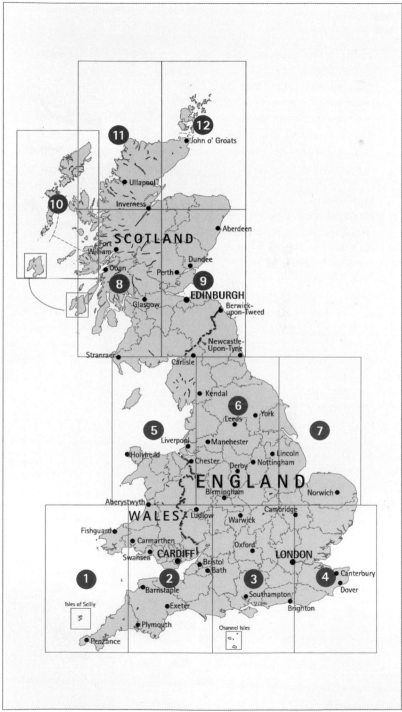

Map 1

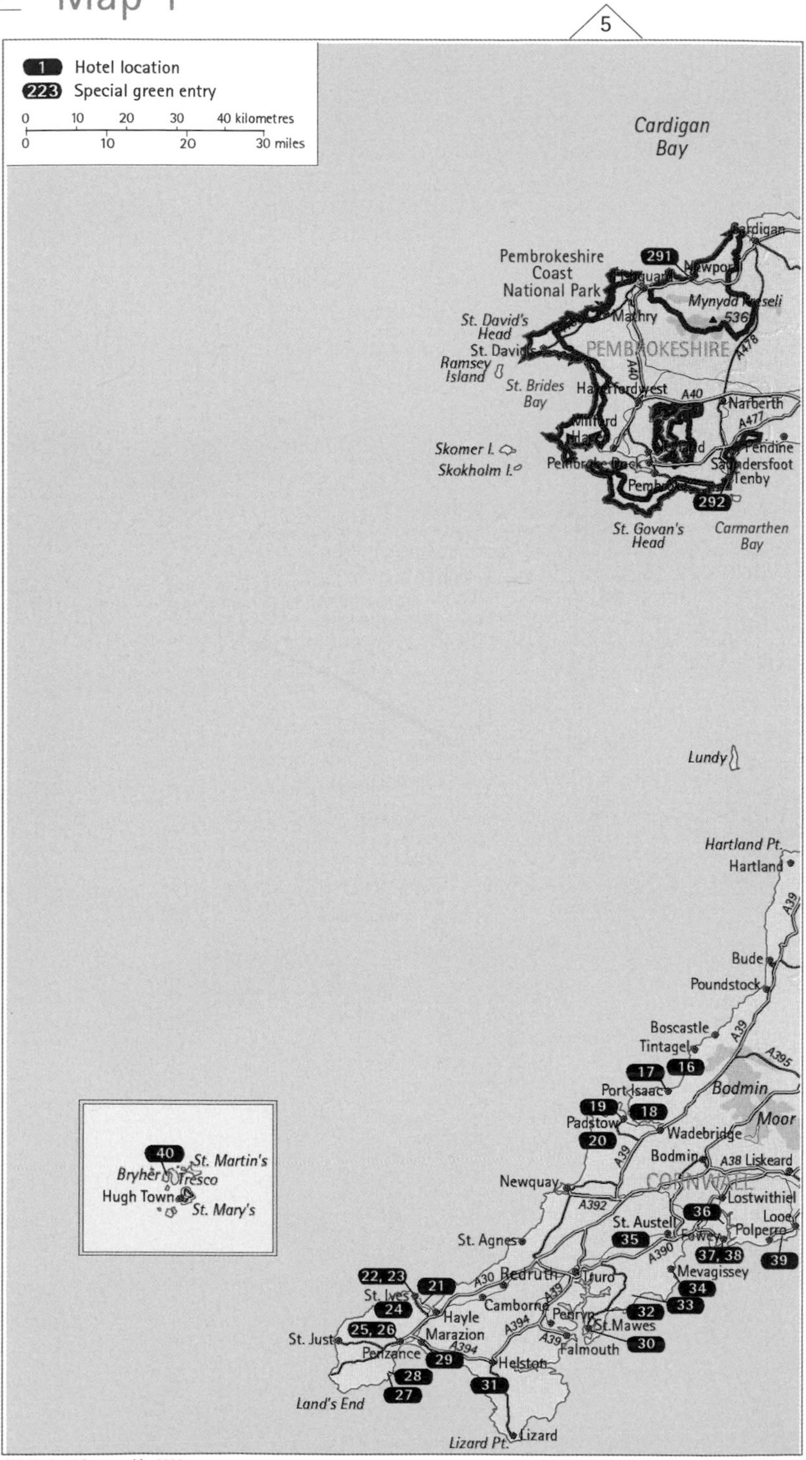

5

Hotel location

223 Special green entry

| 0 | 10 | 20 | 30 | 40 kilometres |

| 0 | 10 | 20 | 30 miles |

Cardigan
Bay

Pembrokeshire
Coast
National Park

291 Newport

Fishguard

St. David's
Head

St. David's

Mynydd Preseli
536

Machry

A487

PEMBROKESHIRE

A478

Ramsey
Island

St. Brides
Bay

Haverfordwest

A40

A40

Narberth

A477

A477

Milford
Haven

Skomer I.

Skokholm I.

Pembroke Dock

Haroun

Pendine

Saundersfoot

Tenby

Pembroke

St. Govan's
Head

292

Carmarthen
Bay

Lundy

Hartland Pt.

Hartland

A39

Bude

Poundstock

A39

Boscastle

Tintagel

17 16

Port Isaac

19 18

Padstow

20

A39

Wadebridge

A38 Liskeard

Bodmin

Bodmin
Moor

A395

A30

40 St. Martin's

Bryher Tresco

Hugh Town

St. Mary's

Newquay

A392

St. Austell

36

Lostwithiel

35 Fowey

Looe

Polperro

St. Agnes

A30 Redruth

Truro

A390

37, 38

39

22, 23

21

A30

Camborne

A39

Mevagissey

34

St. Ives

24

Hayle

A394

Pedryn

32

33

St. Just

25, 26

Marazion

A394

St. Mawes

30

Penzance

29

Helston

A39

Falmouth

28

27

31

Land's End

Lizard

Lizard Pt.

CORNWALL

Map 2

25

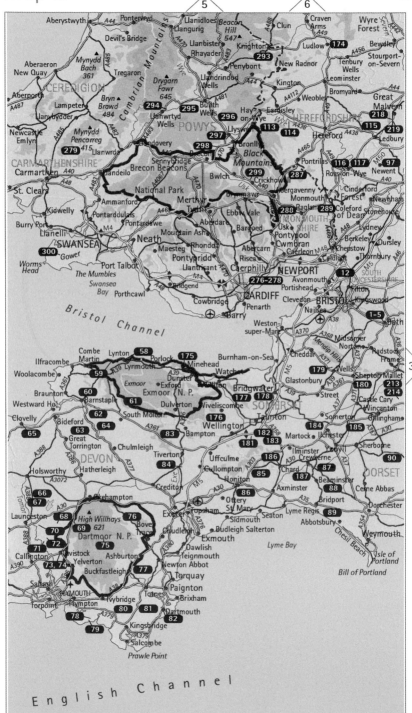

Map 3

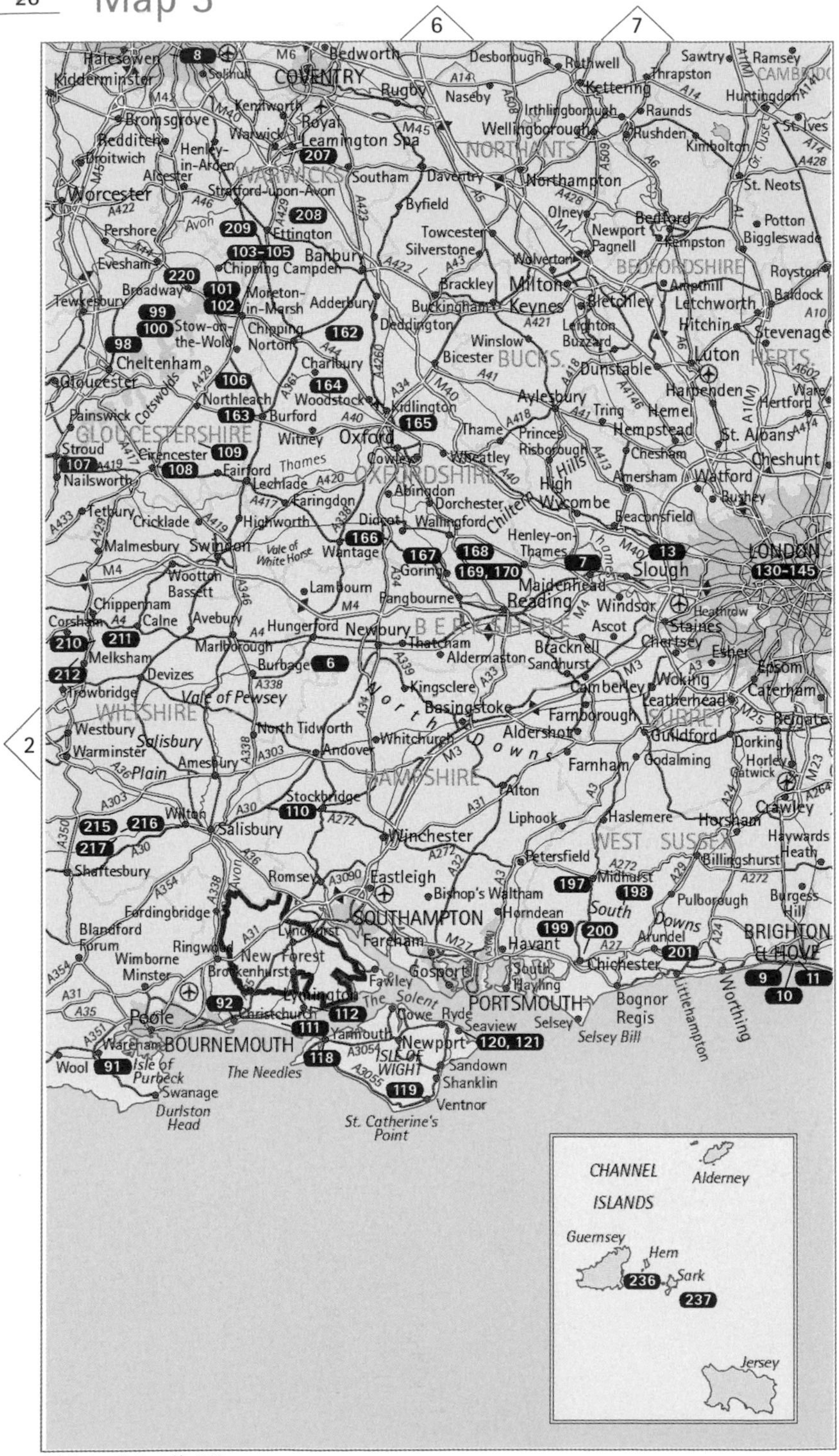
6
7
2
Halesowen
8
Kidderminster
Solihull
M6
Bedworth
COVENTRY
Rugby
Desborough
Rothwell
Kettering
Thrapston
Sawtry
Ramsey
Huntingdon
Bromsgrove
Redditch
Droitwich
Kenilworth
Warwick
Royal Leamington Spa
207
Naseby
Irthlingborough
Wellingborough
Raunds
Rushden
Kimbolton
St. Ives
NORTHANTS
WARWICKS
Henley-in-Arden
Alcester
Worcester
Stratford-upon-Avon
Southam
Daventry
Northampton
St. Neots
208
Byfield
Olney
Bedford
Potton
Pershore
209
Ettington
Towcester
Silverstone
Newport Pagnell
Kempston
Biggleswade
Evesham
103-105
Banbury
Chipping Campden
Wolverton
BEDFORDSHIRE
Royston
220
Broadway
101
102
Moreton-in-Marsh
Adderbury
Brackley
Milton Keynes
Ampthill
Baldock
Tewkesbury
Bletchley
Letchworth
99
100
Stow-on-the-Wold
Chipping Norton
Buckingham
Deddington
162
Hitchin
Stevenage
98
Winslow
Leighton Buzzard
Cheltenham
Charlbury
Bicester
BUCKS.
Luton
HERTS.
Gloucester
106
164
Dunstable
Harpenden
Ware
Northleach
Woodstock
Kidlington
Aylesbury
Tring
Hemel Hempstead
Hertford
Painswick
Cotswolds
163
Burford
165
Thame
Princes Risborough
St. Albans
GLOUCESTERSHIRE
Witney
Oxford
Stroud
109
Cirencester
Cowley
Wheatley
Chesham
Cheshunt
107
108
Fairford
Thames
OXFORDSHIRE
Amersham
Watford
Nailsworth
Lechlade
Abingdon
High Wycombe
Bushey
Tetbury
Faringdon
Dorchester
Chiltern Hills
Cricklade
Highworth
Didcot
Wallingford
Beaconsfield
Malmesbury
Swindon
Vale of White Horse
166
Wantage
Henley-on-Thames
13
LONDON
167
168
7
Slough
130-145
Goring
169, 170
Maidenhead
Wootton Bassett
Lambourn
Reading
Windsor
Heathrow
Chippenham
Pangbourne
Corsham
Calne
Avebury
Hungerford
Newbury
Ascot
Staines
211
BERKSHIRE
Chertsey
210
Marlborough
Thatcham
Bracknell
Esher
Melksham
Aldermaston
Sandhurst
212
Burbage
6
Epsom
Devizes
Woking
Trowbridge
Kingsclere
Camberley
Caterham
Vale of Pewsey
Leatherhead
WILTSHIRE
North Downs
Basingstoke
Farnborough
SURREY
Reigate
Westbury
North Tidworth
Aldershot
Guildford
Salisbury Plain
Whitchurch
Dorking
Warminster
Amesbury
Andover
Farnham
Godalming
Horley
Gatwick
HAMPSHIRE
Stockbridge
Alton
Crawley
110
Liphook
Haslemere
Horsham
215
216
Wilton
Salisbury
Winchester
Haywards Heath
217
WEST SUSSEX
Petersfield
Billingshurst
Shaftesbury
Romsey
Eastleigh
Midhurst
197
198
Bishop's Waltham
Pulborough
Burgess Hill
Fordingbridge
SOUTHAMPTON
Horndean
South Downs
199
200
Blandford Forum
Lyndhurst
Fareham
Havant
Arundel
BRIGHTON & HOVE
Ringwood
New Forest
201
Wimborne Minster
Brockenhurst
Gosport
Chichester
Fawley
South Hayling
9
11
10
The Solent
Lymington
92
Christchurch
112
PORTSMOUTH
Bognor Regis
Littlehampton
Worthing
Poole
Cowes
Ryde
Seaview
Selsey
111
Yarmouth
Selsey Bill
Wareham
BOURNEMOUTH
Newport
120, 121
Wool
91
Isle of Purbeck
118
ISLE OF WIGHT
Sandown
The Needles
Shanklin
119
Swanage
Ventnor
Durlston Head
St. Catherine's Point
CHANNEL ISLANDS
Alderney
Guernsey
Herm
Sark
236
237
Jersey

Map 4

27

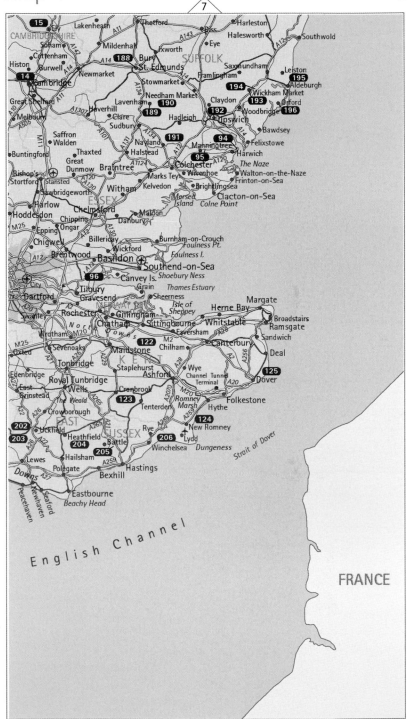

8 9

Stranraer Glenluce Wigtown Gatehouse of Dalbeattie 248
Portpatrick A75 Fleet Carlisle 41
247 The Kirkcudbright Wigton 42
Luce Bay Machars Solway Firth A596 A6
Port William Whithorn Aspatria CUMBRIA
Drummore Wigtown Bay Maryport
Burrow Head Cockermouth 44 45 46 Penrith
Mull of Galloway Workington 43 Keswick A66 Ullswater
Whitehaven Clator Lake Helvellyn 949
St. Bees Head Scafell 47 District Grasmere
St. Bees Pike 48 National Ambleside
Point of Ayre Egremont 978 49 50 Park
Windermere 51
Ramsey District
Isle of Man A3 Broughton- Newby
A2 Furness Bridge
Peel A4 Laxey Millom Milnthorpe
A1 Dalton-in-Furness A590 52
A3 A5 Douglas Carnforth
Port Erin Barrow- Morecambe
Castletown in-Furness Bay Morecambe
Isle of Heysham
Walney
Fleetwood
Irish Sea Cleveleys Garstang
Thornton
Poulton-le-Fylde M55
BLACKPOOL
Lytham St. Anne's Kirkham A59
Southport A570 A59
A565 Ormskirk
Formby Skelmersdale
Liverpool Crosby Kirkby
Amlwch Bay Wallasey St. Helens
Great Hoylake Birkenhead LIVERPOOL
ANGLESEY Ormes 280 Colwyn Prestatyn Heswall Widnes
Holyhead ISLE Head Llandudno Bay Rhyl A548 Runcorn
Holy Valley Benllech 281 Rhuddlan A55 Neston
Island Menai Beaumaris Conwy Abergele Holywell Flint Chester
Rhosneigr Llangefni Bridge Bangor Llanfairfechan St. Asaph Helsby
275 A51
Bethesda Denbigh FLINTSHIRE
Caernarfon A470 CONWY Mold Buckley
Capel Llanrwst Bychau Llay Holt
Caernarfon Curig Betws-y-Coed Ruthin
Bay Snowdon Pentrefoelas DENBIGHSHIRE Wrexham
1085 A5 Malpas
Nefyn Blaenau Dee Llangollen Ruabon Overton
Lleyn Peninsula Ffestiniog Corwen A5 Chirk A495 Ellesmere
Criccieth Ffestiniog 282 Whittington Wem
Pwllheli Snowdonia Bala A5 Oswestry 172
285 Porthmadog Trawsfynydd Lake 283, 284
Abersoch Harlech National Shrewsbury
Aberdaron Tremadog Park GWYNEDD Lake Llanfyllin
Bay Vyrnwy A483 SHROPSHIRE
Bardsey 286 Dolgellau Church
Island Barmouth Welshpool Minsterley Stretton
Barmouth Bay Cader Llanfair A49
Idris Mallwyd Caereinion Bishop's
892 Montgomery Castle
Tywyn Machynlleth Moelfre
Aberdovey A493 468 Caersws A489 Newtown
Borth Talybont 290

Map 6

29

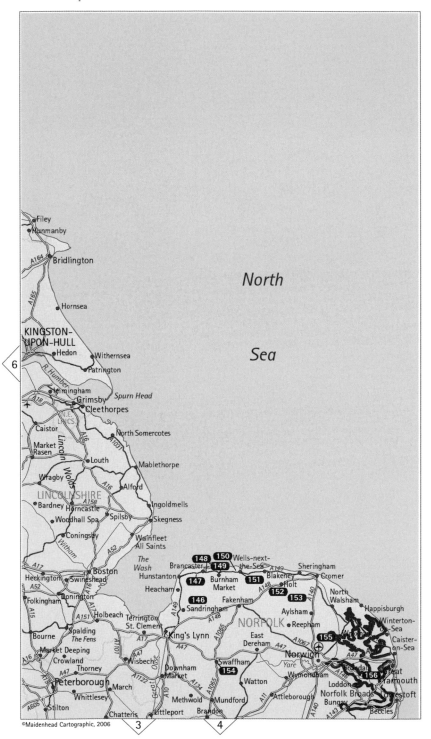

North

Sea

Filey
Hunmanby
A164 Bridlington
A165
Hornsea
KINGSTON-
UPON-HULL
Hedon
Withernsea
6
Patrington
R. Humber
Immingham Spurn Head
A18 Grimsby
Cleethorpes
N.E.
LINCS
Caistor
North Somercotes
Market Rasen
A16
Louth Mablethorpe
Lincoln Wolds
Wragby A16 Alford
LINCOLNSHIRE A158 Ingoldmells
Bardney Horncastle
Woodhall Spa Spilsby Skegness
Coningsby
Witham Wainfleet
A52 All Saints
A17 The Wells-next-
Heckington Swineshead Wash Brancaster the-Sea
A52 Hunstanton **148** **150** A149 Sheringham
Donington Heacham **147** Burnham **151** Holt Cromer
Folkingham Market Blakeney
A15 **146** Fakenham A148 **152** North
A151 Holbeach Sandringham **153** Walsham
Bourne Spalding Terrington Aylsham Happisburgh
The Fens St. Clement A148 Reepham Winterton-
Market Deeping A10 A1065 NORFOLK -Sea
Crowland King's Lynn East **155** Caister-
A16 A47 Dereham A47 on-Sea
Peterborough Thorney A1122 Wisbech Swaffham Norwich Yare
March Downham **154** Watton Wymondham **156** Great
Whittlesey Market Mundford Attleborough A140 Yarmouth
Stilton A605 Crowland A134 A11 Norfolk Broads Loddon Lowestoft
Chatteris Littleport Methwold Brandon Bungay
A143 Beccles

©Maidenhead Cartographic, 2006   3   4

Map 8

31

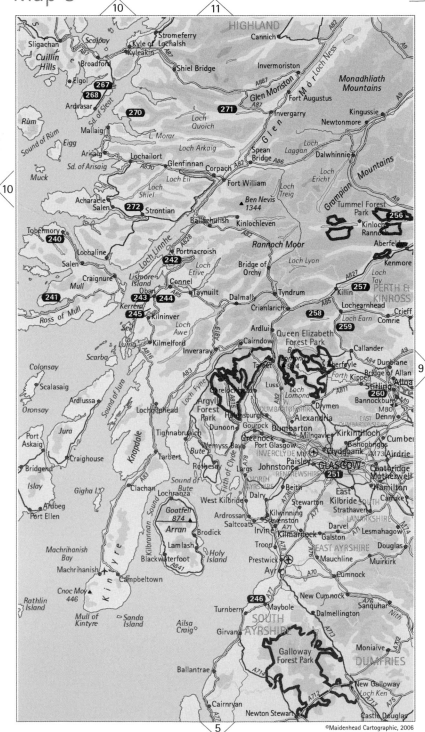

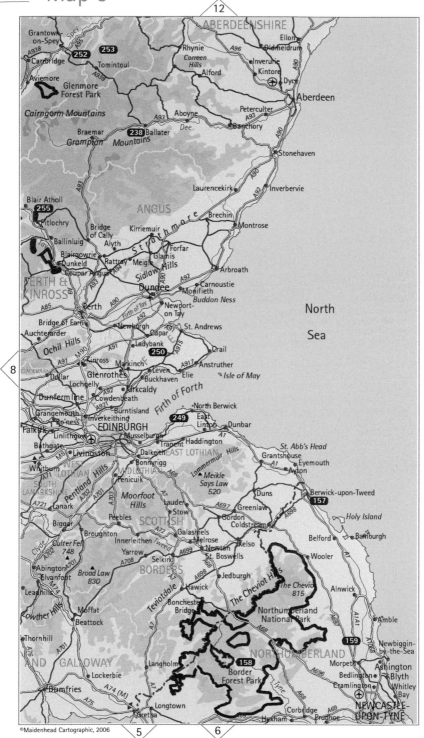

Map 10

33

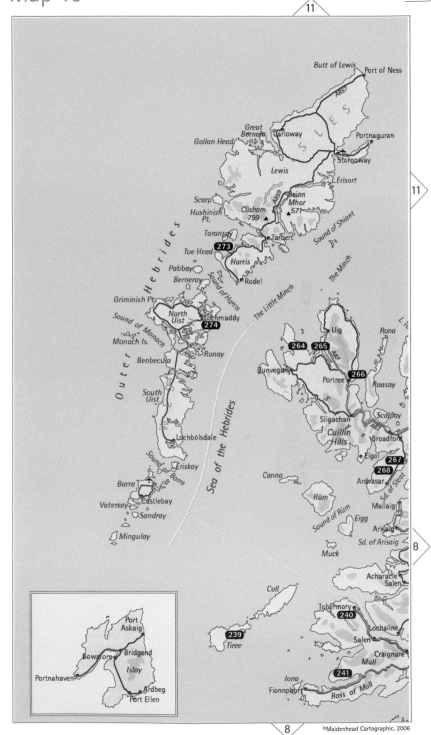

11

11

8

8

Butt of Lewis
Port of Ness
A857
I S L E S
Great Bernera
Carloway
Portnaguran
Gallan Head
Stornoway
Lewis
L.Erisort
Scarp
A859
Beinn Mhor
▲ 571
Hushinish Pt.
Clisham 799 ▲
Sound of Shiant
Taransay
Tarbert
Toe Head
273
Pabbay
Harris
Rodel
Berneray
Sound of Harris
The Minch
Griminish Pt
The Little Minch
North Uist
Lochmaddy
274
Sound of Monach
Uig
Rona
Monach Is.
264 265
A87
Ronay
Dunvegan
Portree
266
Raasay
Benbecula
Scalpay
South Uist
Sligachan
Cuillin Hills
Broadford
Lochboisdale
Sea of the Hebrides
Elgol
267
268
Eriskay
Canna
Ardvasar
Sd. of Sleat
Sound of Barra
Barra
Rùm
Mallaig
Vatersay
Castlebay
Eigg
Arisaig
Sandray
Sound of Rùm
Sd. of Arisaig
Mingulay
Muck
Acharacle
Salen
Coll
Tobermory
240
Lochaline
Tiree
239
Salen
Craignure
Mull
241
Iona
Fionnphort
Ross of Mull

Port Askaig
Bowmore
Bridgend
Islay
Portnahaven
Ardbeg
Port Ellen

©Maidenhead Cartographic, 2006

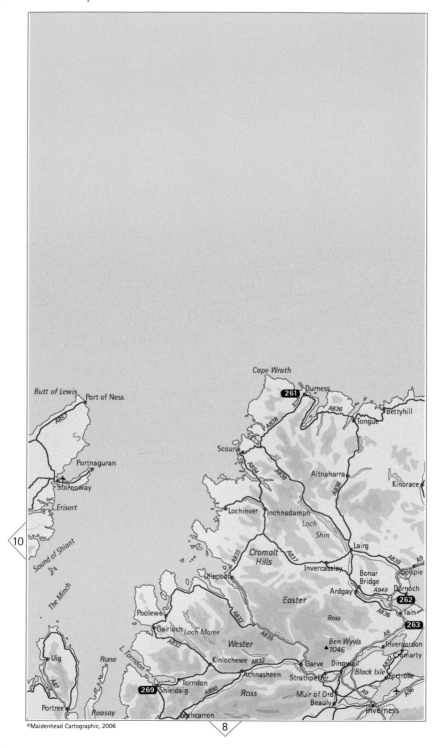

Map 12

35

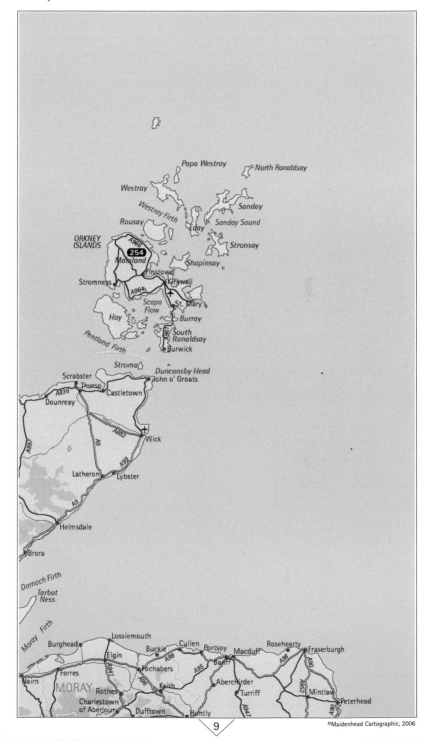

England

The Bath Priory Hotel & Restaurant
Weston Road, Bath, Bath & N.E. Somerset BA1 2XT

An exquisite townhouse hotel, with staff who greet you by your name when you step through the front door. Spin into the drawing room while porters see to your luggage, gaze at exceptional art, warm yourself in front of the fire, then throw open the French windows and explore the four-acre garden for swimming pool, croquet lawn, kitchen garden and an ancient cedar... colour bursts through in summer, and loungers flank the pool. Back inside a Michelin star in the dining room will keep a smile on your face and may offer roasted scallops marinated in lime, slow-poached saddle of fallow deer, nougatine leaves with manuka honey and a lavander-scented truffled goats' cheese. Plush bedrooms are as you'd expect with rich fabrics, warm colours, crisp linen and Roberts radios. Those at the back have garden views, there are shelves of books, proper armchairs, a sofa if there's room. Back downstairs, fresh flowers everywhere and a spa with indoor pool, sauna, steam room, gym and treatment suites. The city is on your doorstep: stroll through the park to the Roman Baths and Royal Crescent.

rooms	31: 27 twins/doubles, 4 suites.
price	£245–£360. Suites £425–£495.
meals	Lunch from £20. Dinner £55.
closed	Never.
directions	From centre of Bath follow red hospital signs west for a mile. Right at far end of Royal Victoria Park. Left at T-junction into Weston Road. Hotel on left.

	Sue Williams
tel	01225 331922
fax	01225 448276
email	mail@thebathpriory.co.uk
web	www.thebathpriory.co.uk

Hotel

Map 2 Entry 1

The Queensberry Hotel & Olive Tree Restaurant
Russel Street, Bath, Bath & N.E. Somerset BA1 2QF

The Queensberry is an old favourite, grand but totally unpretentious and immensely enjoyable. It is rare to find a hotel of this size and elegance still in private hands: owners Laurence and Helen are working hard to complete their ideas, and the staff just couldn't be nicer. Those bedrooms that have had the magic treatment are excellent – contemporary and dramatic, with bold, inspirational colours and huge beds – but all have thick robes and drenching showers in large, sparkling bathrooms. If you have young children, ask for a room that's reachable by lift, and if you feel like spoiling yourself, have breakfast brought up to you: croissants, orange juice, fresh coffee, warm milk and a newspaper. At night, pop down to supper – the restaurant is renowned – and when you get back, your bed will have been turned down, your towels refreshed. As for the homemade fudge after supper... wonderful! All this in a John Wood house in the centre of Bath, a minute's walk from the Assembly Rooms, with reserved on-street parking.

rooms	29: 26 twins/doubles, 1 four-poster, 2 suites.
price	£110-£210. Suites £215-£300.
meals	Breakfast £9-£14. Lunch £13.50. Dinner, à la carte, from £33.
closed	Never.
directions	Into Bath on A4 London Rd to Paragon; 1st right into Lansdown; 2nd left into Bennett St; 1st right into Russel St.

	Laurence & Helen Beere
tel	01225 447928
fax	01225 446065
email	reservations@thequeensberry.co.uk
web	www.thequeensberry.co.uk

Hotel

Map 2 Entry 2

SACO Serviced Apartments

SACO House, St James Parade, Bath, Bath & N.E. Somerset BA1 1UH

Fabulous Bath is England's loveliest city, Georgian to its bone. It's built of mellow golden stone, so wander its streets for elegant squares, beautiful gardens, pavement cafés, delicious delis and the imperious Roman Baths (there's a spa if you want to take a dip). Close to the river, bang in the middle of town, these serviced apartments bask behind a beautifully restored Regency façade – look out for the pillared entrances. Inside you find a collection of airy studios and apartments, all of which come with sparkling kitchens that are fully stocked with ovens, dishwashers, washer/dryers, microwaves, fridges, freezers if there's room. Some are small, some are big, and if you need a bolthole for a night or a cool pad for a week, you'll find one here. You get white walls, Italian designer furniture, flat-screen TVs, CD players and big fluffy towels in spotless bathrooms. There's a lift to whisk you up and away, 24-hour reception, and high-speed broadband connection throughout. Supermarkets are close, but there are masses of great restaurants on your doorstep, too. *Minimum stay two nights at weekends.*

rooms	43 studios & apartments for 2 & 4.
price	Studios: £110-£130. 1-bed apt: £120-£200; 2-bed apt: £190-£230.
meals	Full kitchen facilites. Restaurants within 0.5 miles.
closed	Never.
directions	In centre of town, 5-minute walk from station. Full directions on booking.

	Jo Redman
tel	0845 122 0405
fax	0117 974 5939
email	bath@sacoapartments.co.uk
web	www.servicedapartmentsbath.co.uk

Other Place

Map 2 Entry 3

Dorian House

One Upper Oldfield Park, Bath, Bath & N.E. Somerset BA2 3JX

A cellist with a love of interior design is rare enough, but to find one running a hotel just above beautiful Bath is exceptional. Tim is the London Symphony Orchestra's principal cellist and was once taught by the late and great Jacqueline du Pré. Be yourself in the cosy, spoiling luxury of this converted Victorian house that feels more home than hotel. Everything has been beautifully restored inside; the original tiled hallway is lovely. Sit with afternoon tea in deep sofas in the lounge, or enjoy one of six types of champagne in comfortable bedrooms all named after cellists. No surprise that the most impressive – and the most secluded – is du Pré: its huge four-poster bed is reached up a flight of stairs. Every room is decorated with beautiful fabrics, Egyptian linen, chocolates on the pillow; those on the first floor are traditional, those on the second and third more contemporary, with oak furniture and sloping ceilings (and four new bathrooms). The owners' art collection is everywhere, gathered from their travels abroad. Relaxation assured, and maybe some music, too. *Ten-minute walk to station.*

rooms	11: 3 twins/doubles, 4 doubles, 1 family, 3 four-posters.
price	£72-£150. Singles £60-£78.
meals	Pubs & restaurants within walking distance.
closed	Never.
directions	From Bath centre, follow signs to Shepton Mallet to sausage-shaped r'bout, then A37 up hill, 1st right. House 3rd on left, signed.

	Kathryn & Tim Hugh
tel	01225 426336
fax	01225 444699
email	info@dorianhouse.co.uk
web	www.dorianhouse.co.uk

Hotel

Map 2 Entry 4

Stoke Park Club

Park Road, Stoke Poges, Buckinghamshire SL2 4PG

James Bond played golf with Goldfinger here and nearly lost his head to Odd Job's bowler hat. Whether he stayed for a massage, a game of tennis, a swim in the pool or a meal in the Art Deco-style restaurant is not recorded, but if he didn't, he should have. Stoke Park is a Palladian-style mansion set in 350 acres on an estate that is noted in the Domesday Book. Matchless interiors thrill: Corinthian columns and a cupola dome in the Great Hall, the largest free-standing marble staircase in Europe, and a grand piano opposite a roaring fire. The Orangery, for late breakfasts, is also the members' clubhouse and buzzes with life (ladies in for a hand of bridge, old timers lamenting a missed putt). In summer, life spills onto a balustraded terrace for views across croquet lawn and golf course to the heritage gardens. Expect panelled bars, padded window seats, elaborate wall hangings, even a chapel. Bedrooms are the very best (Hugh Grant and Renée Zellweger stayed in *Bridget Jones's Diary*), with oak four-posters, big fat sofas and fabulous marble bathrooms. The health club, spa and golf club are yours to enjoy.

rooms	21: 18 doubles, 3 suites.
price	£285–£345. Suites £400–£1,100. Half-board £180 p.p.
meals	Breakfast £12.50–£18.50. Lunch from £12. A la carte dinner around £35.
closed	Christmas Day & 1st week in January.
directions	M4, junc. 6, A355 north, then right at 2nd r'about. On right after 1.25 miles.

	Mark Fagan
tel	01753 717171
fax	01753 717181
email	info@stokeparkclub.com
web	www.stokeparkclub.com

Hotel

Map 3 Entry 13

Hotel Felix

Whitehouse Lane, Huntingdon Road, Cambridge, Cambridgeshire CB3 0LX

Hotel Felix is sleekly up to date, a country house with a modern twist and a mere mile (walk in, taxi back?) from the historic city. Centred around a Victorian villa in three acres, two new bedroom wings have been added at right angles to the original building (just four bedrooms in the old part, popular with celebs), thus creating a courtyard with statue and plants in between. Bedrooms are sophisticated and luxurious: huge beds, plump pillows, neutral tones, silk fabrics, feather duvets, generously proportioned bathrooms lined in slate or natural stone; there are CDs and films on demand and every imaginable 'corporate' extra. Overlooking the pleasant terrace and small gardens is the light, airy, elegant Graffiti restaurant, whose chef draws on the flavoursome approach of Mediterranean and Italian cooking... home-smoked salmon with black truffle and celeriac remoulade and russet apple vinaigrette is merely a starter. And there's a Conran-designed health club nearby (with spa) to work off your indulgence – ask for a day pass from reception. Contemporary style without the attitude.

rooms	52 twins/doubles.
price	£168-£275. Singles from £136.
meals	Continental breakfast included; full English £7.50. Bar meals from £4.95. Lunch £12.50-£16.50. Dinner from £30.
closed	Rarely.
directions	A1 north, then A1307/A14 turn-off onto Huntingdon Road into Cambridge. Hotel on left.

Shara Ross
tel	01223 277977
fax	01223 277973
email	help@hotelfelix.co.uk
web	www.hotelfelix.co.uk

Hotel

Map 4 Entry 14

The Anchor Inn

Bury Lane, Sutton Gault, Ely, Cambridgeshire CB6 2DB

A real find, a 1650 ale house on Chatteris Fen. The New Bedford river streams past outside. It was cut from the soil by the pub's first residents, Scottish prisoners of war brought in by Cromwell to dig the dykes that drain the fens. These days cosy luxury infuses every corner. There are low beamed ceilings, timber-framed walls, raw dark panelling and terracotta-tiled floors. A woodburner warms the bar, so stop for a pint of cask ale, then feast on fresh local produce: hand-dressed crabs from Cromer in spring, asparagus and Bottisham hams in summer, wild duck from the marshes in winter; breakfast is equally indulgent. Four spotless rooms above the restaurant fit the mood exactly (not posh, supremely comfy). Expect trim carpets, wicker chairs, crisp white duvets and Indian cotton throws. The suites each have a sofabed and three rooms have fen and river views. Footpaths flank the water; stroll down and you might see mallards or Hooper swans, even a seal (the river is tidal to the Wash). Don't miss Ely (the bishop comes to eat), Cambridge, and Welney for nesting swans by the thousand.

rooms	4: 1 double, 1 twin, 2 suites.
price	£65-£95. Singles from £55. Suites £109.50-£149.50. Extra bed £20.
meals	Lunch £10.95. Dinner £27.
closed	26 December.
directions	West from Ely on A142. Left in Sutton onto B1381 for Earith. On south fringes of Sutton, right signed Sutton Gault. 1 mile north on left at bridge.

	Robin & Heather Moore
tel	01353 778537
fax	01353 776180
email	anchorinn@popmail.bta.com
web	www.anchorsuttongault.co.uk

Restaurant with Rooms

Map 4 Entry 15

Caradoc of Tregardock
Treligga, Cornwall PL33 9ED

Crashing breakers, wheeling gulls, carpets of wild flowers in spring – this place is a dream for artists and a tonic for everyone. Just two fields away from the coastal path, the old farm buildings are set around a grassy courtyard with west-facing patios that catch the setting sun or gathering storm. Some bedrooms look out to sea, all are airy with huge beds, white walls and pretty linen. Caradoc's upstairs drawing room has a magnificent Atlantic view, beams and a woodburner; the farmhouse kitchen with its Rayburn has a large table that seats 12. Janet stocks the fridges with the best of Cornish and lets you cook breakfast whenever you want it, then points you to good restaurants, some within walking distance along the cliffpath; alternatively hire a chef for special occasions. Caradoc and the cottage are ideal for extended families and special-interest groups; for a more secluded break the Seaview apartment is peaceful. There are books, music and videos too if staying in seems like a good idea. *Fully catered painting & yoga holidays available.*

rooms	4 + 1: 4 twins/doubles. Cottage for 4: 1 double, 1 twin, sharing bath (same-party bookings only).
price	£80-£130. Singles £40-£65. Self-catering £375-£1,400 p.w.
meals	Dinner with wine, £35, by arrangement. Private chef available.
closed	Rarely.
directions	South from Delabole; 2 miles right to Treligga; 2nd farm road, signed.

	Janet Cant
tel	01840 213300
fax	01840 213300
email	info@tregardock.com
web	www.tregardock.com

Other Place

Map 1 Entry 16

Mount Haven Hotel & Restaurant

Turnpike Road, Marazion, Cornwall TR17 0DQ

Step into another world – a magical hotel with undisturbed vistas to St Michael's Mount from several decked terraces. The house – originally an 1840s coach house – is both stylish and spiritual at the same time, and Orange and Mike give you a big welcome; most of the staff are in the family. Delight in the beauty of the white marble buddha, framed by a red sunset painting; there's an eclectic mix of local art so wander around and soak it all in. A perfect spot for relaxing and pampering: pad around the large lounge with its wholesome collection of books on art and spirituality, sunbathe on your balcony, book a healing treatment. The dining room is elegant and the food marvellous: little pots of crab and parmesan, whole baked lemon sole, brochette of scallop and pancetta. Big bedrooms have Indian raw silk curtains and throws, contemporary wooden furniture and white bathrooms with seaside smellies. Squashy sofas, chill-out music, funky interiors, family smiles: you may not want to leave. Walk to the Mount, visit the Minnack, or stay put and simply unwind. The views are amazing.

rooms	18: 11 doubles, 5 twins, 2 family.
price	£84–£160.
meals	Lunch about £15. Dinner about £28.
closed	A week before Christmas to 1st Friday in February.
directions	From A30, A394 in Helston direction to r'bout. Tourist sign for Mount Haven, turn right; hotel 400 yds on left. Private parking.

Orange Trevillion

tel	01736 710249
fax	01736 711658
email	reception@mounthaven.co.uk
web	www.mounthaven.co.uk

Hotel

Map 1 Entry 29

Tresanton Hotel

Lower Castle Road, St Mawes, Cornwall TR2 5DR

A carved stone madonna and child guard the entrance from the little road which is all that separates Tresanton from acres of blue sea. A natural hush descends as you walk through the whitewashed opening and into a numinous world of sublime food, perfect service from graceful and intelligent staff, rooms that pretend not to be hotel rooms and modern art that will delight even the most traditional. Mostly large bedrooms come with comfortable bathrooms, simple, neutral colours and the odd stripe of lemon or blue in a blanket, and views – from all but one – of glimmering seas and bobbing boats. The whole point of being here is to unwind and retreat from the outside world, so sprawl in the gorgeous drawing room with a book from the library, bag a deckchair on one of the terraces or simply stay in bed. Heartier folk have oodles of coastal path to ramble or yachts to sail before dinner is served with a gentle breeze overlooking the ocean or in the elegant dining room. However you decide to whimsy away your time here it will not be wasted and Tresanton will be embedded in your soul.

rooms	29 doubles & family suites.
price	£170-£425.
meals	Lunch £21-£28. Dinner, 3 courses, £38.
closed	Two weeks in January.
directions	Drive past the 'St Mawes' welcome sign. Turn right towards St Mawes Castle. Down the hill & Tresanton is at the bottom on the left hand side with four palm trees outside.

Olga Polizzi

tel	01326 270055
fax	01326 270053
email	info@tresanton.com
web	www.tresanton.com

Hotel

Map 1 Entry 30

Halzephron

Gunwalloe, Cornwall TR12 7QB

An opera singer serving real ale in an ancient smuggler's inn: only in Cornwall. But Halzephron (cliffs of hell) is more than that; Harry, Angela's late husband, ran the inn for many years, a much-loved landlord, and a picture of him, pipe in hand, claims its rightful place on the mantelpiece. Come for low ceilings, stone walls, coal fires and polished brass. There are sea views from the roadside terrace, a lively courtyard for summer afternoons, and a small garden overlooking the fields. Lunch on hearty homemade food – perhaps seafood chowder, boeuf bourguignon or Armenian lamb – then walk it all off on cliff-top coastal paths; you can strike out for the Lizard and Church Cove, then catch the bus home. Bedrooms above the bar are country cosy, with antique dressers, quilted eiderdowns, bowls of fruit and restful florals. Both are at the back and come with long views across the fields. One has a bath, one has a shower, and there are books galore, Dickens to Alan Coren. Breakfast is cooked to order and comes with marmalade made by Angela and her niece.

rooms	2 doubles.
price	From £84. Singles £45.
meals	Lunch & dinner: main courses £9-£16.
closed	Christmas Day.
directions	From Helston, A3083, signed The Lizard. Pass Culdrose air base, then right, signed Gunwalloe. 2 miles and inn on left after houses.

Angela Thomas

tel	01326 240406
fax	01326 241442
email	halzephroninn@gunwalloe1.fsnet.co.uk

Hotel

Map 1 Entry 31

Driftwood Hotel
Rosevine, Portscatho, Cornwall TR2 5EW

Cape Cod meets Cape Cornwall. This is a superb place, perfectly positioned, refreshingly understated. It's said the original owner of this 1930s beach villa wandered all over the Roseland Peninsula looking for the right spot and chose here. The views are out of this world: the sun rises over Nare Head, Portscatho village peeks from a small inlet, and boats criss-cross the bay. Fiona and Paul are charming and make the place feel like home. The driftwood theme is everywhere, the colours are restful, the light pours in from every angle. There's a bar with comfy window seats and a lounge with handsome driftwood lamps, deep sofas, piles of books, a log fire. And the food is brilliant, often from the sea, masterminded by a chef who has cooked in top London places; the restaurant is an expanse of white and wooden floor. Mind your head as you go upstairs; bedrooms, including four new, have fabulous linen and sea views from most. Bathrooms are immaculate. Sit on the decked balcony for breakfast and candlelit dinner, or take a hamper to the private beach – you may see a hairy snail.

rooms	15: 11 doubles, 3 twins, 1 cabin.
price	£170–£210.
meals	Dinner £38.
closed	January.
directions	From St Austell, A390 west. Left on B3287 for St Mawes; left at Tregony on A3078 for about 7 miles. Signed left down lane.

	Paul & Fiona Robinson
tel	01872 580644
fax	01872 580801
email	info@driftwoodhotel.co.uk
web	www.driftwoodhotel.co.uk

Hotel

Map 1 Entry 32

The Lugger Hotel
Portloe, Truro, Cornwall TR2 5RD

The Lugger, dipping its toes in the brine, is tucked tightly in to this tiny functioning fishing village where old smuggling tales circulate still. Some of the crisply designed bedrooms and bathrooms are not huge but all have excellent beds, vim-white linen, careful lighting, deep baths, and showers that aim to flatten you. The elegantly shuttered dining room with high-backed black chairs overlooks the harbour and trumpets fresh Cornish fish and locally caught lobster and crab: scope for gluttony of the very best kind. There's a modern seaside feel and sunny terraces to eat outdoors, but staff give good old-fashioned service with impeccable manners and Richard is always on hand to make sure everything is just so. A sitting room with cosy fire and magazines and a little spa room for relaxation treatments could herald a lazy break, but great walking straight onto the wild coastal path (and wellies for guests) may tempt you from idleness. From many rooms the sea can be heard beating out its message – relax, unwind and let the world hurtle on without you for a while. Bliss. *Reductions for longer stays.*

rooms	21 doubles.
price	£150-£310.
meals	Dinner, 3 courses, £37.50.
closed	Rarely.
directions	A390 St Austell to Truro, turn off at B3287 to Tregony. A3078 (St Mawes road); 2 miles on fork left for Portloe; left at T-junc. for Portloe.

	Sheryl & Richard Young
tel	01872 501322
fax	01872 501691
email	office@luggerhotel.com
web	www.luggerhotel.com

Hotel

Map 1 Entry 33

Trevalsa Court Hotel

School Hill Road, Mevagissey, Cornwall PL26 6TH

A big Edwardian country house with sprawling lawns that run down to high cliffs; steps lead down to a sandy beach or you can follow the coastal path to the lighthouse at Mevagissey, an old-fashioned fishing village with a working quay. Don't dally too long. This is the hotel the man who loves hotels bought, and he's made it the perfect seaside retreat: friendly, stylish, young at heart. Mullioned window seats come in cushioned purple, flowers float in a bowl on the wood burner and polished American oak sparkles in the panelled dining room. Bauhaus clocks and lamps add style, black-and-white photos adorn the walls, a bowl of lemons sits on an oak chest. In fine weather, sip drinks on the stone terrace amid beds of colour or hide away with a good book in the summer house. Bedrooms are harmonious and varied, some big, others snug; all but two have sea views. Expect happy colours, crisp linen, Art Deco lamps, perhaps a sofa. Delicious food doesn't try to be too fancy (perfect pasty on a lemon tart), there's no rush in the morning and the Lost Gardens of Heligan and the Eden Project are close.

rooms	11: 6 doubles, 2 twins, 1 single, 2 suites.
price	£98–£150. Singles £65–£90. Suites £150–£200.
meals	Dinner from £27.
closed	December–January.
directions	From St Austell, B3273, signed Mevagissey, for 5.5 miles past beach caravan park, then left at top of hill. Over mini-r'bout. Hotel on left, signed.

Klaus Wagner & Matthew Mainka

tel	01726 842468
fax	01726 844482
email	stay@trevalsa-hotel.co.uk
web	www.trevalsa-hotel.co.uk

Hotel

Map 1 Entry 34

Wisteria Lodge

Boscundle, Tregrehan, St Austell, Cornwall PL25 3RJ

Is it a small, elegant hotel or a posh B&B? The building is 70s modern in a small residential street – and inside, charming interior designer Sally has created a pampering space. Nothing is too much trouble: food can be cooked to order by the resident chef, beauty treatments and massages will be smoothly arranged, you can laze around the lush garden all day or leap in the hot tub. There are enough staff to pander to a small army; this would be great for a house party. Bedrooms (some with whirlpool baths) are neatly dressed in saffrons, mustards and reds, mattresses are huge and expensive, towels are madly fluffy and the Wisteria Room, which is the most private, has its own terrace. There's nothing quirky or unusual, just seamless service, delicious food at tables for two in the conservatory dining room and a comfortable sitting room to slump in. For the idle it is fine and dandy – but you could, possibly, rouse yourself to walk the mile to the Eden Project, or hop in the car for art at the Tate, theatre at the Minack, great surfing or a visit to Rick Stein's.

rooms	5: 3 doubles, 2 twins/doubles.
price	£90–£160.
meals	Dinner, 3 courses, £35.
closed	Rarely.
directions	A390 2 miles east of St Austell, turning to Tregrehan opp. St Austell Garden Centre. First turning on left marked Boscundle Close, just off on right hand side.

	Sally Wilkins
tel	01726 810800
email	info@wisterialodgehotel.co.uk
web	www.wisterialodgehotel.co.uk

Hotel

Map 1 Entry 35

Cormorant on the River

Golant, Fowey, Cornwall PL23 1LL

Golant is well-hidden from Cornwall's tourist trail and the Cormorant is well-hidden from Golant. You drive along the quay, then climb a short, steep hill. The reward is a breathtaking view of the Fowey estuary, flowing through a wooded landscape. Boats tug on their moorings and birds glide lazily over the water – this is a very English paradise. The view is so good the architect made sure it leapt into every room; nine of the 11 bedrooms have picture windows, so they're great to wake up in. Not bad to sleep in either, with comfy beds, pastel colours and spotless bathrooms. From the entrance, steps lead to a huge light-filled sitting room with log fire, colourful pictures and a big map of the estuary to help plan adventures – walks start from the door. There's a small bar with a good smattering of whiskies and a pretty dining room for delicious food. The room is themed on the legend of Tristan, Isolde and jilted King Mark: a nearby 13th-century church once belonged in the king's domain. In summer, have tea under parasols on the terraced lawn and watch the boats zip by.

rooms	11 twins/doubles.
price	£110–£180. Singles from £65 (winter only).
meals	Dinner, 4 courses, from £29.50.
closed	Rarely.
directions	A390 west towards St Austell, then B3269 to Fowey. After 4 miles, left to Golant. Into village, along quay, hotel signed right, up very steep hill.

Carrie & Colin King

tel	01726 833426
email	relax@cormoranthotels.co.uk
web	www.cormoranthotels.co.uk

Hotel

Map 1 Entry 36

Marina Villa Hotel

Esplanade, Fowey, Cornwall PL23 1HY

Follow the accolades to the Marina Villa Hotel. Tucked into a waterfront street in Fowey, it's obvious why this was a favourite of the Bishop of Truro: it promises some of the most gorgeous river views in Cornwall. You have three buildings in all, some grand marble pillars and a subtly nautical décor that mixes antique with modern. Every bed is noteworthy, some are spectacular, all supremely comfortable, and most bedrooms have views – watch the boats glide by from your balcony. The new Fo'csle suite looks out over the mouth of the river past a huge sculpture of a whale's tail, the Marina's insignia. If you prefer to self-cater you can – the apartments are perfect for families – but the stripey-awned restaurant is the reason to come – for caught-that-day halibut and the freshest lobster, served on Villeroy & Boch. New chef Chris Eden is a local and has returned here to make his mark after a spell in London. James's enthusiasm for this place is reflected in a happy supportive team.

rooms	13 + 4: 12 doubles, 1 suite. 4 self-catering apartments for 4.
price	From £134. Singles from £85. Apartments from £130 for 2.
meals	Lunch £26. Dinner £36.
closed	Rarely.
directions	Once in Fowey, hotel parking up hill.

	James Coggan
tel	01726 833315
fax	01726 832779
email	info@themarinahotel.co.uk
web	www.themarinahotel.co.uk

Hotel

Map 1 Entry 37

The Old Quay House Hotel

28 Fore Street, Fowey, Cornwall PL23 1AQ

The Old Quay House has everything going for it: an idyllic waterfront setting, a colourful history dating back to 1889 and an airy architect-designed interior. Add to this owners passionate about good service and a loyal staff determined to deliver and you have a super little hotel. Stylish bedrooms spoil you all the way. You get goose down duvets, Egyptian white cotton, Japanese cabinets and seriously indulging bathrooms (bathrobes, the odd claw-foot bath, maybe a separate shower). Seven have balconies with glittering estuary views and flood with light, those further back look over the rooftops of Fowey. Settle down to delicious modern European dishes in the 'Q' restaurant, smartly decorated in neutral tones, or spill out onto the terrace overlooking the estuary; you can breakfast here in the sun and watch the ferry chug past. Fowey is enchanting, bustles with life and fills with sailors for the August regatta. Come for the best of old Cornwall — narrow cobbled streets, quaint harbour, long-lost ways. A great place to unwind.

rooms	12: 8 doubles, 4 twins/doubles.
price	£160–£210. Singles £130–£210.
meals	Lunch about £15. Dinner about £30.
closed	Rarely.
directions	Entering Fowey, follow one-way system past church. Hotel on right where road at narrowest point, next to Lloyds Bank. Nearest car park 800 yds.

	Jane & Roy Carson
tel	01726 833302
fax	01726 833668
email	info@theoldquayhouse.com
web	www.theoldquayhouse.com

Hotel

Map 1 Entry 38

Talland Bay Hotel
Porthallow, Looe, Cornwall PL13 2JB

You're lost to the world here – the roller-coaster country lanes have seen to that – but what you find is priceless. The sea sparkles through the pines, horses graze in the fields and two acres of lawn and subtropical gardens end in a ha-ha and a 150-foot drop to the bay. The feel is Mediterranean, with French windows opening from the oak-panelled dining room, sitting room, library and bar onto a paved terrace and heated pool. Long views stretch out to the sea, so lie by the pool with a good book, play croquet, badminton and practise your putting, or drift down to the end of the garden and watch the yachts float by. Some bedrooms are traditional, others are warmly contemporary. A refurbishment is underway – four or five rooms a year; ask for one of these. Vibrant colours, crisp fabrics, sofas in the bigger rooms and sparkly marble bathrooms. Two have their own piece of garden, one has a roof terrace, many have sea views. Pull yourself away and link up with the coastal path, but don't stray too far; elegant food is served at white napped tables, with lobster, crab, scallops fresh from the sea.

rooms	22: 17 twins/doubles, 3 suites, 2 singles.
price	£95-£195. Suites £170-£225. Singles from £70. Half-board from £80 p.p.
meals	Light lunch £5-£15. Dinner £32.50.
closed	Rarely.
directions	From Looe, A387 for Polperro. Ignore 1st sign to Talland. After 2 miles, left at x-roads; follow signs.

	George & Mary Granville
tel	01503 272667
fax	01503 272940
email	info@tallandbayhotel.co.uk
web	www.tallandbayhotel.co.uk

Hotel

Map 1 Entry 39

Hell Bay

Bryher, Isles of Scilly, Cornwall TR23 0PR

Nothing stands between Bryher and America. Stand windswept on the edge of the world as the rollers crash in: the autumn gales are thrilling, and those white summer beaches are a flipflop away from your California beachhut room. Hell Bay is a stylishly simple escape for anyone drawn by remote outposts and the promise of a perfect cocktail. The bedrooms are in separate buildings – elegant and fresh with nautical touches. Bleached wood, stripes, checks and pastel shades, views – from most – of the sea and masses of space, inside and out, for relaxing and for children's clutter. The high-ceilinged Lookout Lounge and bar are comfortable with Lloyd Loom furniture, and the whole place vibrant with works from the owners' modern art collection. Come for strawberries and asparagus from local suppliers, lobster and crab from the ocean – all beautifully prepared and presented, with mini dishes for children. Loll by the heated outdoor pool, be pampered by spa and sauna, spot cormorants and seals on an inter-island hop, visit neighbouring island Tresco's world-famous gardens. Special indeed.

rooms	25 suites.
price	Half-board £120-£250 p.p. Child in parent's room £40 (incl. high tea). Under 2s free.
meals	Half-board only. Lunch, 2 courses, from £15.
closed	3 January-11 February.
directions	Ship/helicopter from Penzance, or fly to St Mary's from Bristol, Southampton, Exeter, Newquay or Land's End. Hotel can arrange.

	Philip Callan
tel	01720 422947
fax	01720 423004
email	contactus@hellbay.co.uk
web	www.hellbay.co.uk

Hotel

Map 1 Entry 40

Crosby Lodge
High Crosby, Carlisle, Cumbria CA6 4QZ

Restful, opulent, blissfully detached from the outside world, Crosby Lodge welcomes all. Come to elope (Gretna is close) or just to escape. Patricia is everywhere, always impeccably dressed, never seeming to stop, but never seeming to hurry, either. She used to be a banker – the considerate kind, what else! – and this original 'country-house hotel' remains a laid-back family affair. Michael and Patricia fell in love with the house long before it came on the market – 30-odd years ago now – and the chef has been here since the start; the dining is elaborate and classical. All is warm and cosy within: open fires, polished banisters, family portraits, a wonderful antique chaise longue, a stunning bay window with shutters. Bedrooms are (mostly) big, bright and fun, with flowery fabrics lovingly chosen – even the shower curtains have two layers of ruffles. You get arches and alcoves, ornate lamps and candlesticks, a huge antique wardrobe or a lovely gnarled half-tester. Outside you might sip a pre-prandial glass in the walled garden, or chance upon an artist sketching a pastoral view.

rooms	11: 2 doubles, 5 twins/doubles, 1 single, 3 family.
price	£130-£180. Singles £85-£95.
meals	Lunch from £5. Dinner, 4 courses, £35.
closed	Christmas-mid-January.
directions	M6 junc. 44, A689 east for 3.5 miles, then right to Low Crosby. Through village. House on right.

Michael & Patricia Sedgwick
tel	01228 573618
fax	01228 573428
email	enquiries@crosbylodge.co.uk
web	www.crosbylodge.co.uk

Hotel

Map 5 Entry 41

Number Thirty One

31 Howard Place, Carlisle, Cumbria CA1 1HR

It is difficult to decide which one of these two gems is the best. Is it the fine bow-fronted Victorian house in a quiet, leaf-lined street? Or Pru, who will greet you with an immaculate tray of proper tea-time treats, like homemade banana bread thickly buttered? The sitting room is heaving with Victorian collectibles: brass, pot plants, a ticking grandfather clock, gilt mirrors, tasselled curtains, an ornate glass table and battalions of knick-knacks guarding every buffed surface. Bedrooms are also dressed to the nines, colour-themed and deeply comfortable. Every wall is covered in pictures and old photographs of Carlisle; make the most of Pru and her local knowledge: this is her stomping ground and she knows it inside out. Husband Mike does the cooking – a set menu of mainly British and French dishes with a Mediterranean twang, served at separate tables in a dark red dining room with mahogany bookshelves and a view to a courtyard garden. The start of 81 miles of Hadrian's Wall is right outside the door and Pru will make you a solid packed lunch, probably with a starched linen napkin.

rooms	3: 2 doubles, 1 twin/double.
price	£85–£100. Singles £60-£69.
meals	Packed lunch £7.50. Dinner £20.
closed	Rarely.
directions	From M6 junc. 43, A69 Warwick Rd towards city centre. Right after 5th set of traffic lights into Howard Place. House at far end on left.

	Pru & Mike Irving
tel	01228 597080
fax	01228 597080
email	pruirving@aol.com
web	www.number31.co.uk

B&B

Map 5 Entry 42

White Moss House

Rydal Water, Grasmere, Cumbria LA22 9SE

At the epicentre of Wordsworth country: walk north a mile to his home at Dove Cottage or south to his house at Rydal Mount. The paths are old and you can follow his footsteps up fell and through wood. He knew White Moss, too – he bought it for his son and came here to escape. The Dixons have lived here for a quarter century and they have kept the feel of a home: deep armchairs and heaps of books, flowers on sofas and in vases, a cosy woodburning stove. There's a small bar in an old linen cupboard, and after-dinner coffee in the sitting room brings out the house-party feel. Bedrooms range in size but not comfort and all have good views; those at the back, away from the main road, are the quietest. Expect pretty chintz, a sprinkling of books and magazines, Radox in bathrooms to soothe fell-worn feet. The cottage is in a quiet, beautiful spot further up the hill, with the best view of all right out across Rydal Water. Then there's the small matter of food, all cooked by Peter – five courses of famed indulgence await, and superb wines. *Free use of local leisure centre. Children over five welcome.*

rooms	6: 2 doubles, 3 twins/doubles, 1 cottage for 2-4.
price	£79–£129.
meals	Dinner, 5 courses, £39.50. Not Sundays and Mondays.
closed	December–mid-February.
directions	From Ambleside, north on A591. House signed on right at far end of Rydal Water.

	Susan & Peter Dixon
tel	01539 435295
fax	01539 435516
email	sue@whitemoss.com
web	www.whitemoss.com

Hotel

Map 5 Entry 47

Old Dungeon Ghyll
Great Langdale, Ambleside, Cumbria LA22 9JY

One of England's most famous walking hotels; if you're looking for a night in frontier land, you'll find it here. It's an old favourite of hardy mountaineers – Tenzing and Hilary stayed before scaling Everest – and it stands at the foot of Raven Cragg, surrounded by spectacular peaks. The house was given over to the National Trust in 1928 and has been leased as a hotel/pub every since. Hikers pour off the mountains, ruddy from the day's exertions, full of stories of courage in the face of adversity – mist, driving rain, mobile phone failure and the like. They head for the Walkers' Bar, with cattle-stall seating and a big fire, and feast on decent grub, mugs of tea, and God's own beer: Yates. In wild weather old stone walls keep the wind at bay; when it's fine there are tables outside with Tolkeinian views in every direction. Next door is the hotel, with a crackling fire in the residents' lounge and a dining room for great breakfasts. Bedrooms are simple, not all have their own bathrooms; if you don't mind that, you'll find thick bedspreads, brass beds, good mattresses and fat pillows.

rooms	13: 6 twins/doubles; 5 singles sharing 1 bath & 1 shower; 2 family rooms each with separate bath.
price	£80–£136.
meals	Bar meals from £7.
closed	Christmas.
directions	From Ambleside, A593 for Coniston, right on B5343. Hotel on right after 5 miles, signed, past Great Langdale campsite.

	Neil Walmsley
tel	01539 437272
fax	01539 437272
email	neil.odg@lineone.net
web	www.odg.co.uk

Hotel

Map 5 Entry 48

Gilpin Lodge

Crook Road, Windermere, Cumbria LA23 3NE

One of the loveliest places to stay in the country. Staff are delightful, the house is a treasure trove, and the food, Michelin-starred, is heavenly. Run by two generations of the same family, Gilpin delivers at every turn. Clipped country-house elegance flows throughout: smouldering coals, Zoffany wallpaper, gilded mirrors, flowers everywhere. Afternoon tea, served wherever you want it, comes on silver trays. You're in 20 acres of silence, so throw open doors and sit on the terrace surrounded by pots of colour or stroll through the garden for magnolias, rhododendrons, cherry blossom or climbing roses and a fine copper beech. Bedrooms are predictably divine with crisp white linen, exquisite fabrics, delicious art; nothing is left to chance. Some have French windows that open onto the garden, others have private terraces complete with hot tub, all have sofas or armchairs. As for Chris Meredith's food – the foie gras with a Sauternes jelly was faultless, while a three-page breakfast menu includes nine different teas and strawberry sorbet served with pink champagne. Out of this world.

rooms	20: 4 doubles, 3 twins/doubles, 6 garden rooms, 7 suites.
price	Half-board £120–£165 p.p. Singles from £175.
meals	Half-board only. Lunch £10–£25. Dinner, 5 courses, included; non-residents £42.50.
closed	2 weeks in January.
directions	M6 junc 36, A591 north, then B5284 west for Bowness. On right after 4 miles.

John, Christine, Barnaby & Zoe Cunliffe

tel	01539 488818
fax	01539 488058
email	hotel@gilpinlodge.co.uk
web	www.gilpinlodge.co.uk

Hotel

Map 5 Entry 51

Aynsome Manor Hotel

Cartmel, Grange-over-Sands, Cumbria LA11 6HH

Stand at the front door of Aynsome and look across ancient meadows to Cartmel Priory, still magnificent after 800 years, and still the heart of a small, thriving community. Strike out across the fields to the village – a three-quarter-mile walk – and discover its gentle secrets. The house, too, echoes with history: it was home to the descendants of the Earl of Pembroke; in 1930, it gave up a long-held secret when a suit of chain armour dating back to 1335 was found behind a wall. Dine on the best of local produce in the gorgeous, panelled, candlelit dining room with its ornate tongue-and-ball ceiling. In the hall, a melodious grandfather clock, a wood and coal fire and carved oak panels, the gift of an 1839 storm. A cantilevered spiral staircase with a cupola-domed window leads up to the old-fashioned lounge where fires burn in a marble Adams-style fireplace. Bedrooms are simple, comfortable, and some are small; beamy no. 13, in the attic, was the 'wig room'. Race-goers will love the National Hunt racecourse, and the Varley family is delightful. *No under fives in restaurant.*

rooms	12: 5 doubles, 4 twins, 1 four-poster, 2 family.
price	£85–£110. Singles from £55. Half-board £65–£81 p.p.
meals	Dinner, 4 courses, £25.
closed	January.
directions	From M6 junc. 36 take A590 for Barrow. At top of Lindale Hill, follow signs left to Cartmel. Hotel on right 3 miles from A590.

	Christopher & Andrea Varley
tel	01539 536653
fax	01539 536016
email	info@aynsomemanorhotel.co.uk
web	www.aynsomemanorhotel.co.uk

Hotel

Map 5 Entry 52

Hipping Hall

Cowan Bridge, Kirkby Lonsdale, Cumbria LA6 2JJ

You get a bit of time travel at Hipping Hall: 15th-century bricks and mortar, 21st-century lipstick and pearls. It's all the result of a total refurbishment, and funked-up classical interiors elate. Zoffany wallpaper in a swanky sitting room, red leather armchairs in an airy bar, and varnished floorboards in the old hall – overlooked by a minstrels' gallery, its ceilings open to the rafters. The flagged conservatory is home to an ancient well and opens onto a courtyard where tables and chairs are scattered in summer. Upstairs, fabulous bedrooms in various shades of white contrast with the vibrant colours of the ground floor. Fine ivory carpets, white leather bedheads, muslin canopies and padded window seats. Bathrooms are the best and come in slate or creamy limestone, some with power showers, others with deep baths too, all with fluffy white towels and bathrobes. As for the food, expect something special, perhaps English asparagus with a garlic purée, fillet of veal with glazed sweetbreads, then caramelised pears with a prune and armagnac ice cream. *Minimum stay two nights at weekends.*

rooms	9: 7 doubles, 2 twins/doubles.
price	£140–£210. Singles from £105. Half-board from £110 p.p.
meals	Lunch £15–£25. Dinner, 3 courses, £42.50.
closed	1st two weeks in January.
directions	M6, junc. 36, then A65 east. House on left, 2.5 miles after Kirkby Lonsdale.

Andrew Wildsmith
tel	01524 271187
fax	01524 272452
email	info@hippinghall.com
web	www.hippinghall.com

Hotel

Map 6 Entry 53

Lovelady Shield

Nenthead Road, Alston, Cumbria CA9 3LF

Remote, unspoilt, beguiling – if you want to leave the world behind, the High Pennines is a fine spot to do it. At Lovelady, the River Nent runs through the garden; you can follow it up to Alston, then come home over the fell. The house, hidden down a long and suitably bumpy drive, was rebuilt in 1832, but the cellars date from 1690 and the foundations stretch back to the 14th century when a religious order stood here. No noise, save for sheep in the fields, birds in the trees and the burbling river that you can hear if you sleep with your window open. Peter and Marie run the place with a hint of eccentricity and a relaxed country-house feel: log fires in the sitting room, a well-stocked library in the hall and a snug rag-rolled bar. Long windows bring in the views, but doors fly open in summer for Pimms on the veranda or croquet on the lawn. Dine on super food amid gilt mirrors, sash windows and fresh flowers, then retire to bright, uncluttered bedrooms that come in stylish yellows and whites. You'll find TVs and Scrabble, a sofa if there's room, and most have gorgeous views. Hadrian's Wall is close.

rooms	12: 9 doubles, 2 twins, 1 four-poster.
price	Half-board £110-£145 p.p.
meals	Lunch by arrangement. Dinner, 3 couses, included; non-residents £37.50.
closed	Rarely.
directions	From Alston, A689 east for 2 miles. House on left at junction of B6294, signed.

	Peter & Marie Haynes
tel	01434 381203
fax	01434 381515
email	enquiries@lovelady.co.uk
web	www.lovelady.co.uk

Hotel

Map 6 Entry 54

The Old Rectory

Martinhoe, Exmoor National Park, Devon EX31 4QT

As you quietly succumb to the wonderful sense of spiritual calm, it's hard to conceive that one field away the land skids to a halt and spectacular cliffs drop 800 feet. The Exmoor plateau meets the sea abruptly at the village of Martinhoe – 'hoe' is Saxon for high ground – creating a breathtaking view as you approach. This lovely understated hotel stands next to an 11th-century church in three acres of mature garden. Nurtured by clergy past, the garden now occupies the affection of Chris and Stewart: birdsong, waterfalls, scented azaleas and the bizarre gunnera only hint at its allure. This is a gentle retreat with two elegant drawing rooms, dedicated to food and marvellous hospitality. Expect much local produce on the table: homemade breads, lamb from the moor, West country cheeses; even the water, filtered and purified, is from a local borehole. Traditional bedrooms have Laura Ashley wallpaper and the odd Waring & Gillow antique, and one has a balcony; bathrooms sparkle. Grapes from the 200-year-old vine above your head fill fruit bowls in season.

rooms	9: 5 doubles, 1 twin, 2 twins/doubles, 1 suite.
price	£104–£134. Singles £67–£87. Half-board incl. afternoon tea £80–£100 p.p.
meals	Dinner, 5 courses, £33.
closed	November–February.
directions	A39 for Lynton, by-pass Parracombe, left after 2 miles, for Martinhoe. Across common, left into village, entrance 1st on right by church.

Stewart Willis & Chris Legg

tel	01598 763368
fax	01598 763567
email	info@oldrectoryhotel.co.uk
web	www.oldrectoryhotel.co.uk

Hotel

Map 2 Entry 59

Broomhill Art Hotel & Sculpture Gardens

Muddiford, Devon EX31 4EX

Broomhill is a one off and anyone with the slightest interest in art will love it here. Owner-run and owner-loved, Rinus and Aniet, both wonderfully easy-going, came to fulfil a generous dream: to make art more accessible in the country. Nine years on and you find original pieces on every wall, and a dazzling sculpture garden that's floodlit at night and which defies overstatment; huge bronzes lurk behind trees, paths cut through ten acres of glorious woodland. Back at the hotel, a ten-foot-high red stiletto on the front lawn gives some idea of what to expect, but step inside and find galleries all around (no guest sitting room, just sofas in the galleries). The whole place elates, so even if you don't come to stay, pop in and take a look. Bedrooms, now refurbished, are good value for money. One has a sleigh bed, some overlook the garden, all have pretty linen and original art. The restaurant serves bistro-style food on Friday and Saturday nights; as much as possible is sourced from local farms and markets. Live jazz, lectures and poetry… if it comes along they put it on.

rooms	6: 4 doubles, 2 twins.
price	£70. Singles from £42.50.
meals	Lunch from £5. Dinner from £15. Fridays & Saturdays only. Pubs & restaurants nearby.
closed	20 December-mid-January.
directions	From Barnstable, A39 north towards Lynton, then left onto B3230, following brown signs to Sculpture Gardens & hotel.

	Rinus & Aniet Van de Sande
tel	01271 850262
fax	01271 850575
email	info@broomhillart.co.uk
web	www.broomhillart.co.uk

Hotel

Map 2 Entry 60

Heasley House Hotel
Heasley Mill, North Molton, Devon EX36 3LE

A Georgian dower house in a sleepy hamlet on the southern fringes of Exmoor. Paul and Jan escaped London armed with paint brushes, dispatching the chintz in favour of an airy elegance, and you now get stripped floors, open fires, Farrow & Ball paints and an eclectic collection of art. Best of all is Paul's food — Heasley is pretty much a restaurant with rooms — so come for fresh Devon asparagus, marinated leg of local lamb, then roasted pears with marsala and crème fraîche. Whatever can be is locally sourced, with beef from Exmoor and game from nearby estates, while herbs come from a kitchen garden that will soon supply vegetables and soft fruits. Breakfast is a long lazy affair with freshly-squeezed juice, fresh kippers and no time limits, so dig into bacon and eggs, then set off for the beach at Croyde, imperious walks on Exmoor or a canter across the gallops. Super-comfy rooms have big beds dressed in Egyptian cotton, extra-wide baths or power showers. There are gardens back and front, the sound of running water, and Paul's collection of brandy or armagnac is not to be missed.

rooms	8: 7 twins/doubles, 1 suite.
price	£98. Suite £120. Singles from £75.
meals	Dinner, 3 courses, £21.50.
closed	Christmas Day, Boxing Day & February.
directions	From junc. 27 of M5, A361 to Barnstaple. Turn right at sign for North Molton, then left for Heasley Mill.

	Paul & Jan Gambrill
tel	01598 740213
email	enquiries@heasley-house.co.uk
web	www.heasley-house.co.uk

Hotel

Map 2 Entry 61

Eastacott Barton
Umberleigh, Devon EX37 9AJ

A small, intimate country-house hotel — without the meals but with stacks of special touches. Sue and James used to own fabulously grand Lewtrenchard Manor, and the way they do things is second to none. Log fires in two sitting rooms, three lakes, long views down the lush Taw Valley, a new larch wood and six guinea fowl that preen like super models (long legs, beautifully feathered). The Victorian house, once an estate cottage, has been renovated with no expense spared, and now the Murrays have added a terracotta-floored garden room for morning feasts concocted by Sue: eggs from Eastacott hens, locally made sausages, delicious homemade preserves. Bedrooms are immaculate (crisp linen, thick carpets, south-facing windows, big comfy beds). Those in the house have toile de Jouy quilts, elegantly dressed windows, sumptuous baths; those in the barn are less glam, but have beams and equally lovely views. These 27 acres lie at the end of a lane in deepest Devon, so don't expect to be disturbed. James and Sue can steer you in cultural and gastronomic directions; their welcome is first-class.

rooms	5 doubles.
price	£70–£115. Singles £50–£95.
meals	Pubs/restaurants 3 miles.
	Dinner parties by arrangement.
closed	Rarely.
directions	From South Molton B3227 for Torrington. After 6 miles, left to Eastacott. Continue on lane 1-2 miles. Do not turn left at stone cross (to Eastacott!); go straight; entrance 700 yds on left.

	Sue & James Murray
tel	01769 540545
email	stay@eastacott.com
web	www.eastacott.com

B&B

Map 2 Entry 62

Devon

Northcote Manor
Burrington, Umberleigh, Devon EX37 9LZ

If you're in need of sanctuary then follow the footsteps of those wise 15th-century monks who chose to come to Northcote. The long drive climbs lazily through thick woodland with emerald green valleys and stunning views; the elegant wisteria-clad house with tall chimneys has been lounging here for hundreds of years. The gardens are gorgeous and beautifully kept: good specimen trees, gravel paths, a glassy pond and a newly restored water garden are a must for a gentle stroll. The soundtrack is pure L P Hartley; loud bird song punctuated by the thwack of a tennis ball or crack of a croquet mallet. Cheryl will quietly and professionally show you through the studded oak doors to large, light, comfortable rooms with big windows, cosy chairs, fires in winter. The colours are creams, yellows and blues; some chintzes mixed with stripes and tapestries on deep window seats. Old-fashioned bedrooms with dark antique furniture are a good size, all have lovely views, fresh flowers in tall vases and warm, spotless bathrooms. Eat well in the formal dining room with its hand-painted wall murals.

rooms	11: 4 doubles, 2 twins/doubles, 1 four-poster, 4 suites.
price	£150-£250. Singles from £90. Half-board (min. 2 nights) from £100 p.p.
meals	Dinner £38.
closed	Rarely.
directions	M5, junc. 27, A361 to S. Molton. Fork left onto B3227; left on A377 for Exeter. Entrance 4.1 miles on right, signed.

Cheryl Hinksman

tel	01769 560501
fax	01769 560770
email	rest@northcotemanor.co.uk
web	www.northcotemanor.co.uk

Hotel

Map 2 Entry 63

Halmpstone Manor

Bishop's Tawton, Barnstaple, Devon EX32 0EA

Charles and Jane are preserving a long tradition of farmhouse hospitality at Halmpstone, gently at odds with the 21st century – in 1630, John Westcote described his stay here as "delightful". The handsome Queen Anne manor you see today was completed in 1701, after fire destroyed much of the original house in 1633; its proportions remain charming. Fresh flowers adorn rooms, pink walls cheer, family photos beam from silver frames, china figures stand on parade… all is traditional. Bedrooms in pink and peach are immaculate, with floral coronets, draped four-posters, decanters of sherry, fresh fruit and more flowers. Afternoon tea is included and you can dine by candlelight in the lovely panelled dining room; dig into fresh English asparagus, fillet of ruby red beef, then brûléed lemon tart. Charles was born here and has run the farm for much of his life. Both are 'hands-on' and welcoming. Halmpstone means 'Holy Boundary Stone' and the building faces south to Dartmoor; walk in the pretty garden, or stray further.

rooms	4: 3 twins/doubles, 1 four-poster.
price	£100–£140. Singles £70.
meals	Dinner, 5 courses, £30, by arrangement.
closed	Christmas & New Year.
directions	From Barnstaple, south on A377. Left opp. petrol station, after Bishop's Tawton, signed Cobbaton & Chittlehampton. After 2 miles, right. House on left after 200 yds.

Jane & Charles Stanbury

tel	01271 830321
fax	01271 830826
email	charles@halmpstonemanor.co.uk
web	www.halmpstonemanor.co.uk

B&B

Map 2 Entry 64

The Red Lion Hotel

The Quay, Clovelly, Bideford, Devon EX39 5TF

Clovelly has been spared time's march, partly because of its position – and partly because it is a tenanted estate. It is completely car-free. The houses perch like seagulls' nests on ledges cut into the cliff and many still have original cob walls of red earth and straw. A steep cobbled path snakes down to a small harbour, and there's the Red Lion, right on the quayside, looking out across the Atlantic – you'll hear the sound of the sea from every room. It's an eccentric place but pleasantly so, with laid-back staff and friendly management. Smart bedrooms with nautical touches are up-to-date, thanks to a recent makeover, and every single one has sea or harbour views. Wonderful seafood is delivered straight from the fishing boat to the kitchen. Travel out to Lundy Island, a wildlife sanctuary, or walk along Hobby Drive, a beautiful coastal walk laid out in the early 1800s. The late Christine Hamlyn, anointed 'Queen of Clovelly', restored many of the cottages and is still loved by villagers. There's nowhere quite like it.

rooms	11: 7 doubles, 2 twins, 2 family.
price	£114–£123. Singles from £57. Half-board £77–£82.50 p.p. (min. 2 nights).
meals	Bar lunch from £3.25. Dinner £25.
closed	Rarely.
directions	From Bideford, A39 for Bude for 12 miles, right at r'bout, for Clovelly. Left fork before Visitor Centre, left at white rails down steep hill.

	John Rous
tel	01237 431237
fax	01237 431044
email	redlion@clovelly.co.uk
web	www.redlion-clovelly.co.uk

Hotel

Map 2 Entry 65

Blagdon Manor
Ashwater, Devon EX21 5DF

You'll have the warmest of welcomes from Steve and Liz in their supremely comfortable country house in the middle of nowhere – actually, in 20 acres of woodland and moor – with huge views stretching to Yes Tor. There are doors that open onto the garden in the stone-flagged library, an open fire in the sitting room, a panelled bar in what was the 16th-century kitchen, and a conservatory for breakfast where you can watch the birds flit by. Bedrooms are equiped to spoil. Come for decanters of sherry and fresh flowers, warm country florals and bathrobes. Colours are bold: blues, yellows, lilacs and greens; one room has a fine purple carpet. You get small sofas if there's room, the odd beam, a bit of chintz and comfortably snug bathrooms. All rooms are the same price; the first to book gets the biggest, but none are small. Steve's cooking is not to be missed, perhaps smoked duck breast, local lamb in a rosemary jus, a trio of citrus puddings. Blagdon is dog-friendly (a couple of labradors sleep in front of the fire) and there are towels, blankets, bowls, treats and toys.

rooms	7: 5 doubles, 2 twins/doubles.
price	£120. Singles £85.
meals	Lunch from £17 (Wed–Sun). Dinner from £31.
closed	2 weeks in January; 2 weeks in October; New Year.
directions	A30, then north from Launceston on A388. Ignore signs to Ashwater. Right at Blagdon Cross, signed. Right; right again; house signed right.

	Steve & Liz Morey
tel	01409 211224
fax	01409 211634
email	stay@blagdon.com
web	www.blagdon.com

Hotel

Map 2 Entry 66

The Dartmoor Inn
Lydford, Okehampton, Devon EX20 4AY

There aren't many inns where you can sink into Zoffany-clad winged armchairs in the dining room, snooze on a pink silk bed under a French chandelier, or shop for rhinestone brooches and Provençal quilts while you wait for the wild sea bass to crisp in the pan. Different rules apply at the Dartmoor. This is the template of deep-country chic, a fairytale inn dressed up as a country local. True, there is a snug bar at the front where you can perch on a stool and knock back a glass of ale, but then again the walls are coated in textured wallpaper, gilded mirrors sit above smouldering fireplaces and upstairs a shimmering velvet throw is spread out across a sublimely upholstered sleigh bed. Come for stripped wood floors, timber-framed walls, sand-blasted settles and country-house rugs. Add to this wonderful staff and Philip's ambrosial food (fillet steak for breakfast, ham hock terrine for lunch, free-range duck for dinner) and you have a very special place. Triple-glazed bedroom windows defeat road noise and ensure a good night's rest. The moors are on your doorstep, so walk in the wind, then eat, drink and sleep.

rooms	3 doubles.
price	£90-£115.
meals	Lunch from £5.
	Dinner from £15.
closed	Occasionally.
directions	North from Tavistock on A386.
	Pub on right at Lydford turnoff.

	Karen & Philip Burgess
tel	01822 820221
fax	01822 820494
email	info@dartmoorinn.co.uk
web	www.dartmoorinn.com

Inn

Map 2 Entry 69

The Arundell Arms

Lifton, Devon PL16 0AA

A tiny interest in fishing would not go amiss, though the people here are so kind they welcome everyone. Anne has been at the helm for 45 years; her MBE for services to tourism is richly deserved. This is a *very* settled hotel, with Mrs VB, as staff call her fondly, quietly presiding over all; during a superb lunch – St Enodoc asparagus, scallops, then homemade chocs – she asked after an 80th birthday party, ensuring their day was memorable. Over the years the hotel has resuscitated buildings at the heart of the village: the old police station and magistrates court is a pub, the old school a conference centre. Pride of place is the funnel-roofed cock-fighting pit, one of only two left in England and now the rod room, where local knowledge is shared generously every morning. Anne's late husband wrote about fly-fishing for *The Times* and it's no surprise to discover that this is one of the best fishing hotels in England – or that they own 20 miles of the Tamar and its tributaries. Come to try your luck or merely to search for otter and kingfisher on its banks. As for the hotel, simply divine from top to toe.

rooms	21: 9 doubles, 7 twins, 3 singles, 2 suites.	
price	£155-£180. Singles from £99.	
meals	Bar meals £7-£15. Dinner from £36.	
closed	Christmas.	
directions	A30 south-west from Exeter, past Okehampton. Lifton 0.5 miles off A30, 3 miles east of Launceston & signed. Hotel in centre of village.	

	Anne Voss-Bark
tel	01566 784666
fax	01566 784494
email	reservations@arundellarms.com
web	www.arundellarms.com

Hotel

Map 2 Entry 70

Hotel Endsleigh
Milton Abbot, Tavistock, Devon PL19 0PQ

At the bottom of a long rhododendron-lined drive with heart-stopping views over the Tamar valley, this cottage orné, once home to the 6th Duke of Bedford, is the perfect antidote to bling culture. Step inside to find a grand country house of old, with log fires, a panelled dining room, Herculean vases of garden flowers and rare botanical pictures mixed with modern art and sculpture; only the abundance of discreet, friendly staff reminds you you're in a hotel. Elysian bedrooms, the very best, flood with light and soft colours, crisp white linen, gorgeous fabrics, idyllic views. Bathrooms are just as good: large, coddling and warm. Crests of the Duke's family and friends are embossed in the panelled walls of the dining room, where delicious local produce is served on fine china. Walk off your excess in 108 acres of woodland and exquisite garden (designed by Humphrey Repton), or get up early and cast a fly; the hotel has seven rods on the Tamar. Alternatively, potter around the croquet field, scoff afternoon tea in the library or doze in a deckchair on the terrace. *Minimum stay two nights at weekends.*

rooms	16: 5 doubles, 8 twins/doubles, 2 suites, 1 lodge for 2-4.
price	£200-£300. Singles from £180. Suites £360. Lodge £400.
meals	Lunch £21-£27. Dinner £38.
closed	Never.
directions	A30 to Lauceston, A388 south, then B3362 east for Tavistock. Through Milton Abbott and right at school. After a mile, right at the Lodge. 1.8m down drive.

	Alex Polizzi
tel	01822 870000
fax	01822 870578
email	mail@hotelendsleigh.com
web	www.hotelendsleigh.com

Hotel

Map 2 Entry 71

Tor Cottage
Chillaton, Tavistock, Devon PL16 0JE

At the end of the track, a blissful valley lost to the world. This is an indulging hideaway, wrapped up in 28 acres of majestic country, and those who like to be pampered in peace will find heaven. Hills rise, cows sleep, streams run, birds sing. Bridlepaths lead onto the hill, wild flowers carpet a hay meadow. Big rooms in converted outbuildings are the lap of rustic luxury, each with a wood-burner and private terrace. All are impeccable, one filled with Art Deco, one straight out of *House and Garden*, one whitewashed with ceilings open to the rafters. Best of all is the cabin in its own valley – a wonderland in the woods – with hammocks hanging in the trees and a stream passing below. You can self-cater here and eat on the deck while deer wander in the trees. Breakfasts served in the conservatory promise homemade muesli, local sausages and farm-fresh eggs, but if you get peckish later in the day, wash down smoked salmon sandwiches with a glass of sangria while sunbathing by the pool. Staff couldn't be nicer, guests return. *Minimum stay two nights. Special deals available.*

rooms	5: 3 doubles, 1 twin/double; 1 woodland cabin for 2 (B&B or self-catering).
price	£140–£150. Singles £94. Self-catering from £120 (min. 3 nights).
meals	Supper, 3 courses, £24. On request.
closed	B&B: Christmas & New Year. Self-catering: Never.
directions	In Chillaton keep pub & PO on left, up hill towards Tavistock. After 300 yds, right down bridleway.

	Maureen Rowlatt
tel	01822 860248
fax	01822 860126
email	info@torcottage.co.uk
web	www.torcottage.co.uk

B&B

Map 2 Entry 72

Browns Hotel

80 West Street, Tavistock, PL19 8AQ

The Romans came first and left a well; you can stand on a sheet of glass in the conservatory and peer into it or simply drink its water. Then came the Benedictines, who built an abbey; old carved stones unearthed during renovations are now on show. If tradition holds they'll find Roberts radios, four-poster beds and antique kilims when they rebuild in 200 years. The house dates from 1700 and was Tavistock's first coaching inn. It's still the best place to stay in town, with plump-cushioned armchairs in front of the fire, shiny wood floors and exposed stone walls in the restaurant, and a fine stone-flagged conservatory for bacon and eggs in the morning. Clutter-free bedrooms have a clipped elegance: Farrow & Ball yellows, Egyptian cotton, latticed windows and spoiling bathrobes. Some in the coach house at the back are huge and come with cathedral ceilings. Dine under beams, warmed by open fires, on Cornish scallops, local duck, calvados mousse and apple sorbet. Tavistock is an ancient market town and its famous goose fair takes place in October. Don't miss Dartmoor for uplifting walks.

rooms	20: 11 doubles, 3 twins, 6 singles.
price	£110–£180. Singles from £75.
meals	Bar meals from £7. Lunch from £15. Dinner £35.
closed	Never.
directions	Leave A386 for Tavistock. Right, at statue, for town centre. Left at T-junction, them immediately left into West Street. Hotel on right. Ask about parking.

Peter Brown & Martin Ball

tel	01822 618686
fax	01822 618646
email	enquiries@brownsdevon.co.uk
web	www.brownsdevon.co.uk

Hotel

Map 2 Entry 73

The Horn of Plenty
Gulworthy, Tavistock, Devon PL19 8JD

Wade your way through wild flowers down tiny lanes to this most attractive house built by the Duke of Bedford for a local mine captain. A circular flower bed surrounded by pebbles tinkles with a fountain, a wisteria trails grandly up the side. Step in to a fabulous mix of styles – 17th-century Dutch Master meets 21st-century chic. The Michelin-starred dining room has huge plate-glass walls overlooking miles of the Tamar valley, yellow and cream striped walls, modern art and delightfully un-matched tables. Nibble something homemade and delicious with a glass of wine in the bay-windowed drawing room before a fabulous dinner, perhaps seared squid and king prawns, spring lamb in a red wine sauce, then lemon pannacotta with marinated oranges. Bedrooms and bathrooms are nurturing and spoiling with pale woodwork and walls, large soft beds dressed in smooth white linen, fresh flowers and good antiques. Explore five acres of gardens and orchard, find seats and hide away with a book, toddle back when you want a drink. Staff are young, cheerful and piercingly efficient.

rooms	10 twins/doubles.
price	£140-£230. Singles £130-£220.
meals	Lunch, 3 courses, £26. Dinner, 3 courses, £42.50.
closed	25/26 December.
directions	A386 north to Tavistock. Turn left onto A390, following signs to Liskeard. After 3 miles, right at Gulworthy Cross. Signed.

Paul Roston & Peter Gorton

tel	01822 832528
fax	01822 834390
email	enquiries@thehornofplenty.co.uk
web	www.thehornofplenty.co.uk

Restaurant with Rooms

Map 2 Entry 74

Lydgate House
Postbridge, Dartmoor, Devon PL20 6TJ

You're in 36 acres of heaven, so come for the sheer wonder of Dartmoor: deer and badger, fox and pheasant, kingfisher and woodpecker. A 30-minute circular walk takes you over the East Dart, up to a wild hay meadow where rare orchids flourish, then back down to a 12th-century clapper bridge; sensational. Herons dive in the river by day; you may get a glimpse from the conservatory as you dig into your bacon and eggs. The house is a dream, a nourishing stream of homely comforts: a drying room for walkers, deep white sofas, walls of books, a wood burner and a cat in the armchair. Cindy, a classics teacher, and Peter, a surveyor, somehow find time to double up as host and hostess extraordinaire: expect a good chat, delicious home cooking and peace when you want it. Bedrooms – two are huge – are warmly cossetting: crisply floral with comfy beds and Radox in the bathrooms. Rescued sheep live in the top field and are partial to a slice of toast, while moonwort grows in the hay meadow. Legend says if gathered by moonlight it unleashes magical properties; clearly someone has.

rooms	6: 4 doubles, 1 twin/double, 1 single.
price	£110–£140. Singles from £60.
meals	Dinner, 3 courses, £28.50.
closed	Weekends only November–February.
directions	From Exeter A30 west to Whiddon Down, A382 south to Moretomhampstead, B3212 west to Postbridge. In village, left at pub. House signed straight ahead.

Cindy & Peter Farrington

tel	01822 880209
fax	01822 880202
email	lydgatehouse@email.com
web	www.lydgatehouse.co.uk

Hotel

Map 2 Entry 75

Sandy Park Inn
Sandy Park, Chagford, Devon TQ13 8JW

A small thatched pub in a tiny village on Dartmoor. The river Teign runs through the valley, so follow its path for views that lift the soul. Those of a more sedentary disposition can sit in the beer garden and take in the view while sampling local delicacies. This is a cracking country boozer, loved by locals, and with food that punches above its weight; Barry the butcher brings in slow-grown pork off the moor, the cod comes battered in beer, the cheeses are all local. It's snug, with low ceilings, flagged floors, country rugs and huge knots of wood crackling in an old stone fire. Standing room only at the bar at weekends; local musicians occasionally drop in to play on Sunday nights. Bedrooms sparkle with unexpected treats – flat screen TVs, CD players, padded headboards, colourful throws – but the bar is lively, and a night here will only suit those who want to have some fun. Most rooms have pretty views over the village; some are en suite, others not, so come to practice the dying art of smiling at strangers on the landing. Also: kippers at breakfast, maps for walkers and dog biscuits behind the bar.

rooms	5: 1 twin, 1 double; 3 doubles with separate bath or shower.
price	£80. Singles £55.
meals	Lunch from £5. Dinner from £8.
closed	Never.
directions	A30 west from Exeter to Whiddon Cross. South 2 miles to Sandy Park. Pub on right at x-roads.

	Nick Rout
tel	01647 433267
email	sandyparkinn@aol.com
web	www.sandyparkinn.co.uk

Inn

Map 2 Entry 76

Burgh Island

Bigbury-on-Sea, Devon TQ7 4BG

The walk over the sand with a golden beach to either side is dramatic and at high tide you must arrive by sea tractor. On the island, the little Pilchard Inn seems cowed by the rocks; towering over it all is the splendid white building that was Archie Nettlefold's playpen for naughty theatrical folk in the 1930s. Inside is no less impressive: the Peacock Bar with its intricate ceiling, the cool, dazzling Palm Court, the glamorous Ballroom and the charming Captain's Cabin – all have been rescued and there's more to do. Everything is in the Art Deco style, meticulously restored or painstakingly tracked down by Tony, who understands and adores the era, and Deborah who fizzes with fun and organises great balls and evenings of dance. Bedrooms, some of which are not huge, are totally authentic and delightful with plenty of room for bathing and perfecting make-up. Stacks to do, from tottering down to the freshwater pool to a game of tennis or a brisk walk. At night, plenty of frothy dash and glamour, a touch of decadence and a jolly good dinner. Very Agatha Christie. *Minimum stay two nights at weekends.*

rooms	23 doubles & suites.
price	Half board £300-£480 per room.
meals	Half-board only. Non-residents lunch £30; dinner £50.
closed	Rarely.
directions	Drive to Bigbury-on-sea. At high tide you are transported by sea tractor, at low tide by Landrover. Walking takes three minutes.

Deborah Clark & Tony Orchard

tel	01548 810514
fax	01548 810243
email	reception@burghisland.com
web	www.burghisland.com

Hotel

Map 2 Entry 79

Hazelwood House

Loddiswell, Kingsbridge, Devon TQ7 4EB

A relaxed, unpretentious country house wrapped up in 67 acres of wild river valley. Hazelwood is no ordinary hotel and not the smartest place in the book, but its spirit is second to none, and those who want to hide away in the country with minimum fuss will find just that. It's a place of exceptional peace and natural beauty – you can strike out from the front door and follow the river through the valley, or take to the hills and disappear from the day. Come back to lectures, courses and evenings of music, all of which play a big part. They have a knack for attracting the best and it's all carried off with a friendly approach. Delicious food is organic where possible, so come for avocado and walnut salad, barbecued leg of local lamb, then chocolate and rum torte. Spring-fed water is as fresh as can be, but there's a good wine list too. Cream tea on the veranda is wonderful. You can roam past ancient rhododendrons and huge camellias, cut through fields of wild flowers and stroll past grazing sheep. Bedrooms are warmly coloured and have fabulous views of the valley. You can even get married here.

rooms	15: 4 doubles, 2 twins, 1 family room; 2 doubles, 3 twins, 2 family rooms, 1 single, all sharing 4 baths.
price	£70-£150. Singles £47-£112.
meals	Lunch £14. Dinner £30-£35.
closed	Never.
directions	From Exeter, A38 south; A3121 south. Left onto B3196 south. At California Cross, 1st left after petrol station. After 0.75 miles, left.

Janie Bowman, Gillian Kean
& Anabel Watson

tel	01548 821232
fax	01548 821318
email	info@hazelwoodhouse.com
web	www.hazelwoodhouse.com

Hotel

Map 2 Entry 80

Fingals
Dittisham, Dartmouth, Devon TQ6 0JA

Richard miraculously combines a laissez-faire management style with a passionate commitment to doing things well. He is ever-present without intruding, fun without being challenging, spontaneous without being demanding. This is his place, his style, his gesture of defiance to the rest of the hotel world. He does things his way, and most people love it. And he is backed by Sheila, whose kindness and perennial good nature are a constant source of wonder. The food is good, with a Gallic appeal, and the meals around the big table memorable. This is a place to mingle with kindred spirits into the early hours; though the accent is on conviviality, you can eat at separate tables if you prefer. You find children wandering freely, happy adults, mooching dogs, and Sheila's ducks being marshalled home in the evening. Ask for rooms in the main house – they're bigger. The indoor pool beckons, and sauna and jacuzzi, ping-pong and croquet for all, perhaps tennis on the lawn and cosy conversation in the bar. But don't be misled, you can do peace and quiet here, too. Perfect for the open-hearted.

rooms	10 + 1: 8 doubles, 1 twin, 1 family. Self-catering barn for 4.
price	£75–£160. Barn £500–£800 per week.
meals	Dinner £27.50.
closed	2 January–26 March.
directions	From Totnes, A381 south; left for Cornworthy. Right at x-roads for Cornworthy; right at ruined gatehouse for Dittisham. Down steep hill, over bridge. Signed on right.

	Richard Johnston
tel	01803 722398
fax	01803 722401
email	richard@fingals.co.uk
web	www.fingals.co.uk

Hotel

Map 2 Entry 81

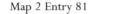

Browns Hotel

27-29 Victoria Road, Dartmouth, Devon TQ6 9RT

Bang in the centre of bustling Dartmouth, this painted Georgian townhouse with pretty windows appears unremarkable. But inside is a large, airy space with vibrant James Stewart paintings on otherwise unadorned cream and lilac walls, cast-iron fireplaces, squashy sofas, books and magazines and no reception desk — it's very friendly, very relaxed, and there are loads of places to sit and sip something delicious while you ponder which of the fresh tapas dishes to order. James has his pick of Devon's finest fish, meat and veg, so your taste buds will be thrilled. Bedrooms vary in size — none are huge — but all have pocket-sprung mattresses, plain colours with the odd funky headboard or zebra-striped screen, super snazzy bathrooms and modern art. Georgous breakfasts, fantastic cocktails, board games for rainy days, sailing for sunny ones. There are arduous walks too, great beaches and all the shops and restaurants of pretty Dartmouth. Check their web site before you come: it's packed with good advice about what you can do. One night may not be enough.

rooms	10: 8 doubles, 1 twin, 1 four-poster.
price	£80-£165. Singles £60 (Sunday-Thursday).
meals	Tapas £2.50-£8.50 (not Sunday/Monday).
closed	January.
directions	From M5 A38 for Plymouth; A385 for Totnes then to Dartmouth. There, 3rd right (Townstal Road) & down into town. On right hand side. Free parking permit (small doubles exempt).

	James & Clare Brown
tel	01803 832572
email	enquiries@brownshoteldartmouth.co.uk
web	www.brownshoteldartmouth.co.uk

Restaurant with Rooms

Map 2 Entry 82

Devon

Bark House Hotel

Oakfordbridge, Bampton, Devon EX16 9HZ

The comfort of a country hotel – a cosy lounge with books and magazines, a candlelit dining room serving fabulous food – yet here you have the personal touch. The service is superb for a place this size: Alastair takes your luggage and ushers you in, Justine offers irresistible homemade cake and tea. These are people who love what they do and their old-fashioned courtesy is reassuring and hugely appreciated. Behind the wisteria-strewn façade all is pristine: pale velvety sofas, candles and fresh flowers, crisp flowered chintz. Proper-sized bedrooms have floral covers on firm beds, a touch of noise from the road, but nothing to worry about, vases of garden flowers and sweet meadow views, and exquisite new showers in some rooms. As for the food, you'll be bowled over by it. Alastair orchestrates it all, from the canapés to the truffles. There are 50 bins from the old and new worlds, while breakfast here is as good as it gets, one of the best in Britain. A garden to relax in, steamers for sunbathing, seats for afternoon tea, and bird tables to coax the locals out of the woods for a bite of lunch. Wonderful.

rooms	5: 2 doubles, 2 twins/doubles; 1 double with separate bath.
price	£95–£119. Singles £50–£57.50. Half-board from £76 p.p.
meals	Dinner £29.50.
closed	Occasionally.
directions	From Tiverton, A396 north towards Minehead. Hotel on right, 1 mile north of junction with B3227.

Alastair Kameen & Justine Hill
tel 01398 351236
email bark.house.hotel@btinternet.com
web www.barkhouse.co.uk

Hotel

Map 2 Entry 83

Bickleigh Castle
Bickleigh, Tiverton, Devon EX16 8RP

The bride gets to stay in the castle, you stay in the cottages – they're thatched, just-renovated and gorgeous. With its 15th-century film set looks, Bickleigh is one of the south-west's most beautiful castles – and its 1096 chapel the oldest place in Devon in which to exchange vows. The Hays have swept in full of energy and ideas – for speciality dinners, charity balls, wine weekends, country fairs, vintage car rallies, and the occasional talk about matters ghostly. You get 30 acres of grounds, five of which are landscaped (great banks of rhododendrons with fine views to the Exe, a knot garden just planted) and terrific food; organic Devon pork in west country cider with honey apples and cream caught our eye. The Great Hall (perfect for big functions) has a fireplace of carved stone, the bridal suite a four-poster clothed in rich yellow. Cottage bedrooms couldn't be prettier: walls freshly painted, curtains and cushions strewn with flowers, soft lamps, embroidered quilts, the odd fireplace or beam. There's history here in bucketloads – and peace, romance and fabulous food.

rooms	15: 10 doubles, 2 twins, 2 family; 1 four-poster with separate bath (by special arrangement only).
price	£110–£130. Singles from £55.
meals	Dinner from £25, by arrangement.
closed	Rarely.
directions	M5 junc. 27 to Tiverton. Clearly signposted 'Bickleigh Castle' on the road.

	Sarah & Robert Hay
tel	01884 855363
fax	01884 855783
email	info@bickleighcastle.com
web	www.bickleighcastle.com

Hotel

Map 2 Entry 84

Kings Arms
Stockland, Honiton, Devon EX14 9BS

A 16th-century coaching inn on what was the main London to Penzance road. These days lively locals fill the bar, the skittles team play three times a week and farmers come to chew the cud. If you miss the gossip amid the all the chatter, staff will post it on the notice board so you can catch up later. Jazz bands play on the last Sunday of the month, there's a slightly tatty lounge for rugby and *Coronation Street* and if you fancy a game of darts, you'll get one; there's a piano, too, so come to belt out a tune. Exposed stone walls, low beamed ceilings and open fires in the dining room and front bar; in summer you can pop out onto the sprawling terrace/garden at the front and watch village life slide by. Rooms are simple, maybe a walnut bed or a cushioned window seat, but bear in mind that this is a lively local and won't be quiet until about 11pm; come to join in, not to crash out. Seemingly endless boarded menus offer crispy roast duck, rack of lamb, fillet of ostrich and monkfish Marseillaise; a full menu for vegetarians is available and there's fried bread at breakfast. The Blackdown hills await.

rooms	3: 2 doubles, 1 twin.
price	£70. Singles £45.
meals	Lunch from £8.50. Dinner, 3 courses, from £22.50.
closed	Christmas Day.
directions	From centre of Honiton, head north-east out of town. Stockland signed right just before junction with A30. Straight ahead for 6 miles to village.

Paul Diviani, John O'Leary & Heinz Kiefer

tel	01404 881361
fax	01404 881732
email	reserve@kingsarms.net
web	www.kingsarms.net

Inn

Map 2 Entry 85

Combe House Hotel & Restaurant
Gittisham, Honiton, Exeter, Devon EX14 3AD

A sensational setting: 3,500 acres with a 'lost' arboretum and a long and meandering approach; darting pheasants and galloping Arabian horses add to the romance. Globe-trotting hoteliers Ruth and Ken Hunt have settled here and made this mullion-windowed Grade I manor into a special place to stay without giving it a hotel look or atmosphere and the staff are delightful. The Georgian kitchen where private parties dine by the glow of the Tilley lamps and candles is celebrated in a Richard Adams picture called 'Making Jam'. Here, and in the charmingly frescoed, award-winning, dining room, you will be treated to some fine, creative cooking with the emphasis on the best Devon produce. Bedrooms are mostly a good size and the master suites sport silk-hung wallpapers, antiques and large beds; one has a huge Indian copper bath. Most atmospheric of all is the entrance hall with its carved fireplace, oak panelling, worn slate flagstones and ancestral portraits – grab a book and settle here on one of the many comfy sofas. Then head for the coast; it's nearer than you might think.

rooms	15: 10 twins/doubles, 1 four-poster, 4 suites.
price	£164-£254. Singles from £134. Suites £308. Half-board from £115 p.p.
meals	Lunch £20-£26. Dinner £39.50. Private parties in Georgian kitchen from £39.50 p.p. plus room hire.
closed	Rarely.
directions	M5 junc. 28 or 29 to Honiton, then Sidmouth. A375 south for a mile. House signed right through woods.

	Ruth & Ken Hunt
tel	01404 540400
fax	01404 46004
email	stay@thishotel.com
web	www.thishotel.com

Hotel

Map 2 Entry 86

The Fox Inn

Corscombe, Dorchester, Dorset DT2 0NS

This is Hardy's Wessex at its loveliest: deeply rural, blisteringly pretty. As for the Fox, a 17th-century thatched inn – it's one of Dorset's seven wonders. Its position is dreamy; a stream runs past outside, horses graze in the fields and the odd flock of geese has been known to waddle up the lane. In the old days drovers on the way to market would wash their sheep in the stream and stop for a pint of cider (the inn only received a full licence 40 years ago). These days it remains true to its earthy roots; huge shafts of wood still smoulder in the original fireplace, thirsty footsteps still scuttle across ancient stone floors, and farm cider still pours from the tap (albeit at slightly higher prices). A saddle sits on a stool by the bar, stuffed owls peer out from glass cases, hunting cartoons hang on stone walls and old pine tables are dressed in gingham tablecloths. Don't miss the flower-filled conservatory, its long table made from a single piece of oak that fell in the storm of '87. Bedrooms are simple and the one in the loft is reached via stone steps; expect pine beds, uneven floors and window seats.

rooms	4: 3 doubles, 1 twin.
price	£80–£100. Singles £55–£75.
meals	Lunch from £10. Dinner, à la carte, around £30.
closed	Christmas Day.
directions	From Yeovil, A37 for Dorchester for 1 mile, then right, for Corscombe, for 5.5 miles. Inn on left on outskirts of village. Use kitchen door to left of main entrance if arriving before 7pm.

	Clive Webb
tel	01935 891330
fax	01935 891330
web	www.thefoxinn.co.uk

Inn

Map 2 Entry 87

Bridge House Hotel

3 Prout Bridge, Beaminster, Dorset DT8 3AY

There is much here to make one happy – an engaging old property in a country town, the inestimable beauty of Dorsetshire, delightful young owners. The Donovans have swapped the worlds of media and fashion for hospitality in Hardy country; given their energy and talents they will make a grand job of it. The bedrooms – go for those in the main house – have stacks of space, the best overlooking the garden at the back. Traditional florals are being gradually replaced by chic fabrics, flat-screen TVs and stylish bathrooms. At the heart of Bridge House is the food – local, organic, delicious – served in the panelled Georgian dining room on crisp linen. Then retire to one of two sitting rooms cosy with log-filled inglenooks and hundreds of candles. As for the house, it's laden with history. It started out as an ancient monument, was home to a priest in the 13th-century, became a dwelling house in Tudor times (hence the variety of mullioned windows) and a priest's hole was added sometime after. There are river walks for kingfisher-spotters, llama-trekking should you crave adventure and Dorset's Jurassic coast.

rooms	14: 7 twins/doubles, 1 four-poster, 1 single. Coach House: 3 doubles, 1 family room, 1 single.
price	£122-£174. Single £60-£92. Half-board (min. 2 nights) from £81 p.p.
meals	Lunch from £3.95. Dinner, 3 courses, £31.50.
closed	Never.
directions	From Yeovil, A30 west; A3066 for Bridport to Beaminster. Hotel at far end of town, as road bends to right.

	Mark & Joanna Donovan
tel	01308 862200
fax	01308 863700
email	enquiries@bridge-house.co.uk
web	www.bridge-house.co.uk

Hotel

Map 2 Entry 88

The Priory Hotel
Church Green, Wareham, Dorset BH20 4ND

Come for a slice of old England. The lawns of this 16th-century priory run down to the river Frome. Behind, a church rises, beyond, a neat Georgian square; in short, a little bit of time travel. A stone-flagged courtyard leads up to the hotel, where comfortable country-house interiors include a first-floor drawing room with views of the garden and a stone-vaulted dining room in the old cellar. Best of all is the terrace; 200 yards of dreamy English gardens front the river, so sit in the sun and watch yacht masts flutter. Bedrooms in the main house come in different sizes, some cosy under beams, others grandly adorned in reds and golds. Also: mahogany dressers, padded window seats, bowls of fruit, the odd sofa. Bathrooms — some new, some old — come with white robes. Eight have river views, others look onto the garden or church. Rooms in the boathouse, a 16th-century clay barn, are opulent, with oak panelling, stone walls, the odd chest and sublime views. Four acres of idyllic gardens have climbing roses, a duck pond and banks of daffs. Wonderful. *Minimum two nights at weekends in summer.*

rooms	18: 14 twins/doubles. Boat House: 1 double, 3 suites.
price	£210–£280. Suites from £340. Half-board (obligatory at weekends) from £130 p.p.
meals	Lunch from £20. Dinner from £35.
closed	Never.
directions	West from Poole on A35, then A351 for Wareham and B3075 into town. Through lights, 1st left, right out of square, then keep left and entrance on left beyond church.

	Jeremy Merchant
tel	01929 551666
fax	01929 554519
email	reservations@theprioryhotel.co.uk
web	theprioryhotel.co.uk

Hotel

Map 3 Entry 91

Lord Bute Hotel

Lymington Road, Highcliffe, Christchurch, Dorset BH23 4JS

Tucked behind the original entrance lodges to Highcliffe Castle (itself worth a visit), a hotel that stands head and shoulders above the rest. The restaurant is glamorous – black carpets, white linen – and you book in advance for its award-winning menu. Settle back with a pre-dinner drink in the relaxing conservatory-orangery for blissful garden views – oriental pots sprout bamboo and colourful acers sit on well-groomed terraces leading to a pretty grassed area. Air-conditioned, double-glazed bedrooms are smartly contemporary with big suede headboards and subtle colours (oatmeals, beiges, a touch of mustard or crimson). The bridal suite is sumptuous and bathrooms are awash with Molton Brown goodies; the family suite has a kitchenette. Best of all: Gary and Simon, full of enthusiasm for this place and working hard to give you a good time; there are monthly cabaret evenings with famous names and live music on most weekends. If you have any energy left over, take the path down to the beach behind the castle, or head for the New Forest. Bournemouth is nearby for shopping.

rooms	13: 10 twins/doubles, 2 suites. Coach House: 1 family suite.
price	From £98. Singles from £65. Suite from £140. Family suite from £120.
meals	Lunch £8. Dinner £29.95 & à la carte. Closed Monday.
closed	Never.
directions	From Christchurch, A337 towards Lymington to Highcliffe. Hotel 200 yds past castle.

	Gary Payne & Simon Box
tel	01425 278884
fax	01425 279258
email	mail@lordbute.co.uk
web	www.lordbute.co.uk

Hotel

Map 3 Entry 92

The Mistley Thorn

High Street, Mistley, Colchester, Essex CO11 1HE

In Constable country: an unexpectedly chi-chi village with some red-bricked and some painted Georgian cottages gathered around the river estuary with its wide, light views of water, bobbing boats and green hills beyond. David and Sherri (who has a cookery school next door) run the place beautifully: staff are young and very good, there are plenty of locals tossed into the mix downstairs and some impeccably behaved children too. The mood is laid-back city wine bar rather than country pub. Colours are soft and easy, the tables are of various shapes, candles flicker, modern art rubs along well with the odd antique and food is taken seriously but with no grim reverence. There's lots of good local fish and seafood – perhaps cooked with an Italian or Asian twist – and a pudding list that includes cheesecake from Sherri's mum. Bedrooms are calm with cream carpets, big beds, pale green paintwork and some have views over the water. Bathrooms have a Turkish feel with tiny beige and cream tiles, spotless white baths and overhead showers. It's all entirely charming.

rooms	5: 3 doubles, 2 twins/doubles.
price	From £80.
meals	Dinner, 2 courses, £12.80–£25.90.
closed	Christmas Day.
directions	From A12 take Hadleigh/East Bergholt exit north of Colchester. Go through East Bergholt to A137. Follow signs to Manningtree, drive through to Mistley High Street.

	David McKay & Sherri Singleton
tel	01206 392821
fax	01206 390122
email	info@mistleythorn.co.uk
web	www.mistleythorn.co.uk

Inn

Map 4 Entry 95

The Bell Inn & Hill House

High Road, Horndon-on-the-Hill, Essex SS17 8LD

Christine is an original fixture of this Great Inn of England: her parents ran the Bell for years. John is a key figure, much admired in the trade, as is Joanne, their loyal manager of many years. The flagstoned bar, with oak panelled walls and French wood carvings, bustles at lunchtime. Bare flags or boards covered in rugs, an open fire, a grandfather clock, fine prints, ancient hot-cross buns hanging from beams – all bring warmth and gregariousness. In contrast the breakfast room is light and airy, with elegant creamy covers for tables and chairs. In the evenings, waiters dressed in black serve an interesting array of dishes under the watchful eye of Master Sommelier Joanne. You could have Parma ham with figs poached in red wine, pan-fried John Dory with buttered spinach, then bitter chocolate tart with Chantilly sauce. Fat chips come with balsamic mayonnaise and the food picks up awards, as do Christine's flower baskets in the courtyard. As for the bedrooms, go for one of the suites: cosy, traditional, individual, rather wonderful.

rooms	15: 7 doubles, 3 twins, 5 suites.
price	£50-£60. Suites £85.
meals	Breakfast £4.50-£9.50. Bar meals from £8.50. Dinner, à la carte, around £26. No food bank holidays.
closed	Christmas Day & Boxing Day.
directions	M25 junc. 30/31. A13 towards Southend for 3 miles, then B1007 to Horndon-on-the-Hill. On left in village.

	Christine & John Vereker
tel	01375 642463
fax	01375 361611
email	info@bell-inn.co.uk
web	www.bell-inn.co.uk

Inn

Map 4 Entry 96

Three Choirs Vineyards
Newent, Gloucestershire GL18 1LS

A fondness for cooking and wine-making will equip you for the full-bodied and very English experience of Three Choirs. Thomas has run the pesticide-free vineyard with thoughtful and gentle reserve for over a decade. There are 100 acres of grounds of which 75 grow 16 varieties of grape; the rest have been left to encourage wildlife, including birds of prey. The wine from here went to the wedding of Charles and Diana and still lubricates British embassies; the hotel and restaurant evolved more recently as an addition to the winery; weddings are welcomed. The bedrooms are in a purpose-built building and are crisply clean and comfortable, each with French windows opening to a small patio with cast-iron furniture: relax with a glass of wine and enjoy the peaceful views that produced it. At breakfast, don't be embarrassed to ask for more wine with your smoked salmon and scrambled eggs – it's a house special. Chef Darren cooks like a dream, has won many accolades and runs monthly cookery courses. Dick Whittington was born up the road – you may wonder why he ever left.

rooms	8 twins/doubles.
price	£95–£115. Singles £75–£85. Half-board £155–£165 per room per night (min. 2 nights).
meals	Lunch from £21. Dinner, à la carte, around £35.
closed	Christmas & New Year.
directions	From Newent, north on B4215 for about 1.5 miles, follow brown signs to vineyard.

	Thomas Shaw
tel	01531 890223
fax	01531 890877
email	info@threechoirs.com
web	www.threechoirs.com

Hotel

Map 2 Entry 97

Hotel on the Park

Evesham Road, Cheltenham, Gloucestershire GL52 2AH

Symmetry and style to please the eye in the centre of the spa town of Cheltenham. The attention to detail is staggering – everything has a place and is just where it should be. The style is crisp and dramatic, a homage to the Regency period in which the house was built, but there's plenty of good humour floating around, not least in Darryl and Jo, who are brilliant at encouraging people to dive in and enjoy it all. There are lovely touches too: piles of fresh hand towels in the gents' cloakroom, where there's a sink with no plug hole – you'll work it out; newspapers hang on poles, grab one and head into the drawing room where drapes swirl across big windows. Lose yourself in Scrabble (on the rotating games table) in the library, tuck into pan-fried scallops, noisette of lamb or red mullet escabèche on the terrace or in the brasserie: wooden tables, planked floor, modern dishes. Upstairs, bedrooms are fabulous, crisp and artistic, all furnished to fit the period. One has an infinity bath, others aromatherapy baths, jacuzzis and walk-in showers. A huge treat.

rooms	12: 7 doubles, 4 twins/doubles, 1 suite.
price	£126-£186. Singles £99-£106.50. Suite £154.
meals	Breakfast £6.95-£10.50. Starters from £4.95; main courses from £13.95.
closed	Never.
directions	From town centre, join one-way system, & exit signed Evesham. On down Evesham Road. Hotel on left opposite park, signed.

	Darryl Gregory
tel	01242 518898
fax	01242 511526
email	stay@hotelonthepark.co.uk
web	www.hotelonthepark.com

Hotel

Map 3 Entry 98

Lower Brook House

Lower Street, Blockley, Gloucestershire GL56 9DS

The village is a Cotswold jewel, saved from the tourist hordes by roads too narrow for coaches. Lower Brook is no less alluring. It was built in 1624 to house workers from one of the 16 silk mills that made Blockley rich. Step inside to find country rugs on flagged floors, Farrow & Ball paints on timber framed walls, mullioned windows, vases of flowers and piles of vintage luggage. Winter logs smoulder in a huge inglenook in the sitting room – slide onto the leather sofa and roast away. Bedrooms are crisply stylish with beautiful fabrics, pristine linen, bowls of fresh fruit and handmade soaps in super little bathrooms. All but one overlooks the garden; views fly up the hill. Outside, colour bursts from the beds in summer and a small lawn runs down to a shaded terrace for afternoon tea in good weather. Walks start from the door: you can be deep in the country within half a mile. Come back to Anna's delicious cooking, perhaps mustard and cress soup, roast loin of lamb, rhubarb crumble; breakfast treats include smoothies, croissants and freshly-squeeze juice. *Minimum stay two nights at weekends.*

rooms	6: 2 doubles, 2 twins, 2 four-posters.
price	£95–£165.
meals	Dinner, 3 courses, £25.
closed	Christmas.
directions	A44 west from Moreton in Marsh. At top of hill in Bourton on the Water, right signed Blockley. Down hill to village, on right.

Julian & Anna Ebbutt

tel	01386 700286
fax	01386 701400
email	info@lowerbrookhouse.com
web	www.lowerbrookhouse.com

Hotel

Map 3 Entry 101

Horse and Groom
Bourton-on-the-Hill, Moreton-in-Marsh, Gloucestershire GL56 9AQ

You're at the top of the hill, so grab the window seats for views that pour over the Cotswolds. This is a hive of youthful endeavour, with brothers at the helm; Will cooks, Tom pours the ales, and a cheery conviviality flows throughout. The public spaces, recently refurbished, mix the old (open fires, exposed stone walls and beamed ceilings) with the new (warm halogen lighting, crisp coir matting and a cool marble bar), making this a fine place in which to hole up for a night or two. There are settles and boarded menus in the bar, stripped wooden floors and old rugs in the dining room. Tuck into homemade soups, Cornish sardines, Cotswold lamb, then sinful chocolate puddings. In summer you can eat in the back garden under the shade of a damson tree and watch the chefs raid the kitchen garden for raspberries and strawberries, onions, fennel and broad beans. Bedrooms are nicely plush, smart but uncluttered, and those at the front are sound-proofed to minimise noise from the road. The red room is huge and comes with a sofa, while the garden room has doors that open onto the terrace.

rooms	5 doubles.
price	£90–£115. Singles from £65.
meals	Bar meals all day from £9.50. Dinner, à la carte, from £25. Pub closed Sunday night & Monday.
closed	New Year's Eve & New Year's Day.
directions	West from Moreton in Marsh on A44. Climb hill in Bourton on the Hill and pub at top on left.

	Tom & Will Greenstock
tel	01386 700413
fax	01386 700413
email	info@horseandgroom.info
web	www.horseandgroom.info

Inn

Map 3 Entry 102

Gloucestershire

The Eight Bells
Church Street, Chipping Campden, GL55 6JG

A pristine Cotswold village with a market place that dates from 1627 and a church for Evensong on Sunday nights. As for the tiny Eight Bells, it dates back to the 14th century and is made of flat-faced stone, thus was once an important building. These days old beams, flagged floors and walkers in socks by the open fire add a mellow country warmth; those in search of rustic comfort in a bright and breezy traditional inn will be happy. Flower baskets hang against golden stone outside, old cobbles in the entrance lead towards the bar. Rooms up in the eaves (there are two on the ground floor) are snug with beams, exposed timber frames and uneven floors. You might have a stone wall, a cast-iron bed, a leather bedhead or faux-fur blankets. Some have compact showers, others have generous bathrooms. Good food downstairs includes tapas at lunch, excellent Sunday roasts and beer-infused, local sausages. There are fruit wines and Hook Norton ales (tours of the brewery can be arranged). Best of all is the decked garden that overlooks the alms houses, perfect for lazy summer evenings. Stratford is close.

rooms	7: 6 doubles, 1 single.
price	£85–£120.
meals	Lunch & dinner from £9.50.
closed	Christmas Day.
directions	A44 north from Oxford, then right on B4081 into village. Up high street, loop round one-way system, and pub on right.

Neil & Julie Hargreaves
tel	01386 840371
fax	01386 841669
email	neilhargreaves@bellinn.fsnet.co.uk
web	www.eightbellsinn.co.uk

Inn

Map 3 Entry 103

The Cotswold House Hotel

The Square, Chipping Campden, Gloucestershire GL55 6AN

Few brochures quite capture the spirit of a place; Cotswold House's is one exception. It pulls out like a concertina, revealing a tantalising glimpse of what to expect behind the impressive colonnaded entrance of the 19th-century wool merchant's house. Ian and Christa's philosophy was to create a hotel where the bedrooms felt better than your own room at home. Whether you go for a cosy cottage room or a sumptuous suite (with hot tubs in private gardens!) you'll find stylishness and contemporary colour, cashmere throws on giant-sized beds, TVs in bathrooms and tubs for two, fresh coffee percolators, top of the range entertainment systems, remote controls to fine-tune your viewing and listening pleasure... even a bedding menu. Downstairs, relax in red leather armchairs in the bar or dine – extremely well – in one of two restaurants: one elegant, one informal. Outside: two acres of walled garden with tumbling borders and secluded spots. Wine, music and celebrity events are held through the year, and the immaculate town has boutiques to browse. Spoil yourself!

rooms	30: 20 doubles, 7 suites, 3 cottage rooms.
price	£140–£725.
meals	Brasserie meals from £9. Dinner £45.
closed	Never.
directions	From Oxford, A44 north for Evesham. 5 miles after Moreton-in-Marsh, right on B4081 to Chipping Campden. Hotel in square by town hall.

	Ian & Christa Taylor
tel	01386 840330
fax	01386 840310
email	reception@cotswoldhouse.com
web	www.cotswoldhouse.com

Hotel

Map 3 Entry 104

The Malt House
Broad Campden, Chipping Campden, Gloucestershire GL55 6UU

In the middle of a refreshingly untouched Cotswold village, a place that so echoes to the past you almost expect the vicar to call for tea. Still much in evidence is that very English ritual of sipping gin in a lovely setting: the garden has its own 'gin and tonic' bench! And a thatched summer house for afternoon tea, a walled kitchen garden that grows figs and soft red fruits, and a perfect croquet lawn by a sweet stream. The house has a mellow grandeur: polished wooden floors, walls of shimmering gold and an inglenook fireplace at its heart. Bedrooms, all enticing, have mullioned windows, sloping floors, gilt mirrors, elegantly refurbished bathrooms, a collection of exotic *objets trouvés* and… perhaps a fireplace or doors onto the garden. This is a quintessential English country house with a personal feel – everything ticks over beautifully, Judi's smile is warm and her breakfasts will keep you smiling for days. For lunch and dinner you can't do better than the Churchill Arms at Paxford, two miles up the road.

rooms	7: 1 double, 4 twins/doubles, 1 four-poster, 1 suite.
price	£128-£135. Singles from £85. Suite from £150.
meals	Pub 1 mile. Dinner by arrangement (min. 12 people).
closed	Christmas.
directions	From Oxford, A44 through Moreton-in-Marsh; right on B4081 north to Chipping Campden. Entering village, 1st right for Broad Campden. Hotel 1 mile on left.

	Judi Wilkes
tel	01386 840295
fax	01386 841334
email	info@malt-house.co.uk
web	www.malt-house.co.uk

Hotel

Map 3 Entry 105

The Dial House

The Chestnuts, Bourton-on-the-Water, Gloucestershire GL54 2AN

In a quiet corner of the ever-popular 'Venice of the Cotswolds', with sandstone Georgian houses and the slow, meandering Windrush drifting by, is the lovely Dial House built in 1698 by architect Andrew Paxford – his and his wife's initials are carved on the front. Originally The Vinehouse, it was renamed after the large sundial above the front door. Inside, Jane and Adrian have created an oasis of old world charm, with Jacobean-style furniture, wonderful four-posters, old portrait paintings and impressive stone fireplaces. Elegant yet friendly, it epitomises the traditional country-house hotel. Easily the best bedrooms are in the main house, with lovely antiques, a refreshing lack of chintz, Penhaligon smellies and organic chocolates – views are of the busy town and peaceful river through leaded window panes. Rooms in an extension look out onto the walled garden, which is a lovely spot to keep the world at arm's length for a while, and the classic English menu takes a lot of beating.

rooms	13: 9 doubles, 3 four-posters, 1 four-poster suite.
price	£110–£120. Suite £175. Half-board (min. 2 nights) £75 p.p.
meals	Dinner, 3 courses à la carte, from £30. Packed lunch available.
closed	Never.
directions	From Oxford, A40 to Northleach, right on A429 to Bourton. Hotel set back from High St opp. main bridge.

	Jane & Adrian Campbell-Howard
tel	01451 822244
fax	01451 810126
email	info@dialhousehotel.com
web	www.dialhousehotel.com

Hotel

Map 3 Entry 106

Heaven's Above at The Mad Hatters

3 Cossack Square, Nailsworth, Gloucestershire GL6 0DB

In Carolyn's words, you "never know what's coming next" at this exceptional, fully organic restaurant with rooms. Arrive to a bowl of cherries one day, some fragrant sweet peas picked from the garden the next. She and Mike were smallholders once. They lived at the top of the hill, worked the land, kept livestock, made bellows and earned next to nothing. In the early Nineties they came down the hill to open a restaurant. Locals flocked in, and still do. The food is delicious, consistently so, some still grown back up the hill: try fabulous fish soup, lamb with garlic and rosemary, and a mouth-puckering lemon tart. *Cotswold Life* has given it 'chef of the year' award but it's a place with heart, not designed to impress, which is probably why it does, and full of rustic charm: cookery books squashed into a pretty pine dresser, mellow stone walls, big bay windows, stripped wooden floors, simple ash and elm tables and exceptional art. Bedrooms are delightful – huge, like an artist's studio, with wooden floors, whitewashed walls and rag-rolled beams.

The folk at the Mad Hatters are as organic as can be. Mike works two allotments when he's not running the restaurant, growing beans, courgettes, tomatoes and raspberries, while Michael Watts (mentor to Matthew Fort the food critic) provides every potato; Carolyn goes up on Fridays to plunder his beds, pulling up the freshest of English vegetables while she's there. Lamb comes from local smallholders; chicken, pork and bacon from award-winning Adey's Organic Farm; and Wiltshire's Global Organics supply the more exotic produce – peppers, chillies, oranges and lemons.

rooms	3: 1 double; 1 double, 1 twin sharing bath.
price	£60-£70. Singles £35-£45.
meals	Lunch £15. Dinner, à la carte, from £25. Not Sunday evenings, Mondays & Tuesdays.
closed	Rarely.
directions	M5, junc. 13, A419 to Stroud, then A46 south to Nailsworth. Right at r'bout & immed. left; restaurant & house opp. Britannia Pub.

Carolyn & Mike Findlay

| tel | 01453 832615 |
| email | mafindlay@waitrose.com |

SPECIAL GREEN ENTRY
see page 21

Restaurant with Rooms

Map 3 Entry 107

No. 12
Park Street, Cirencester, Gloucestershire GL7 2BW

No. 12 is another of those pleasing British phenomena, not a hotel but a small place run with enormous thought and care. (The offer of tea and homemade cake on arrival is a typical touch.) Sarah has lavishly converted this splendid, listed Georgian townhouse, with its beams dating back to the early 1600s, right down to the last detail. Bedrooms mix antique and contemporary furniture, while heaped feather pillows, merino wool blankets and fine bed linen spoil further... extra-long beds include a *bateau lit* and a leather sleigh bed. Ultra-modern bathrooms, almost minimalist in style, come with dressing gowns and Molton Brown goodies. Cranberry-red walls and white china make a striking contrast in the dining room at breakfast, while checked sofas, fresh flowers and *Condé Nast Traveller* and *Vogue* in the sitting room encourage you to linger. It is quietly immaculate. As is old Cirencester, 'capital of the Cotswolds', a favourite destination for travellers since Roman times and civilised in every way. *Children over 12 welcome.*

rooms	3 doubles.
price	£80. Singles £60.
meals	Restaurants in Cirencester.
closed	Rarely.
directions	M4 junc. 15, A419 to Cirencester. M5 junc. 11a, for Cirencester. Free parking nearby.

Sarah Beckerlegge
tel	01285 640232
email	no12cirencester@ukgateway.net
web	www.no12cirencester.co.uk

B&B

Map 3 Entry 108

Bibury Court Hotel
Bibury, Gloucestershire GL7 5NT

A Jacobean mansion that stands next to the church in one of Gloucestershire's loveliest villages. The six-acre garden is reason enough to come; it's utterly English, with croquet on the lawn, clipped yew hedges, a rose arbour flanked by beds of lavender and the serene river Coln ambling past on one side. You can fish from its banks or follow the footpath into glorious country; just wonderful. A very friendly place, grand, but not stuffy. There's a panelled drawing room for afternoon teas, a conservatory for indulgent breakfasts and a smart dining room for serious dinners, so don't expect to lose weight; in summer, life spills out onto the stone terrace for sundowners in a scented garden. Handed-down antiques are scattered about: oak chests, mahogany dressers, writing desks and oil paintings by the score. A refurbishment is underway to remove all trace of the 1980s, but it wouldn't matter if it wasn't; what wins here is the relaxed atmosphere and the kind staff. Bedrooms tend to be large, with mullioned windows, old radiators, parkland views, crisp linen, the odd four-poster and a grand piano in the suite.

rooms	18: 15 doubles, 1 suite; 2 doubles, each with separate bath.
price	£140–£190. Suite £240. Singles £125.
meals	Lunch from £12.50. A la carte dinner from £30.
closed	Never.
directions	West from Burford on B4425. Cross bridge in village and house signed right along high street.

Robert Johnston & Sam Pearman

tel	01285 740337
fax	01285 740660
email	info@biburycourt.com
web	www.biburycourt.com

Hotel

Map 3 Entry 109

The Greyhound
31 High Street, Stockbridge, Hampshire SO20 6EY

There's a Michelin star in the restaurant, an easy elegance in the bedrooms and jumping brown trout in the river Test, which flanks one side of the garden. It's one of the loveliest chalkstreams in the country, a site of pilgrimage for those who like to cast a fly on lazy afternoons. The inn has a couple of rods on its 200-yard stretch; have some luck and they'll smoke your catch or cook it for supper. No hot food in the garden; instead, wonderful hampers of terrine, charcuterie, salad and wine that are brought to you with crisp white napkins and proper crockery. Chef Helene Schoeman offers year-round treats, perhaps black bream, Gressingham duck or fillet of beef – the best of English perfectly cooked. Open fires smoulder under low beamed ceilings, so pick up a newspaper and flop into a sofa. Bright and airy bedrooms upstairs fit the bill perfectly: exposed brick and timber walls, crisp Egyptian cotton, mohair blankets, beautifully upholstered amrchairs and smart monsoon showers. Stockbridge is a delight, the sort of country town you find in a Jane Austen novel.

rooms	8: 4 twins, 3 doubles, 1 single.
price	£75–£110. Singles from £65.
meals	Lunch & dinner £6–£36.
closed	Christmas Day & New Year's Day.
directions	A303, A34 south, then A30 into Stockbridge. Pub on right on west end of high street.

Helene Schoeman
tel 01264 810833
web www.thegreyhound.info

Restaurant with Rooms

Map 3 Entry 110

Westover Hall

Park Lane, Lymington, Hampshire SO41 0PT

A swish hotel, but family-run and without the slightest hint of stuffiness. It was designed for the German industrialist Siemens in 1897 – the most luxurious house on the south coast. A fortune was lavished on wood alone. It is still vibrant with gleaming oak and exquisite stained glass and it's hard to stifle a gasp when you enter the vast hall: a controlled explosion of wood. The Mechems and their staff are generous and open-minded, keen that people should come to unwind and treat the place as home – private parties can take over completely. Bedrooms are grandly contemporary and bathrooms sparkle; some have sea views, all are furnished with a mix of the antique and the new. Spacious opulence, fine art, discreet pampering: sheer indulgence. Romantics can take to the bar or restaurant and, over food that has you purring with pleasure, gaze out to sea.
The more active can dive outside, walk up the beach to Hurst Castle, or stroll to their Mediterranean beach hut. Alternatively, sink into a sofa on the balcony for great views of the Needles.

rooms	12: 8 doubles, 2 twins, 1 family, 1 single.
price	£200–£260.
meals	Light lunch £10–£15. Dinner £38.50.
closed	Rarely.
directions	From Lymington, B3058 to Milford-on-Sea. On through village. House on left up hill.

Nicola & Stewart Mechem

tel	01590 643044
fax	01590 644490
email	info@westoverhallhotel.com
web	www.westoverhallhotel.com

Hotel

Map 3 Entry 111

Master Builder's House Hotel

Bucklers Hard, Beaulieu, Hampshire SO42 7XB

By the river Beaulieu, in timeless, end-of-the-road, postcard-pretty Buckler's Hard, the Master Builder's has the feel of a well-heeled yacht club. The hotel shares this blissful spot with two rows of cottages still lived in by workers of the nearby Montagu Estate, and was the modest home of Master Shipwright Henry Adams who built many of the warships that fought at Trafalgar. The ancient slipways that launched the ships still survive; now yachts and sailing boats glide past on their way to the Solent following the route taken by Nelson's fleet two centuries before. Bedrooms in the modern wing are lavish; pricier rooms in the older, more characterful part of the hotel have river views (bring the binoculars). There's a traditional pub full of yachties in summer, a hall that seems to tumble down to the water, a restaurant with a view and a terrace for summery meals. The staff are excellent and the food is quite something. Work off lunch with a one-hour walk upstream past marshland and birdlife to Beaulieu. Wonderful.

rooms	25 twins/doubles.
price	£175–£235. Singles £130.
meals	Lunch from £19.95; bar lunch from £4.95. Dinner from £32.50.
closed	Rarely.
directions	From Lyndhurst, B3056 south past Beaulieu turn, then 1st left, signed Bucklers Hard. Hotel signed left after 1 mile.

	Samantha Brinkman
tel	01590 616253
fax	01590 616297
email	res@themasterbuilders.co.uk
web	www.themasterbuilders.co.uk

Hotel

Map 3 Entry 112

Kilverts Hotel

The Bullring, Hay-on-Wye, Herefordshire HR3 5AG

Those wanting to stay in the thick of this literary outpost bang on the Welsh border could do no better than check into Kilverts. The hotel sits in narrow streets teeming with bookshops, art galleries and antique shops… they wind round the town's crumbling castle which peers over all. Hay is the secondhand bookshop capital of Britain and holds an internationally famous literary festival the last week in May. The front terrace of the hotel is the place to people-watch with a drink or a meal; the bar is a cosy retreat if the weather drives you inside with its stone floor, wooden tables, local ales, Welsh lamb in season and homemade pizzas. The more formal restaurant has a mural of a ballroom in chaos, the menu is the same wherever you eat and the specials board changes daily. There's also a peaceful half acre of lawns and flower beds out back. We'd go for one of the cosy beamed attic rooms at the top; the rest hold few surprises but are comfortable and clean. Colin is a likeable chap and the countryside seduces.

rooms	12: 7 doubles, 4 twins/doubles, 1 twin.
price	£70–£110. Singles £55.
meals	Bar meals from £3.95. Lunch & dinner, à la carte, from £21.
closed	Christmas Day.
directions	A438 from Hereford, then B4350. Pass clock tower, left after Blue Boar pub, past castle then left. Hotel on right 200 yds, parking at rear.

	Colin Thomson
tel	01497 821042
fax	01497 821580
email	info@kilverts.co.uk
web	www.kilverts.co.uk

Hotel

Map 2 Entry 113

Moccas Court
Moccas, Hereford, Herefordshire HR29LH

Glorious Moccas. Sweep down the drive, plunge into ancient parkland, pass a 12th-century Norman church and discover this thrilling mansion. The river Wye flows past serenely behind; you can fish from its banks, or follow a path down to the red cliffs and spy on peregrine falcons. As for the interiors, enormous stately rooms come in classical design: stripped wood floors and a Broadwood piano forte in the music room (Handel played here); library steps and a moulded marble fireplace for open fires in the sitting room; original wallpaper in the circular dining room. Windows open onto balustraded terraces that lead down to the river. Bedrooms (two big, three huge) have Zoffany wallpapers, Jane Churchill fabrics, gigantic beds, mahogany dressers, padded window seats, the original 1785 shutters... the very best. Those at the front look towards the deer park where an enclosed fallow herd have run since Norman times (now they eat the garden) and the Moccas beetle is found nowhere else. Ben's cooking hits the spot: perhaps goat's cheese salad, rack of lamb, lemon tart. Exceptional.

rooms	5: 4 twins/doubles, 1 double.
price	£140-£195.
meals	Dinner, 3 courses, £30, Picnic lunches by arrangement £7.
closed	Christmas and New Year.
directions	South from Hereford on A465, then west on B4352 to Moccas. Right by stone cross in village, 200 yds to drive, signed.

	Ben & Mimi Chester-Master
tel	01981 500019
fax	01981 500095
email	info@moccas-court.co.uk
web	www.moccas-court.co.uk

Other Place

Map 2 Entry 114

The Verzon

Hereford Road, Trumpet, Ledbury, Herefordshire HR8 2PZ

You're on the Ledbury to Hereford road; views to the back stretch across miles of open country to the Malvern Hills. Step into this late-Georgian red-brick farmhouse for warm contemporary interiors and a top-to-toe refurbishment. Expect timber-framed brick walls, creamy limestone tiles, Farrow & Ball paints and stripped wood floors. Bottles of wine fill an alcove, big mirrors lean against walls in the airy restaurant. Hanging baskets and bay trees add colour at the front, and in summer life spills onto a decked terrace (bamboo flares, potted palms) in the garden. Rooms — go for the big ones — are a real surprise, nicely over-the-top. Expect funky designer wallpaper, the odd claw-foot bath behind a screen in the room, faux leopard-skin cushions, a colonial-style four-poster or an imitation crocodile-skin bedhead. All are away from the road, none are above the bar, so a peaceful night's sleep is assured. Excellent food — steak sandwiches, steamed mussels, breast of guinea fowl — can be eaten wherever you want, and there are Gloucester old spot sausages and freshly squeezed local apples for breakfast.

rooms	8: 4 doubles, 3 suites, 1 single.
price	£88–£150. Singles from £65.
meals	Lunch from £9.95. Dinner from £12.50.
closed	24-26 December.
directions	A438 west from Ledbury for 4 miles. On right, signed.

	Justin Pinchbeck
tel	01531 670381
fax	01531 670830
email	info@theverzon.co.uk
web	www.theverzon.co.uk

Hotel

Map 2 Entry 115

Glewstone Court Country House Hotel & Restaurant

Glewstone, Ross-on-Wye, Herefordshire HR9 6AW

Grand, yet relaxed enough to have no rule book. Bill does front of house, Christine cooks brilliantly, both are charming and fun. There's faded elegance and an easy conviviality in the drawing room bar, with squashy sofas and an open log fire in front of which resident dogs lie. The centre of the house is early Georgian, with a stunning staircase that spirals up to a galleried and porticoed landing; some of Christine's award-winning textile art pieces are on display here, as well as in the art gallery restaurant. Good-sized bedrooms are warm, comfortable and traditional with pleasant furniture and excellent lighting. The Rose Room is wonderful, the Victoria Room is magnificent. All look over fruit orchards to the Wye Valley and the Forest of Dean beyond, while in the garden an ancient cedar of Lebanon shades the croquet lawn and an antique fountain quietly serenades. Dine in the art gallery restaurant or outside in good weather. Most food is locally sourced – the Hereford beef is exceptional – some organic, some from the potager garden. Heaven for those in search of the small and friendly.

rooms	8: 5 doubles, 1 four-poster, 1 single, 1 suite.
price	£115-£132. Singles £58-£99.
meals	Lunch & dinner à la carte. Sunday lunch £17.50.
closed	25-27 December.
directions	From Ross-on-Wye, A40 towards Monmouth, right 1 mile south of Wilton r'bout, for Glewstone. Hotel on left after 0.5 miles.

Christine & Bill Reeve-Tucker

tel	01989 770367
fax	01989 770282
email	glewstone@aol.com
web	www.glewstonecourt.com

Hotel

Map 2 Entry 116

The Bridge at Wilton

Wilton, Ross-on-Wye, Herefordshire HR9 6AA

Built in 1740, the large white-painted house with partially walled gardens slopes down to the river with views of Ross-on-Wye and an abundance of trees. At the front, a fairly busy road – but once inside you won't notice it. Mike and Jane have worked hard over the last two years and have (almost) rid the place of woodchip. Now there are wide elm planks and newly-laid slate on the floor, leather sofas and cheery yellow walls hung with modern oils. A small conservatory overlooks the garden – two acres with a mainly cottage feel and a well-kept lawn and tables with parasols running down to the river where you can fish. The food here is superb: lamb from the next village, Herefordshire beef, Gloucester Old Spot belly and cheek, and vegetables and fruit, home or locally grown. Smart (but not swish) bedrooms over two floors of rather wonky walls and beams have some antique beds, new mattresses, patchwork quilts, easy chairs and pristine slate-floored bath and shower rooms. There are endless outdoor water sports to hurl yourself into, lovely walks and delightful snoops around town. Then back for tea and cakes.

rooms	9 twins/doubles.
price	£96-£120.
meals	Lunch & dinner, 3 courses, £24-£30.
closed	Never.
directions	End of M50, follow A40. At 3rd roundabout take left marked Ross-on-Wye. Approx 150 yds on left.

	Michael & Jane Pritchard
tel	01989 562655
email	info@bridge-house-hotel.com
web	www.bridge-house-hotel.com

Hotel

Map 2 Entry 117

The George Hotel

Quay Street, Yarmouth, Isle of Wight PO41 0PE

The position is fabulous, with the old castle on one side, the sea at the end of a lovely lawn dotted with umbrellas, and the centre of the island's oldest town just beyond the front door. Handy if you're a corrupt governor intent on sacking passing ships: Admiral Sir Robert Holmes moved here for that very reason in 1668, demolishing a bit of the castle to improve his view. The house has been rebuilt since Sir Robert's day but a grand feel most definitely lingers: the entrance is large, light and stone-flagged, the drawing room is beautifully traditional – tapestry cushions, velvet drapes, big old oils, a stag's head, a roaring fire. Bedrooms refurbished in Colefax and Jane Churchill are smartly panelled and immaculate; one has a huge four-poster, two have timber balconies with views out to sea. You dine in the brasserie – busy, bright – or in the sumptuous, burgundy dining room from a lavish menu. Dig even deeper into your pocket and charter a private boat to take you to lunch at their other hotel on the mainland. A gracious and atmospheric hotel, perfectly run.

rooms	15 twins/doubles.
price	£180-£255. Singles from £130.
meals	Brasserie lunch & dinner from £25. Dinner, 3 courses, £46.50. Restaurant closed Sundays & Mondays.
closed	Rarely.
directions	Lymington ferry to Yarmouth, then follow signs to town centre.

	Jacki Everest
tel	01983 760331
fax	01983 760425
email	res@thegeorge.co.uk
web	www.thegeorge.co.uk

Hotel

Map 3 Entry 118

The Hambrough

Hambrough Road, Ventnor, Isle of Wight PO38 1SQ

You look out on a carpet of sea rolling off towards France. Splash out on the best rooms and you get a balcony — the Hambrough's equivalent of the royal box. There are loungers and tables and they'll bring up your breakfast, freshly juiced oranges and a plate of peeled fruits, then bacon and eggs with coffee and toast. Rooms are exquisite with huge beds, high ceilings, espresso machines and LCD TVs. Mosaic bathrooms are faultless (underfloor heating, thick white bathrobes, the deepest baths); from those on the top floor you can gaze out to sea as you bathe. Despite all this the Hambrough's chief passion is its food. Come down for champagne cocktails at the bar, then dig into seared scallops with a pea bavoise, fillet of pork with a ravioli of braised cheek, chocolate clafoutis with white chocolate ice cream. Back upstairs you'll find your bed turned down and a bowl of popcorn in case you want to watch a movie. Ventnor, an old-fashioned English seaside town, is worth exploring. Don't miss the botanic gardens or Osborne House, Queen Victoria's favourite home.

rooms	7 doubles.
price	£130–£200.
meals	Lunch from £7. Dinner from £25; 8-course tasting menu £45.
closed	Never.
directions	A3055 into Ventnor. On western edge of town, south into Hambrough Rd, following blue sign to police station. House on left overlooking sea.

	Frederic Sol
tel	01983 856333
fax	01983 857260
email	info@thehambrough.com
web	www.thehambrough.com

Hotel

Map 3 Entry 119

Priory Bay Hotel
Priory Drive, Seaview, Isle of Wight PO34 5BU

Medieval monks thought Priory Bay special, so did Tudor farmers and Georgian gentry; all helped to mould this tranquil landscape. Parkland rolls down from the main house and tithe barns to a ridge of trees. The land then drops down to a long, clean sandy beach and a shallow sea, ideal for families; fishermen land their catch here for the freshest grilled seafood. Huge rooms in the house mix classical French and contemporary English styles. The sun-filled drawing room has tall windows; exquisite rococo-style chairs obligingly face out to sea, and afternoon cream teas by the winter log fire are a treat. There's a lovely brasserie for breakfast — tall windows, old parquet floors, fine murals on the wall. Bedrooms in the main house are luxurious; some have a fresh and modern feel, others oak panelling, maybe a crow's nest balcony and telescope. Bedrooms in the outbuildings are less enticing but less pricey. Andrew is a humorous host, and a supporter of the organic movement. The swimming pool is floodlit and the grounds support falcon and red squirrel, and the odd golfer.

rooms	25: 16 twins/doubles, 2 family, 7 cottages for 2, 4 or 6.
price	£90–£270. Singles from £65. Half-board £65–£125 p.p.
meals	Lunch £18.50. Dinner £25. Picnic hampers available.
closed	Rarely.
directions	From Ryde, B3330 south through Nettlestone, then left up road, signed to Nodes Holiday Camp. Entrance on left, signed.

	Andrew Palmer
tel	01983 613146
fax	01983 616539
email	enquiries@priorybay.co.uk
web	www.priorybay.co.uk

Hotel

Map 3 Entry 120

Seaview Hotel and Restaurant
High Street, Seaview, Isle of Wight PO34 5EX

A seaside hotel that draws a devoted crowd. Locals pop in for super food, Londoners come to escape the city, yachtsmen abandon cramped cabins for a night of comfort. The Seaview's reputation has spread across the seven seas and rightly so; it's smart, lively and welcoming, with a touch of seaside chic. The terrace, with railings, mast and flag, is like the prow of a ship; inside you pass portholes, sails and lanterns. The local's bar is one of the oldest on the island; pop in for its famous hot crab ramekin, then wash it down with a pint of island-brewed ale. You can eat all over the place – bar, terrace, conservatory – but if you want to tuck into fresh local produce in some style head for the restaurants; one is elegantly old-fashioned, the other contemporary. You get sea views in a super first-floor sitting room and lots of colour in warm bedrooms. Watch boats zip by from those at the front, those at the back are nice and quiet. Exemplary service – beds are turned down, breakfast can be brought to your room – and membership of a nearby health club, with pool, is on the house. Great for families.

rooms	17 + 2: 3 doubles, 13 twins/doubles, 1 family suite. 2 self-catering cottages, 1 for 10, 1 for 4.
price	£74–£179. Singles from £58. Suites £194–£252. Cottages from £240 for 4 nights.
meals	Lunch & dinner £5–£30.
closed	Christmas.
directions	From Ryde, B3330 south for 1.5 miles. Hotel signed left.

	Andrew Morgan
tel	01983 612711
fax	01983 613729
email	reception@seaviewhotel.co.uk
web	www.seaviewhotel.co.uk

Hotel

Map 3 Entry 121

Romney Bay House

Coast Road, New Romney, Kent TN28 8QY

The library look-out upstairs has a telescope so you can spy France on a clear day. Designed by Clough Williams-Ellis – creator of Portmeirion – for American film star Hedda Hopper, this ethereal dreamscape is as stunning as the photograph suggests. Inside, the whole place has a lingering 1920s house-party feel. Rooms are not huge but filled with chintzy cushions, sofas to sink into, frills and flowers, an honesty bar, a drawing room with a merry fire in winter, a conservatory for cream teas, and a dining room where Clinton prepares locally-caught fish – some home-smoked – and meat reared in Kent. He and Lisa swapped jobs in London hotels for the 'good life' in Kent; they have impeccable pedigrees and know what works... whether you're here for a conference, a wedding or a great escape, you'll appreciate their relaxed perfectionism. Bedrooms are the best feature; all are elegant, with pretty furniture, half-testers, sleigh beds and long views – some to the links, some to the sea. Go for a bracing shingleside walk, try your hand at croquet or drive the fairways on the neighbouring green.

rooms	10: 8 doubles, 2 twins.
price	£90-£150. Singles £65-£95.
meals	Dinner, 4 courses, £37.50. Cream teas from £5.75.
closed	One week at Christmas.
directions	M20, junc. 10, A2070 south, then A259 east through New Romney. Right to Littlestone; left at sea & on for 1 mile.

Clinton & Lisa Lovell

tel	01797 364747
fax	01797 367156

Hotel

Map 4 Entry 124

Wallett's Court Country House Hotel

Westcliffe, St Margaret's at Cliffe, Dover, Kent CT15 6EW

Wallett's Court is *old*. Odo, half-brother of William the Conqueror, lived on the land in Norman times, then Jacobeans left their mark in 1627 but it still retains the feel of a small country house without any pretension. Gorgeous architectural features have been retained; ancient red-brick walls in the drawing room, an oak staircase with worn, shallow steps in the hall and a huge log fire on chilly days. Bedrooms in the main house are big with four-posters and heaps of character, those in the barn and cottages are smaller and quiet. Above the spa complex – indoor pool, sauna, steam room and massage, aromatherapy and treatment suite – four excellent, contemporary suites have been added. There are tennis, a terrace with views towards a distant sea and white cliffs within a mile for breezy walks, rolling mists and wheeling gulls. First class cooking from Steven Harvey is a delight; try caramelised Rye Bay scallops with medallions of wild rabbit or Folkestone-landed sea bass. Walk it off with a stroll around the lovely garden.

rooms	16: 12 twins/doubles, 4 suites.
price	£119-£159. Singles £99-£119.
meals	Lunch £19.50. Dinner £35.
closed	Christmas.
directions	From Dover, A2/A20, then A258 towards Deal, then right, signed St Margaret's at Cliffe. House 1 mile on right, signed.

	Chris, Lea & Gavin Oakley
tel	01304 852424
fax	01304 853430
email	stay@wallettscourt.com
web	www.wallettscourt.com

Hotel

Map 4 Entry 125

The Inn at Whitewell

Whitewell, Clitheroe, Lancashire BB7 3AT

You'll be hard-pressed to find anywhere better. The inn sits just above the river Hodder with views across parkland to rising fells in the distance. Merchants used to stop at this old deerkeeper's lodge and fill up with wine, food and song before heading north through notorious bandit country; superb hospitality is still assured but the most that will hold you up today is a stubborn sheep. Back at the inn the bar is welcoming and the fire roars; grab a paper and a pint and watch the world from here. Bedrooms are large, warm and cosy, some with fabulous Victorian showers, others with deep cast-iron baths and Benesson fabrics; all have art and Bose music systems, some have peat fires; the biggest look onto the river. Families and dogs are welcome here and the food is a treat; Whitewell fish pie is their most famous dish and the restaurant – with fabulous views – serves à la carte treats like fillet of beef for two. There are also seven miles of private fishing, even their own well-priced Vintner's. Mildly eccentric, great fun.

rooms	23: 9 twins/doubles, 13 four-posters, 1 suite.
price	£94-£125. Singles £77-£114. Suite £114-£150.
meals	Bar meals from £5.50. Dinner, à la carte, from £25.
closed	Never.
directions	M6, junc. 31a, then B6243 east through Longridge, then follow signs to Whitewell for 9 miles.

	Charles Bowman
tel	01200 448222
fax	01200 448298
email	reception@innatwhitewell.com
web	www.innatwhitewell.com

Hotel

Map 6 Entry 126

Northcote Manor

Northcote Road, Langho, Blackburn, Lancashire BB6 8BE

This old Victorian manor house has been famous as a great place to eat and a super place to stay for over 20 years – now it is having a grand refurbishment. The location is pretty fabulous; the Ribble Valley, the trough of Bowland, historic castles, monuments and history surround you and there's great walking from the door. Downstairs, new checked carpets dazzle, there are plenty of comfortable places to sit and relax with a drink, and a crisp, formal dining room for Nigel's special creations. Try heather-fed free range Bowland lamb or breast of Goosnargh duckling; many of the vegetables, leaves and herbs are organically grown in the garden, eggs are from their own hens and Craig's wine list is long. Bedrooms vary in size but none are really small; all have huge beds with Egyptian cotton sheets and excellent bathrooms. The newly-decorated rooms have a more contemporary feel and there's a lovely old marble bath in one. Extensive lawns, mature trees and pretty flower beds are perfect for a stroll and great for wedding pictures.

rooms	14 twins/doubles.
price	£155–£190.
meals	Lunch, 3 courses, from £20. Dinner, à la carte, from £45.
closed	Christmas Day, New Year's Day and bank holiday Mondays.
directions	From the A6119 bypass take A666 towards Clitheroe for 4 miles. At large roundabout take 1st exit for Langho, then 1st right into Northcote Road.

	Craig Bancroft & Nigel Haworth
tel	01254 240555
email	sales@northcotemanor.com
web	www.northcotemanor.com

Restaurant with Rooms

Map 6 Entry 127

The Queen's Head

2 Long Street, Belton, Leicestershire LE12 9TP

This old village pub now sparkles in contemporary splendour, and at the bar the art of mixing cocktails is practised with flair – come for a Manhattan or a martini. But there's more than just a cool interior here; ales from a local microbrewery satisfy the cravings of die-hard traditionalists, while walls of wine rise in the airy bistro, making this a very inclusive watering hole. All this draws a devoted crowd: for jazz nights, wine tastings, cookery demonstrations and delicious food. Sunday lunch is hugely popular (make sure you book). There are boarded menus and tasty bar meals in the bistro or you can dive into the dining room for something a little more formal – perhaps cream of artichoke soup, fillet of wild salmon, rhubarb and custard soufflé. The feel throughout is warm and vibrant – cream walls, blond wood, chrome bars, leather sofas; in summer, doors open onto a side terrace. Big bedrooms are nicely stylish with crisp white linen, leather bedheads, pine dressers, perhaps a cast-iron sofa. Two on the second floor share a bathroom and are perfect for families.

rooms	6: 4 doubles; 2 twins sharing bath.
price	£70–£100. Singles £60.
meals	Lunch from £6.50. Sunday lunch £13. A la carte dinner £15–£30.
closed	Christmas & New Year.
directions	M1 junc. 23, then A512 west. North to Belton after 2 miles, signed.

	Henry & Ali Weldon
tel	01530 222359
fax	01530 224860
email	enquiries@thequeenshead.org
web	www.thequeenshead.org

Inn

Map 6 Entry 128

Allington Manor
Allington, Grantham, Lincolnshire NG32 2DH

Minutes from the old A1 but as quiet as a mouse, the village has a pub, a post office and the Viking Way; the walking is stunning. The Dutch-influenced Jacobean manor house is elegant yet solid, and filled with suits of armour, ancient weaponry and old oak furniture. Walk straight into the large square hall with flagstone floor (this part of the house goes back to 1630) and Garth or Joanne will bring you tea or a drink in an elegant sitting room, complete with twinkling fire on cold days. There isn't a trace of fuss or pomposity so you'll quickly feel at home. Proper home cooking (local beef or lamb) is served in a long dining room with ancient brick walls and lovely stone mullioned windows overlooking the garden. Bedrooms are large with soothing colours (blues, greens, creams), one with an enormous wooden bâteau bed, another with a four-poster; two have free-standing roll top baths to pamper yourself in. Curtains and fabrics are thickly lined and generous – not that there's any noise to mask. Walk, cycle, visit Lincoln or Nottingham, see Belvoir Castle or Burleigh House – all are near.

rooms	3: 2 doubles, 1 four-poster.
price	£95–£140. Singles from £85.
meals	Dinner with wine, £22.50–£27.50.
closed	Never.
directions	From Nottingham, A52 to Sedgebrook; left into Allington. House on right, just before pub & post office.

Garth Vincent

tel	01400 282574
fax	01400 282658
email	enquiries@allingtonmanor.co.uk
web	www.allingtonmanor.co.uk

B&B

Map 6 Entry 129

base2stay

25 Courtfield Gardens, Earl's Court, London SW5 0PG

Stylish rooms and attractive prices make this is a brilliant base for those in town for a night or two. Part hotel, part serviced apartments, the idea here is to keep things simple and pass on the savings to guests. You won't find a bar or a restaurant, you will find a tiny kitchen cleverly concealed behind cupboard doors in each room. You get fridges, kettles, sinks and microwaves, so chill drinks, make your own breakfast or zap up an evening meal. Super rooms come in a cool contemporary style and offer a lot for the money: halogen lighting, crisp white linen, air conditioning – and flat-screen TVs through which you can surf the internet at no cost (there are points for laptops too). Watch movies on demand, or raid the hotel's music library for 1,500 tracks. Bathrooms are equally good and come with limestone tiles, big white towels and power showers. There's a directory of local restaurants that deliver to the door, 24-hour reception, good security, a daily maid service. Some rooms interconnect, and a continental breakfast box can be delivered to your door. Bars, clubs and restaurants are close.

rooms	67: 32 twins/doubles, 13 triples, 18 singles, 4 suites, all with kitchenettes.
price	£99-£110. Triples £135. Singles £80. Suites £175.
meals	Continental breakfast £4.50.
closed	Never.
directions	Tube: Earl's Court (3-minute walk). Bus: 74, 328, C1, C3. Parking £30 a day, off-street.

	Nassar Khalil
tel	0845 262 8000
fax	0845 262 8001
email	info@base2stay.com
web	www.base2stay.com

Hotel

Map 3 Entry 130

The Rockwell

181 Cromwell Road, Earls Court, London SW5 0SF

An impeccably renovated designer hotel that oozes style at every turn. Step in off the road and the clipped contemporary elegance will elate you. Flames leap from pebbles in the fireplace, big sofas wait to take the strain, high windows flood the rooms with light. Follow the breeze onto an immaculate terrace, where olive trees shimmer and bamboo erupts from vast urns; come for breakfast in good weather or pop down for a cocktail after a hard day in town – it's floodlit at night. A lift sweeps you up to understatedly gorgeous bedrooms. Expect modish wallpapers and solid oak cabinets, capacious beds dressed in Egyptian linen, warmed by merino wool, Philippe Starck shower rooms (no baths), waffled bathrobes and White Company lotions. Rooms at the front are triple-glazed which defeats traffic noise entirely, while three rooms at the back have French windows that open onto small private terraces. You can stop for delicious lunch and dinner – fois gras, rack of lamb, fig and almond tart – but there are hundreds of restaurants on your doorstep and friendly staff will advise.

rooms	40: 15 doubles, 5 twins, 16 singles, 4 suites.
price	£150–£180. Singles £100–£140. Suites £200.
meals	Breakfast £12.50; continental £9.50. Lunch & dinner £5–£30.
closed	Never.
directions	Tube: Earl's Court (3-minute walk). Bus: 74, 328, C1, C3. Parking £30 a day, off-street.

Anna Swainston

tel	020 7244 2000
fax	020 7244 2001
email	reservations@therockwell.com
web	www.therockwell.com

Hotel

Map 3 Entry 131

Twenty Nevern Square
Earl's Court, London SW5 9PD

This is a great place, a fusion of classical and minimalist styles, with a clean, cool contemporary interior and beautiful things all around: Victorian birdcages, gilt mirrors, porcelain vases, a bowl full of dried rose petals. There's a real flow to the downstairs, all the way though to the conservatory-bar, with its stained glass, ceiling fans, cane chairs and glass tables. Bedrooms are equally stylish, with natural colours on the walls, cedar-wood blinds and rich fabrics throughout: silks, cottons and linens – nothing here is synthetic. CD players and TVs have been cleverly hidden away in pretty wooden cabinets so there is no clutter. Rooms come in different shapes and sizes, each with something to elate: an Indonesian hand-carved wooden headboard, an Egyptian sleigh bed, a colonial four-poster, some sweeping blue and gold silk curtains. A couple of the rooms have balconies, there are marble bathrooms and room service, too. An open fire warms the sitting room in winter. Good value for money, very friendly staff, and close to the tube.

rooms	20: 13 doubles, 3 twins, 3 four-posters, 1 suite.
price	£99-£140. Four-posters from £120. Singles £80-£110. Suite £160-£190.
meals	Continental breakfast included; full English £5-£9.
closed	Never.
directions	Tube: Earl's Court (2-minute walk). Bus: 74, 238, C1, C3. Parking: £20 a day off-street (2pm-11am).

	Sadik Saloojee
tel	020 7565 9555
fax	020 7565 9444
email	hotel@twentynevernsquare.co.uk
web	www.twentynevernsquare.co.uk

Hotel

Map 3 Entry 132

The Mayflower Hotel

26-28 Trebovir Road, Earl's Court, London SW5 9NJ

Excellent value for London with original art and colonial-style furniture. Harry's Bar in New York was the inspiration for the interior of the juice bar, while in reception an enormous wood carving from Jaipur frames a sculpted waterfall. Wander at will and come across creamy stone floors, leather sofas, American walnut and original art. Bedrooms are not huge but wonderfully designed, with shiny red marble bathrooms and exceptional walk-in showers. Most are filled with unusual antiques from India and the Far East, with lots of carved wood, gorgeous Andrew Martin fabrics and light wood floors. You get swish curtains, merino wool blankets, Egyptian cotton and ceiling fans. The technology is state-of-the-art, the use of space is clever. Rooms at the front flood with light and a couple have balconies. Family rooms are super-funky with bunk beds and good lighting. The tube is a two-minute walk and Earl's Court is on your doorstep. Don't miss the Troubadour for live music and great food; Bob Dylan, Jimi Hendrix and Joni Mitchell all played there in the 60s.

rooms	47: 28 doubles, 11 twins, 5 family, 3 singles.
price	£79-£99. Family room £120. Singles £59-£79.
meals	Continental breakfast included; English breakfast £5-£10.
closed	Never
directions	Tube: Earl's Court (2-minute walk). Bus: 74, 328, C1, C3. Parking: £20 a day, off-street (2pm-11am).

	Faisal Saloojee
tel	020 7370 0991
fax	020 7370 0994
email	info@mayflower-group.co.uk
web	www.mayflowerhotel.co.uk

Hotel

Map 3 Entry 133

Imperial College London

Accommodation Link, 58 Princes Gate, Exhibition Road, South Kensington, London SW7 2PG

Here's something outstanding. The campus accommodation of Imperial College (five Nobel prizewinners) is open to all during the summer holidays, and the rooms in Beit Hall, 200 yards from the Albert Hall, are exceptionally comfortable – big, bright, well-decorated, spotlessly clean. Many in the east wing have views of the Albert Hall. Extraordinarily, they keep the whole place running for you – cafés, bars, restaurants, shops, even a state-of-the-art sports centre in which you can swim, work out or stop for a juice. There's a full cleaning service, linen and towels are thrown in and you can expect barbecues in a shaded quad. The beer is subsidised, there's free internet access, airport pick-up, banks, whatever you need. A full breakfast is served in the Senior Common Room that overlooks the Queen's Lawn, and there are peaceful gardens in which to escape the city. All the big museums are around the corner and private tours led by curators can be arranged for groups. Hyde Park is on your doorstep, and it's great for the Proms (August and September).

rooms	580: twins & singles, some with showers, others sharing baths & showers.
price	£80-£85. Singles £42-£65.
meals	Lunch from £3.95. Dinner from £5.95.
closed	Late-September-May (limited availablity all year).
directions	Tube: South Kensington (5-minute walk). Bus: 9, 10, 14, 52, 74, C1. Parking: £25 a day, off-street.

	Marie Wilcox
tel	020 7594 9507
fax	020 7594 9504
email	accommodationlink@imperial.ac.uk
web	www.imperial-accommodationlink.com

Other Place

Map 3 Entry 134

The Cranley Hotel

10 Bina Gardens, South Kensington, London SW5 0LA

In a charming quiet London street of brightly painted Georgian houses, the Cranley has a neat front garden with wooden tables and chairs, clipped bay trees and wide steps up to the front door. The hall leads straight into a calm drawing room with deep Wedgewood-blue walls, original fireplaces, good antiques, coir carpets and the odd lively rug. Bedrooms are extremely comfortable: pale carpets, lilac walls, embroidered headboards over huge beds, plain cream curtains with bedspreads to match, pretty windows and cream-tiled snazzy bathrooms. Robes and slippers, state-of-the-art technology, air conditioning, prettily-laid tables for continental breakfast if you don't want it in bed and lovely Penhaligon smellies as a link back to the family who once owned the house. A cream tea with warm scones and clotted cream in the afternoon comes with the package, along with champagne and canapés at 7pm before you go off to an excellent local restaurant booked by the friendly staff. *24-hour room service. Weekend rates from £130.*

rooms	39: 15 doubles, 10 twins, 9 four-posters, 4 singles, 1 suite.
price	£165-£300. Singles £130-£165. Suite £300.
meals	Continental breakfast £9.95.
closed	Rarely.
directions	Tube: Gloucester Road (4-minute walk). Bus: 49, 74, C1. Parking: £30 a day, off-street.

	Lory Caprioli
tel	020 7373 0123
fax	020 7373 9497
email	info@thecranley.com
web	www.thecranley.com

Hotel

Map 3 Entry 135

Knightsbridge Green Hotel
159 Knightsbridge, London SW1X 7PD

This hotel has a battalion of faithful guests who return for the central position, the reasonable prices, the unfussy rooms and the ever-present Paul. He aims to greet everyone personally during their stay, and if you meet him by the lift, he'll chauffeur you up to your room. This is a family-owned hotel and you can expect to be welcomed genuinely and warmly. Spotlessly clean bedrooms tend to be fairly standard but they are surprisingly big, and while the design may be simple it is also pleasing. There are marble bathrooms, off-white walls, canvas curtains, air-conditioning and flat-screen TVs. The hotel doesn't have a bar, but it is licensed and drinks are brought to your room, as is breakfast: croissants, freshly-squeezed orange juice, and bacon and sausages from Harrods if you pay the extra. Rooms at the back have been vibrantly decorated to make up for the lack of light in the stairwell and a couple of them are nicely old-fashioned with warm floral fabrics and big beds (ever-popular with long-standing guests). All things Knightsbridge are on your doorstep, and the tube is a hop and a skip across the road.

rooms	28: 4 twins, 5 doubles, 7 singles, 12 suites.
price	£140-£160. Singles £105-£120. Suites £160-£185.
meals	Breakfast £4-£12.
closed	Never.
directions	Train: Victoria (to Gatwick); Paddington (to Heathrow). Tube: Knightsbridge (2-minute walk). Bus: 9, 10, 14, 19, 22, 52, 137. Parking: £30 a day, off-street.

	Paul Fizia
tel	020 7584 6274
fax	020 7225 1635
email	reservations@thekghotel.com
web	www.thekghotel.co.uk

Hotel

Map 3 Entry 136

L'Hotel

28 Basil Street, Knightsbridge, London SW3 1AS

L'Hotel is well-named – it has the feel of a small Parisian hotel, but chief among its many bounties is Isabel, who has proved it is not only what you do, but how you do it that matters. Her way is infectious; she is kind and open and nothing is too much trouble. The hotel's not bad either. No lounge, but a great little restaurant/bar – the social hub of the place – where the odd note of jazz rings out and where wines come direct from the hotel's French vineyard. You can have breakfast down there (excellent coffee in big bowls, pains au chocolat and hot croissants from the hotel bakery – lovely), or up in your room, while you laze about on vast beds that are covered in Egyptian cotton, with Nina Campbell fabric on the walls, little box trees on the mantlepiece and original art on the walls. Turn left on your way out and Harvey Nicks is a hundred paces; turn right and Harrods is closer. If you want to eat somewhere fancy, try the Capital next door. It has a big reputation, is owned by the same family (the Levins), and Isabel will book you in. A very friendly – and popular – hotel.

rooms	12: 11 twins/doubles, 1 suite.
price	£180–£200. Suite £215.
meals	Continental breakfast included; full English from £6.50. Lunch & dinner £5–£20.
closed	Rarely.
directions	Train: Victoria (to Gatwick). Tube: Knightsbridge (2-minute walk). Bus: 14, 19, 22, 52, 74, 137. Parking: £30 a day, off-street.

	Isabel Murphy
tel	020 7589 6286
fax	020 7823 7826
email	reservations@lhotel.co.uk
web	www.lhotel.co.uk

Hotel

Map 3 Entry 137

Searcy's Roof Garden Bedrooms

30 Pavilion Road, Knightsbridge, London SW1X 0HJ

A one-off, the sort of place you could only find in England. From the street you enter directly a 1927 freight elevator (it's had a facelift), then ascend three floors – by-passing Searcy's, the 160-year-old catering company whose headquarters these are. Step out of the lift and into comfy bedrooms decorated in country-house style – Laura Ashley wallpaper, canopied beds, fresh flowers, a smattering of antiques. Bathrooms can be eccentric – two rooms have baths in the actual bedroom – but most are tucked away snugly and all come with waffled robes, big white towels and Molton Brown treats. Breakfast is brought to you with a complimentary newspaper and is occasionally accompanied by the sound of the Household Cavalry passing below. In summer, you can move outside and scoff croissants on a very pretty roof garden surrounded by pots of colour. Air-conditioning and wireless internet run throughout, dry cleaning can be arranged, and if you want to eat in, local restaurants will deliver. Excellent value close to Harrods, and Hyde Park a short stoll.

rooms	10: 7 twins/doubles, 2 singles, 1 family suite.
price	£160. Singles £110. Suite £200.
meals	Continental breakfast included. Restaurants nearby.
closed	Christmas & New Year.
directions	Train: Victoria (to Gatwick). Tube: Knightsbridge (5-minute walk). Bus: 9, 10, 14, 19, 22, 52, 74, 137. Parking: £35 a day, off-street.

Demitrius Neofitidis

tel	020 7584 4921
fax	020 7823 8694
email	rgr@searcys.co.uk
web	www.30pavilionroad.co.uk

Hotel

Map 3 Entry 138

The Goring

Beeston Place, Victoria, SW1W 0JW

The Goring is a London institution, an epitome of Englishness, with a dining room for Dover sole or breast of pheasant and a bar for oysters and champagne. Ninety-six years a hotel with a Goring ever at the helm, it is the oldest family-run hotel in London (built in 1910) and the first hotel in the world to have central heating and a bathroom in every room. It is both grand and charming, proud of its traditions – there's still a cocktail party for guests on Sunday evenings – and, thanks to its warm, professional staff, is a happy ship indeed. Enter a world of marble floors, yellow walls and chandeliers by the dozen. Liveried doormen at reception dress like (friendly) Napoleonic generals; one of them, Peter, has worked here for 30-odd years. The restaurant has recently been refurbished by David Linley, good-sized bedrooms are smart and traditional with a dash of flair: crisp linen, woollen blankets, plush carpets and fresh flowers; bathrooms are wood-panelled, rooms at the back have gorgeous garden views. Two minutes from Buckingham Palace – yet Beeston Place is peaceful for such a central position.

rooms	71: 47 twins/doubles, 17 singles, 7 suites.
price	£260–£505. Singles £210–£325. Suites £345–£620.
meals	Breakfast £18.50. Lunch £29.75. Dinner £40.
closed	Never.
directions	Train: Victoria (to Heathrow). Tube: Victoria (2-minute walk). Bus: 2, 8, 16, 36, 38, 52, 73, 82. Parking £30 a day, off-street.

	Jeremy Goring
tel	020 7396 9000
fax	020 7834 4393
email	reception@goringhotel.co.uk
web	www.goringhotel.co.uk

Hotel

Map 3 Entry 139

Five Maddox Street
Mayfair, London W1S 2QD

This is the epitome of London cool, a zen-sleek, highly discreet, central London wonderland. The style is effortless. Terrazzo stone stairs sweep you up past polished plaster walls sealed with beeswax. In reception, tropical fish laze behind a wall of glass; in other rooms, you can lounge on leather cushions in front of a fire. Every suite is an apartment; two have planted terraces, several have decked balconies and the one in the loft has a leather staircase. Be seduced by pressed-bamboo floors, waffled bathrobes, oil-burners throughout. There are glass tables, chenille sofas, creamy leather headboards, lacquered walls. Beds are dressed in crisp Egyptian cotton and faux-fur blankets, limestone bathrooms delight. Every conceivable electronic gadget: CD and DVD players, fax machines, private lines… think of it, they've got it. And there are four different types of breakfast (including 'Vitality' for hangovers), great room service from local restaurants, private kitchens stuffed with goodies (from ice cream to champagne) and chefs who come in to cook for you. Bond Street and Soho are on the doorstep.

rooms	12 suites: 9 for 2, 2 for 4, 1 for 6, all with living rooms & kitchens.
price	£295-£440. 2-bed £540. 3-bed £730.
meals	Breakfast £10-£20. Room service.
closed	Never.
directions	Train: Paddington (to Heathrow). Tube: Oxford Circus (4-minute walk). Bus: 3, 6, 8, 12, 15, 23, 88, 159. Parking: £30 a day, off-street.

	Tracy Lowy
tel	020 7647 0200
fax	020 7647 0300
email	no5maddoxst@living-rooms.co.uk
web	www.no5maddoxst.com

Hotel

Map 3 Entry 140

22 York Street
Marylebone, London W1U 6PX

The Callis family live in two 1820s, Georgian-style townhouses in W1 – not your average London residence and one that defies all attempts to pigeon-hole it. There may be 18 bedrooms but you can still expect the feel of home. Michael keeps things friendly and easy-going, which might explain the salsa dancing lessons that once broke out at breakfast – a meal of great conviviality taken around a curved wooden table in a big, bright kitchen. Here, a weeping ficus tree stands next to the piano, which, of course, you are welcome to play. There's always something to catch your eye, be it the red-lipped oil painting outside the dining room or the old boots on the landing. Wooden floors run throughout. Each house has a huge sitting room (original high ceilings, shuttered windows), one with a grand piano, the other with sofas, books and backgammon. Bedrooms, spotless and comfy, have Provençal eiderdowns, good beds, country rugs, perhaps a piano or a chaise longue. There's a computer for guests to use, wi-fi throughout. Madame Tussaud's, Regent's Park and Lord's are close. A very friendly place.

rooms	18 twins, doubles, family & single rooms (3 with separate bathrooms).
price	£100–£120. Family rooms £145. Singles £89.
meals	Pubs/restaurants nearby.
closed	Never.
directions	Train: Paddington (to Heathrow). Tube: Baker Street (2-minute walk). Bus: 2, 13, 30, 74, 82, 113, 139, 274. Parking: £25 a day, off-street.

	Michael & Liz Callis
tel	020 7224 2990
fax	020 7224 1990
email	mc@22yorkstreet.co.uk
web	www.22yorkstreet.co.uk

Other Place

Map 3 Entry 141

The Royal Park Hotel

3 Westbourne Terrace, Lancaster Gate, Hyde Park, London W2 3UL

Paddington is just round the corner – and Hyde Park a three-minute stroll – yet there is none of the sleaze that surrounds many railway stations. The houses here are dignified and handsome; in this case, three houses newly rolled into one in a grand gesture of solidarity – but so discreetly that you would hardly know there was a hotel here at all. It is easy to imagine the carriages trundling up to the door in Victorian times. Staff are attentive and kind and charmingly multi-national. If you arrive at tea-time you will be served complimentary scones and jams in one of the two small drawing rooms, where you may pretend to be grander than you feel. (If the company is uninspiring, bury yourself in a newspaper or gaze studiously at the flickering gas fire.) Later, champagne and canapés will be served too, all 'on the house' – a lovely touch that encourages guests to chat. The bedrooms are serenely impeccable, generous with their beds, handmade mattresses, crisp sheets, woollen blankets, plump pillows and elegant bathrooms – and with almost every conceivable minor luxury.

rooms	48: 28 doubles, 5 twins, 2 four-posters, 2 singles, 11 suites.
price	£170-£300. Singles £130-£170. Suite £265-£300.
meals	Continental breakfast £9.95.
closed	Rarely.
directions	Train: Paddington (to Heathrow). Tube: Lancaster Gate; Paddington (both 4-minute walk). Bus: 7, 12, 15, 23, 27, 36, 94. Parking: £30 a day, off-street.

	Lisa Stewart
tel	020 7479 6600
fax	020 7479 6601
email	info@theroyalpark.com
web	www.theroyalpark.com

Hotel

Map 3 Entry 142

Miller's

111a Westbourne Grove, London W2 4UW

This is Miller's, as in the antique guides, and the collectibles on show in the first-floor drawing room make it one of the loveliest rooms in this book. Continental breakfast is taken around a 1920s walnut table, while at night, cocktails are served on the house, a fire crackles in the carved-wood fireplace and a couple of hundred candles flicker around you. It is an aesthetic overdose, exquisitely ornate, every wall stuffed with gilt-framed pictures. An eclectic collection of regulars include movie moguls, fashion photographers, rock stars, even a professional gambler. An opera singer once gave guests singing lessons at breakfast. Wander at will and find an altar of Tibetan deities (well, their statues), a 1750s old master's chair, busts and sculptures, globes, chandeliers, plinths, rugs and a three-legged chair stuffed on top of a Regency wardrobe. Things get moved around all the time, so expect the scene to change. Muralled walls in the hall were inspired by the Pope's palace at Avignon. Bedrooms upstairs are equally embellished; some bathrooms are minute. Wild extravagance in cool Notting Hill.

rooms	8: 6 doubles, 2 suites.
price	£175–£270.
meals	Continental breakfast included.
closed	Never.
directions	Train: Paddington (to Heathrow). Tube: Notting Hill Gate, Bayswater. Bus: 7, 23, 28, 31, 70. Parking: £25 a day, off-street.

	Martin Miller
tel	020 7243 1024
fax	020 7243 1064
email	enquiries@millersuk.com
web	www.millersuk.com

Hotel

Map 3 Entry 143

Portobello Gold

95-97 Portobello Road, Notting Hill Gate, London W11 2QB

A fun little place off Ladbroke Grove – a bar, a restaurant, a gallery and a place to stay. Sit out on the pavement in wicker chairs and watch the fashionistas stroll by, or hole up at the bar with a pint of ale and half a dozen oysters. Tiled floors, an open fire and monthly exhibitions of photography or art fill the walls while, at the back, the conservatory restaurant with its retractable roof feels comfortably 'jungle'. Dine – to the sweet song of canaries – on roast sea bass with rosemary and garlic (seafood's a speciality), Aberdeen Angus steak, sashimi or wild boar sausages. Recently refurbished bedrooms have good beds, a chair, a desk, and flat-screen TVs; the roof terrace apartment comes with putting green and barbecue, the new suite has an open fire and – a world first – a foldaway four-poster! Ideal if the hippy in you is still active, or you're after a quirky little place to stay where you also eat and drink. The cyber café is free to hotel guests, there are Trappist ales, Belgian beers and great wines available by the glass.

rooms	8: 4 doubles, 2 twins/doubles, 1 suite, 1 apartment for 6.
price	£60-£90. Suite £120. Apartment £150-£170.
meals	Continental breakfast included; full English £7.50. Bar meals from £6. Dinner £20-£25.
closed	Never.
directions	Train: Paddington (to Heathrow). Tube: Notting Hill (5-min walk). Bus: 12, 27, 28, 31, 52, 328. Parking meters outside.

Michael Bell & Linda Johnson-Bell

tel	020 7460 4910
fax	020 7229 2278
email	reservations@portobellogold.com
web	www.portobellogold.com

Restaurant with Rooms

Map 3 Entry 144

Europa House

79A Randolph Avenue, Maida Vale, London W9 1DW

Half a mile south, the Grand Union Canal sweeps through Little Venice, but you may wish to spurn it for these idyllic communal gardens: three acres of weeping willows, well-kept lawns and absolute peace. The apartments are equally divine: big and airy, extremely comfy, nicely private (John Malkovich stayed here when filming *The Libertine*), all with sitting rooms, fully-equipped kitchens and marble bathrooms. The style is crisply uncluttered – glass tables, big sofas, spacious halls, trim carpets – and there's a refreshingly open-plan feel. Creamy walls soak up the light; comfortable beds wear Egyptian cotton. Two apartments have terraces, all come with hi-fis, DVD players, wireless internet connection and video entrance phones. You could cook for yourself (there are stores close by), but Clifton Road has an easy-going village feel and is stuffed with delis, cafés and irresistible shops… stroll down for beakfast at Vicki's, coffee at the Clifton Road Nursery, lunch at Raoul's. Maid service daily (Monday-Friday) and Regent's Park is close.

rooms	11 apartments: 1 for 2, 8 for 4, 1 for 6, 1 for 8, all with living rooms & kitchens.
price	£175. 2-bed £260-£285. 3-bed £425. 4-bed 500.
meals	Self-catering.
closed	Never.
directions	Train: Paddington (to Heathrow). Tube: Warwick Road; Maida Vale (both 5-minute walk). Bus: 6, 16, 46, 98. Parking: £15 a day, off-street.

	Linda Campbell
tel	020 7724 5924
fax	020 7724 2937
email	linda@westminsterapartments.co.uk
web	www.westminsterapartments.co.uk

Hotel

Map 3 Entry 145

The White Horse

Brancaster Staithe, Norfolk PE31 8BY

The setting is magical. Fabulous views reach across the marshes and the water with its moored boats, and dinghies sailing on the evening high tide. The coastal path starts right outside this neat inn with its benches, parasols and troughs of plants and flowers: the perfect spot for a pint after a stroll. Inside, the fishy theme continues but in a modern, crisp way: seascape colours, natural materials, pictures of boats, bowls of pebbles and shells, big windows to the views. Bedrooms are beautiful. Those upstairs capture the ever-changing light; those on the ground floor have wide doors which open onto flower-filled terraces and are decorated in duck-egg blues, with tongue and groove and a New England feel. From here you can spot oyster catchers, ringed plovers, several species of tern and, in winter, geese; don't forget your binoculars. Dine by candlelight on mussels and oysters from yards away, homemade bread and ice creams, all of it as local and seasonal as possible. Watch the sun slide over the marshes as you unwind, slowly.

rooms	15: 9 doubles, 6 twins.
price	£90–£135.
meals	Lunch & dinner, 2 courses, from £15.
closed	Never.
directions	Midway between Hunstanton & Wells-next-the-Sea on the A149 coast road.

	Kevin Nobes
tel	01485 210262
fax	01485 210930
email	reception@whitehorsebrancaster.co.uk
web	www.whitehorsebrancaster.co.uk

Inn

Map 7 Entry 148

The Hoste Arms

The Green, Burnham Market, Norfolk PE31 8HD

Nelson was once a local. Now it's farmers, fishermen and film stars who jostle at the bar and roast away on winter evenings in front of a roaring fire. In its 300-year history the Hoste has been a court house, a livestock market, a gallery and a brothel. These days it's more a pleasure dome than an inn and even on a grey February morning it was buzzing with life, the locals in for coffee, the residents polishing off leisurely breakfasts, diligent staff attending a wine tasting. The place has a genius of its own with warm bold colours, armchairs to sink into, panelled walls, its own art gallery. Fabulous food can be eaten anywhere and anytime, so dig into honey-glazed ham hock, fillet of English beef or seared sea bass with fennel. In summer, life spills out onto tables at the front or you can dine on the terrace in the garden at the back. Rooms are all different: a tartan four-poster, a swagged half-tester, leather sleigh beds in the Zulu wing and Fired Earth bathrooms. Burnham Market is gorgeous, the north Norfolk coast is on your doorstep (bring your shrimping net). And don't miss the ladies' loo!

rooms	36: 12 twins/doubles, 4 four-posters, 5 singles, 7 suites. Zulu wing: 5 doubles, 3 suites.
price	£117–£206. Singles from £88. Suites £150–£260. Half-board from £74 p.p.
meals	Lunch from £10. Dinner from £25.
closed	Rarely.
directions	A148 east from King's Lynn for Fakenham. Left after 2 miles onto B1153, then right at Great Bircham; onto B1155 for Burnham Market.

Paul & Jeanne Whittome

tel	01328 738777
fax	01328 730103
email	reception@hostearms.co.uk
web	www.hostearms.co.uk

Hotel

Map 7 Entry 149

The Victoria at Holkham

Park Road, Wells-next-the-Sea, Norfolk NR23 1RG

Come for Rajasthan colour and the prettiest rooms on the north Norfolk coast. On the Holkham Hall estate, owned by the Earl of Leicester, Tom (Viscount) Coke and his wife Polly have taken on the old Vic and turned it into a boutique hotel – with three luscious self-catering 'follies' in the grounds. Families and city folk are drawn to the rare mix of escapism and boho chic… splashes of aubergine, lime-green and pink mingle with the old colonial feel, in homage to the pub's royal namesake. Stone flags and seagrass floors, velvet sofas and leather armchairs, huge bowls of lemons and limes, a buzzing bar, a feel of anticipation… not your usual retreat. In a dining room redolent with lilies, friendly staff ferry in crabs from Cromer, game from the estate and great steaming puddings; children get their own two-course menu – and outdoor swings. Bedrooms vary in size but all are serene in their Indian garb, the quietest away from the bar, with views to marshes, pinewoods, dunes and sea. Sands and skylarks are a stroll away – at their finest, and quietest, out of season. And the Big Hall is magnificent.

rooms	10 + 3: 9 doubles, 1 attic suite. 3 self-catering lodges for 2-4.
price	£110-£200. Singles £90-£110. Lodges £160-£200. Children in parents' room £15.
meals	Lunch & dinner £20-£35.
closed	Rarely.
directions	On A149, 2 miles west of Wells-next-the-Sea.

Tom Coke

tel	01328 710206
fax	01328 713249
email	globe@holkham.co.uk
web	www.victoriaatholkham.co.uk

Hotel

Map 7 Entry 150

The Globe Inn

The Buttlands, Wells-next-the-Sea, Norfolk NR23 1EU

Set back a few hundred yards from the bustling harbour at Wells, the Globe sits on leafy Buttlands Green. The 19th-century coaching inn has been given a thorough makeover by Tom and Polly Coke, who transformed the Victoria on their family estate at Holkham: expect the best. They've been especially clever to attract visitors and locals, and the bar – fire, coastal photographs, wooden floor – emanates a happy buzz. The restaurant, in New England style, already has a good reputation for food that's unstuffy, fresh, modern; lots comes from the estate. Only the season's finest will do: spring lamb with fresh asparagus, roasted seabass, game pie. On sunny days you can take your plates and your pints (Adnams and Woodfordes) out into the sunny red-brick courtyard, bordered on one side by a vast, as yet, unused, ballroom. Bedrooms are a treat – as fresh and un-traditional as can be, with oak floors, blinds, sumptuous velvet cushions and terrific bathrooms with big baths and monsoon showers. Children and dogs love it too, what with child-size pies, crabbing on the quay and walks on the hugest beach ever.

rooms	7: 5 doubles, 2 twins.
price	£55–£115.
meals	Lunch & dinner, 2 courses, from £14.
closed	Two weeks in February.
directions	North from Fakenham on B1105. Hotel on green in centre of village.

	Peter Hudson
tel	01328 710206
fax	01328 713249
email	globe@holkham.co.uk
web	www.globeatwells.co.uk

Inn

Map 7 Entry 151

Byfords

1-3 Shirehall Plain, Holt, Norfolk NR25 6BG

The bustling market town of Holt is filled with unusual and interesting shops and buildings. In the middle of it all sits Byfords, its oldest building, made of brick and flint. Pass the tables and chairs on the pavement and walk in to the delicatessen, its wooden shelves brimming with wines, oils, jams, chutneys and coffees. The place hums with shoppers, here for the local meat and cheeses, and the coffee and homemade cakes in the busy café. Iain and Clair have gone for the wow factor in the bedrooms: enormous Vi-sprung mattresses on oak bed frames, sumptuous linen and plump silky cushions, soft leather chairs on polished wood floors. Modern music systems and Bang & Olufsen TVs abound, views of higgledy-piggledy roof tops are an unexpected surprise, and bathrooms are luxurious with underfloor heating, fluffy towels and drenching showers. Downstairs windows and doors are flung open for outdoor dining when it's warm, and there's a green oak conservatory with open-plan kitchen, so you can watch your supper being cooked. Evenings are peaceful, with candles and log fires on winter nights.

rooms	9 + 1: 7 doubles, 2 twins. 1 self-catering apartment for 5.
price	From £130. Singles from £90.
meals	Dinner, 3 courses, from £21.
closed	Christmas Day.
directions	A148 to Cromer. Holt is approx. a 20-minute drive past Fakenham. Car parking available for residents.

	Iain Wilson
tel	01263 711400
email	queries@byfords.org.uk
web	www.byfords.org.uk

B&B

Map 7 Entry 152

Saracens Head
Wolterton, Erpingham, Norfolk NR11 7LX

A true country inn with nourishing food, real ale, good wines, an enchanting old courtyard walled garden, Norfolk's bleakly lovely coast – this is why people come here. But the food is the deepest seduction. Robert and his team cook up "some of Norfolk's most delicious wild and tame treats". Tuck into Morston mussels with cider and cream, pigeon, Cromer crab, venison. Vegetarians are pampered too. Then Robert works his own magic on old favourites such as bread and butter pudding... The bar is as convivial as a bar could be, a welcome antidote to garish pub bars with their fruit machines – Robert will have none of them. There's a parlour room for residents, decidedly civilised: terracotta walls with friezes, candles in bottles, a black leather banquette, open log fires. Retire to lovely bedrooms with bold colours, sisal floors, linen curtains, pretty touches; wake to a fabulous breakfast. The whole mood is of quirky, committed individuality – slightly arty, slightly unpredictable and in the middle of nowhere. *Minimum stay two nights & half-board only at weekends.*

rooms	6: 5 doubles, 1 twin.
price	£90. Singles £50. Half-board from £70 p.p.
meals	Bar meals from £4.95. Dinner, 2 courses, about £17.
closed	Christmas Day.
directions	From Norwich, A140 past Aylsham, then left, for Erpingham. Don't bear right for Aldborough, go straight through Calthorpe. Over x-roads. On right after about 0.5 miles.

	Robert & Rachel Dawson-Smith
tel	01263 768909
fax	01263 768993
email	saracenshead@wolterton.freeserve.co.uk
web	www.saracenshead-norfolk.co.uk

Inn

Map 7 Entry 153

Strattons

4 Ash Close, Swaffham, Norfolk PE37 7NH

Nowhere is perfect, but Strattons — one of the country's most eco-friendly hotels — comes close. Silky bantams strut on the lawn, funky classical interiors thrill. Les and Vanessa met at art school and every square inch of their Queen Anne villa is crammed with mosaics and murals, marble busts, cow-hide rugs on stripped wood floors, art packed tight on the wall. It is an informal bohemian country-house bolthole of French inspiration in a small market town. Bedrooms are exquisite: a carved four-poster, a tented bathroom, Indian brocade and stained glass. There's trompe l'œil panelling, sofas by a log fire and Botticelli's *Venus* hanging on a bathroom wall. Wonderful food in the candlelit restaurant (turn right by the chaise longue) is all organic, perhaps pea ice cream, leg of lamb, then hazelnut parfait. Les talks you through the cheese board with great panache, and breakfast (toasted stilton, goat's cheese omelette) is equally divine. Don't miss The Brecks for cycle tracks through Thedford forest and a neolithic flint mine. E M Forster dreamt of "a holy trinity of soil, soul and society." This is it.

rooms	8: 1 twin/double, 3 doubles, 4 suites.
price	£130–£140. Singles from £85. Suites from £200.
meals	Dinner, 4 courses, £40.
closed	Christmas.
directions	Ash Close runs off north end of market place between W H Brown estate agents & fish & chip restaurant.

Vanessa & Les Scott

tel	01760 723845
fax	01760 720458
email	enquiries@strattonshotel.com
web	www.strattonshotel.com

Hotel

Map 7 Entry 154

The Norfolk Mead Hotel

Coltishall, Norwich, Norfolk NR12 7DN

The setting is enchanting and you can paddle your canoe from the bottom of the garden to the Broads. But make time for these eight acres – lawns, trees, walled garden, swimming pool, fish-stocked lake and dinghy for messing about on the river. The sugar planter's house was built in 1740 – big, gracious and beautifully proportioned. Come for the people, the food and the easy-going comforts of a country-house hotel. A coronet bedhead, a Victorian bath with brass fittings, a striped attic snug... each bedroom is individual, super-comfortable and full of special touches: be-ribboned sheaves of Norfolk lavender, a teddy on the pillows, a basket of primroses, scrumptious linen. There are a fine entrance hall with sofas and log fire, a bar that opens to the garden, and menus from a creative young chef who loves his kitchen. Food is light, delicate and sophisticated – partridge from Norfolk, mussels from Morston, whisky and orange jelly with hazelnut tuiles, perfect cheese biscuits (homemade). Jill is lovely and full of ideas, daughter Nicky can massage or manicure you, and the barn owl may hoot you to sleep.

rooms	13: 7 doubles, 3 twins, 1 garden suite. Cottage suite: 1 double, 1 twin.
price	£85–£160. Singles £70–£95. Suites from £160. Half-board from £72 p.p.
meals	Sunday lunch £16.95. Dinner £31.50.
closed	Rarely.
directions	From Norwich, B1150 to Coltishall, over bridge; after 600 yds, bear right at petrol station, 1st right before church; down drive, signed.

Jill & Don Fleming

tel	01603 737531
fax	01603 737521
email	info@norfolkmead.co.uk
web	www.norfolkmead.co.uk

Hotel

Map 7 Entry 155

Fritton House Hotel

Church Lane, Fritton, Norfolk NR31 9HA

A small, chic, country-house hotel on the Somerleyton estate. Walks start from the back door, where paths lead out through sublime parkland and run down to Fritton lake. You can walk round it, row on it or take to the skies above it in a hot-air balloon. The building is 16th-century and was once a smuggler's inn; these days, warmly groovy interiors excite. Come for stripped wood floors, Cole & Son wallpapers, Farrow & Ball paints, sand-blasted beams. There's a smart drawing room at the front with super sofas, old shutters, country rugs and fresh flowers, then an airy bar and restaurant with leather armchairs, exposed brick walls and doors onto a gravelled terrace for views of the estate. Seriously indulging bedrooms flood with light and come with timber-framed walls, padded bedheads and mahogany dressers. Beds are dressed in crisp white linen and warmed with Welsh wool blankets, while funky bathrooms have colourful resin floors, deep baths and power showers. Sheep graze in the fields around you, brasserie food keeps you happy and visits to Somerleyton can be arranged. Brilliant.

rooms	9: 5 doubles, 2 twins/doubles; 1 double, 1 twin/double sharing bath (same-party bookings only).
price	£110–£160. Singles from £80.
meals	Lunch from £8. Dinner, 3 courses, about £27.
closed	Never.
directions	From Beccles A143 north for Great Yarmouth. In Fritton, right, signed Fritton Lake. Hotel on right before lake.

	Sarah Winterton
tel	01493 484008
email	frittonhouse@somerleyton.co.uk
web	www.frittonhouse.co.uk

Hotel

Map 7 Entry 156

No. 1 Sallyport

Off Bridge Street, Berwick-upon-Tweed, Northumberland TD15 1EZ

A boutique B&B that stands a stone's throw from Berwick's Tudor ramparts. Tiny lanes and cobbled alleyways sweep up to this 17th-century listed townhouse; step inside and you find seriously funky interiors. Bedrooms are wild – a fire and huge plasma screen in one, cherubs in a bay window in another. Wander at will and find leather sleigh beds, beautifully upholstered armchairs, shimmering Osborne & Little wallpaper, shiny hardwood floors. All rooms come with DVD players and a selection of films, Bose sound systems (bring some CDs), fridges in which to chill your wine (the house isn't licensed, so you're encouraged to bring your own). Super-cool bathrooms, most with deluge showers, come with Fired Earth tiles and waffle bathrobes to pad about in. Dinner can be arranged. Elizabeth used to have her own restaurant and will whisk up a feast, perhaps Dublin Bay prawns, leg of lamb casserole, warm orange tart; breakfast, served communally in a cool country dining room, is equally seductive. And medieval Berwick, built by an Italian architect from Lucca, is far prettier than you might imagine.

rooms	5 doubles.
price	£90–£140.
meals	Packed lunches £7.50. Dinner £35, by arrangement. BYO.
closed	Never.
directions	Leave A1 for A1167. Right at T-junc and over bridge into Berwick. Right into Marygate, right into West St, left into Bridge St and house on right.

Elizabeth Middlemiss

tel	01289 308827
fax	01289 308827
email	info@sallyport.co.uk
web	www.sallyport.co.uk

B&B

Map 9 Entry 157

The Pheasant Inn

Stannersburn, Kielder Water, Northumberland NE48 1DD

A really super little inn, the kind we all hope to chance upon: not grand, not scruffy, just right. The Kershaws run it with passion and an instinctive understanding of its traditions. The stone walls hold 100-year-old photos of the local community; from colliery to smithy, a vital record of its past. The bars are wonderful: brass beer taps glow, anything wooden – ceiling, beams, tables – has been polished to perfection and the clock above the fire keeps perfect time. The attention to detail is a delight, the house ales expertly kept: Timothy Taylor's and Theakston's Black Sheep. Robin cooks with relish, again nothing too fancy, but more than enough to keep a smile on your face – cider-baked gammon, grilled sea bass with herb butter, wicked puddings, Northumbrian cheeses; as for Sunday lunch, *The Observer* voted it the best in the North. Bedrooms in the old hay barn are as you'd expect: simple and cosy, good value for money. You are in the glorious Northumberland National Park – no traffic jams, no rush. Hire bikes and cycle round the lake, canoe or sail on it, or saddle up and take to the hills.

rooms	8: 4 doubles, 3 twins, 1 family.
price	£70-£80. Singles from £45. Half-board from £60 p.p.
meals	Bar meals from £8.95. Dinner, 3 courses, £16-£26.
closed	Mon & Tues November-March.
directions	From Bellingham, follow signs west to Kielder Water & Falstone for 7 miles. Hotel on left, 1 mile short of Kielder Water.

	Walter, Irene & Robin Kershaw
tel	01434 240382
fax	01434 240382
email	thepheasantinn@kielderwater.demon.co.uk
web	www.thepheasantinn.com

Inn

Map 9 Entry 158

Eshott Hall
Morpeth, Northumberland NE65 9EN

Slip into graceful inertia for a weekend, or longer; take the slog out of a drive up to Scotland; or ramble and yomp to your heart's content through (some say) the finest countryside in Britain with its dreamy castles and white beaches. Whatever the excuse, you will be indulged in this listed Palladian house. Bedrooms flourish fine linen, thick fabrics, restful colours; warm bathrooms have power showers, large baths and grand views over the estate and its medieval woodland. You are only 20 minutes from Newcastle with all the fun of shops, restaurants, galleries and theatres, but you are surrounded by wildlife (bats, deer, badgers and red squirrels). Ho and Margaret are passionate conservationists: ceramic floors, working shutters, a rare staircase and a stained-glass window designed by William Morris are just a few of the stunning architectural features. The garden is delightful with rare old trees, a Victorian fernery, a covered pergola and oodles of woodland trails. Enjoy local and seasonal food and vegetables from the walled garden — by candlelight in the formal dining room or in the Lost Wing.

rooms	5: 3 doubles, 2 twins/doubles.
price	£108. Singles £68.
meals	Dinner, 3 courses, £27.50. By arrangement.
closed	22 December-5 January.
directions	East off A1, 7 miles north of Morpeth, 9 miles south of Alnwick, at Eshott signpost. Hall gates approx. 1 mile down lane.

	Ho & Margaret Sanderson
tel	01670 787777
fax	01670 787999
email	thehall@eshott.com
web	www.eshott.com

Hotel

Map 9 Entry 159

Lace Market Hotel

29-31 High Pavement, Nottingham, Nottinghamshire NG1 1HE

Follow the cobbled streets to the heart of the old town and there's the Lace Market Hotel, perfectly carved out of three Georgian houses next to St Mary's church. On Sunday mornings you can lie in bed and listen to heavenly voices soar. Swish, contemporary interiors are crisp and warm – not minimalist, just stylish. Bedrooms come in different sizes, all have American oak furniture, crisp white linen, clean lines and smoked glass. In several you can soak in the bath and look out on the old court house opposite, while suites come with chrome banisters, wraparound windows and raised platforms for big beds. Head downstairs for cocktails at a marble bar, then wander through to a mirrored restaurant and dine on the best of British – or pop in next door to the hotel's funky alehouse, where you can sit in comfy wing-backed armchairs under a red-brick vaulted roof and dine on bistro food. Work off any excess free of charge at Holmes Place Health Club down the road, a stunning conversion of a Victorian railway station. Trendy bars, restaurants, shops and clubs are on your doorstep – come to have fun.

rooms	42: 33 doubles, 6 singles, 3 suites.
price	£119-£139. Singles from £90. Suites £185-£239.
meals	Continental breakfast £8.95; full English £12.95. Lunch (Tues-Fri) from £11.95. Dinner, 3 courses, around £27 (not Sun).
closed	Rarely.
directions	From city centre follow brown signs for Lace Market, Galleries of Justice & St Marys Church. NCP behind hotel: £7 per 24 hours.

Mark Cox

tel	0115 8523232
fax	0115 8523223
email	stay@lacemarkethotel.co.uk
web	www.lacemarkethotel.co.uk

Hotel

Map 6 Entry 160

Langar Hall
Langar, Nottinghamshire NG13 9HG

Langar Hall is one of the most engaging and delightful places in this book – reason enough to come to Nottinghamshire. Imogen's exquisite style and natural joie de vivre make this a mecca for those in search of a warm, country-house atmosphere. The house sits at the top of a hardly noticeable hill in glorious parkland, bang next door to the church. Imo's family came here over 150 years ago. Much of what fills the house arrived then and it's easy to feel intoxicated by beautiful things; statues and busts, a pillared dining room, ancient tomes in overflowing bookshelves, a good collection of oil paintings. Bedrooms are wonderful, some resplendent with antiques, others with fabrics draped from beams or trompe l'œil panelling. Heavenly food, simply prepared for healthy eating, makes this almost a restaurant with rooms – you'll need to book if you want to enjoy Langar lamb, fish from Brixham, game from Belvoir Castle and garden-grown vegetables. In the grounds: medieval fishponds, canals, a den-like adventure play area and, once a year, Shakespeare on the lawn.

rooms	12: 7 doubles, 2 twins, 1 four-poster, 1 suite, 1 chalet for 2.
price	£90–£210. Singles £65–£100.
meals	Lunch from £10. A la carte dinner about £30.
closed	Never.
directions	From Nottingham, A52 towards Grantham. Right, signed Cropwell Bishop, then straight on for 5 miles. House next to church on edge of village, signed.

	Imogen Skirving
tel	01949 860559
fax	01949 861045
email	langarhall-hotel@ndirect.co.uk
web	www.langarhall.co.uk

Hotel

Map 6 Entry 161

Falkland Arms

Great Tew, Chipping Norton, Oxfordshire OX7 4DB

In a perfect Cotswold village, the perfect English pub. Five hundred years on and the fire still roars in the stone-flagged bar under a low-slung timbered ceiling that drips with jugs, mugs and tankards. Here, the hop is treated with reverence; ales are changed weekly and old pump clips hang from the bar. Tradition runs deep; they stock endless tins of snuff with great names like Irish High Toast and Crumbs of Comfort. In summer, Morris Men jingle in the lane outside and life spills out onto the terrace at the front and into the lovely big garden behind. This lively pub is utterly down-to-earth and in very good hands. Dig into pork pies and plates of cheese in front of the fire or hop next door to the tiny beamed dining room for Paul's home-cooked delights. Bedrooms are cosy, some verging on snug; the attic room is wonderfully private. Brass beds and four-posters, maybe a bit of old oak and an uneven floor; you'll sleep well. The house is blissfully short on modern trappings, nowhere more so than in the bar, where mobile phones meet with swift and decisive action. Very special, book early for weekends.

rooms	5 doubles.
price	£80–£110.
meals	Lunch & dinner: main courses £8–£15. Must book for dinner. Not Sunday evenings.
closed	Never.
directions	North from Chipping Norton on A361, then right onto B4022, signed Great Tew. Inn by village green.

Paul Barlow-Heal
& Sarah-Jane Courage

tel	01608 683653
fax	01608 683656
email	sjcourage@btconnect.com
web	www.falklandarms.org.uk

Inn

Map 3 Entry 162

Burford House

99 High Street, Burford, Oxfordshire OX18 4QA

Burford House is a delight, intensely personal, full of elegant good taste, relaxing, and small; small enough for Simon and Jane to influence every corner, which they do with ease and good cheer. Classical music and the scent of fresh flowers drift through beautiful rooms, all of which have been stylishly upgraded: oak beams, leaded windows, good fabrics, antiques, simple colours, log fires, immaculate beds, roll top baths and a little garden for afternoon teas. And there's an honesty bar, with homemade sloe gin and cranberry vodka to be sipped from cut-glass tumblers. Hand-written menus promise ravishing breakfasts and tempting lunches, and they will recommend the best places for dinner. Both are happy in the kitchen: Simon cooks and Jane bakes, and Cotswold suppliers provide honey, jams, smoked salmon and farmhouse cheeses. Jumble the cat is 'paws on', too. Unwind, then unwind a little more. Enchanting river walks start in either direction through classic English countryside. Guests return time after time. A perfect little find in a perfect Cotswold town.

rooms	8: 3 doubles, 2 twins, 3 four-posters.
price	£125-£155. Singles from £85.
meals	Light lunch & afternoon tea (not Sundays). Pubs/restaurants in Burford.
closed	Rarely.
directions	In centre of Burford. Free on-street parking, free public car park nearby.

	Jane & Simon Henty
tel	01993 823151
fax	01993 823240
email	stay@burfordhouse.co.uk
web	www.burfordhouse.co.uk

B&B

Map 3 Entry 163

The Kings Head Inn

The Green, Bledington, Oxfordshire OX7 6XQ

About as Doctor Dolittle-esque as it gets. Achingly pretty Cotswold stone cottages around a village green with quacking ducks, a pond and a perfect pub with a cobbled courtyard. Archie is young, affable and charming with locals and guests, but Nic is his greatest asset – a milliner, she has done up the bedrooms on a shoestring and they look fabulous. All are different, most have a stunning view, some family furniture mixed in with 'bits' she's picked up, painted wood, great colours and lush fabrics. The bar is lively – not with music but with talk – so choose rooms over the courtyard if you prefer a quiet evening. Breakfast and supper are taken in the pretty flagstoned dining room (exposed stone walls, Farrow & Ball paints, pale wood tables), while you can lunch by the fire in the bar on devilled kidneys, sausage and mash, or perhaps fish pie; there are homemade puds and serious cheeses, too. Lovely unpompous touches like jugs of cow parsley in the loo. There's loads to do, antiques in Stow, golf at Burford, walking and riding in gorgeous country, even a music festival in June.

rooms	12: 10 doubles, 2 twins.
price	£70-£125. Singles from £55.
meals	Lunch & dinner: main courses £9.95-£17.95. Bar meals from £4.
closed	Christmas Day & Boxing Day.
directions	East out of Stow-on-the-Wold on A436, then right onto B4450 for Bledington. Pub in village on green.

	Archie & Nic Orr-Ewing
tel	01608 658365
fax	01608 658902
email	kingshead@orr-ewing.com
web	www.kingsheadinn.net

Inn

Map 3 Entry 164

Old Parsonage Hotel

1 Banbury Road, Oxford, Oxfordshire OX2 6NN

A stylish old Oxford favourite that's not just for well-heeled Mums and Dads.
The 400-year-old house – the parsonage to St Giles church – couldn't be better
placed for exploring. Through an ancient door find warmth from a log fire that
burns all day, old stone flags, dark red walls, comfortable sofas and window seats;
country-house but with a fresh, contemporary feel. Bedrooms are off winding
old corridors and stairs: they differ in size but all have Vi-sprung mattresses,
muted colours, excellent linen and modern, swish bathrooms. The suites have
plenty of room for lounging, downstairs rooms have their own little patio, there's
even a charming roof terrace. The bar/restaurant is the place for a lazy breakfast
or a snazzy lunch; try proper steak and chips or great seafood, including lobster,
from Jersey. Later, mooch out to the terrace on fine evenings for a barbecue or jig
to the jazz on a Friday night. Gee's Restaurant up the road also belongs to the
hotel and you can eat food served by young, cosmopolitan staff who are also
poets, artists, philosophers. Ah, the pleasures of Oxford.

rooms	30: 25 twins/doubles, 4 suites, 1 single.
price	£160-£200. Suites £225.
meals	Breakfast from £10.50. Lunch & dinner from £10.
closed	Never.
directions	From A40 ring road, south at Banbury Road r'bout to Summertown city centre. On right next to St Giles Church.

	Marie Jackson
tel	01865 310210
fax	01865 311262
email	info@oldparsonage-hotel.co.uk
web	www.oldparsonage-hotel.co.uk

Hotel

Map 3 Entry 165

The Boar's Head
Church Street, Ardington, Wantage, Oxfordshire OX12 8QA

A dapper estate village with a church, a pub and a post office, the pub being the home of the village cricket club. It's a friendly place with a battalion of locals who come for the open fires, the daily papers, the local ales and the gorgeous food. Sunday lunch rolls on to six and the bar is lively most evenings, making it the hub of a small community. Gilt mirrors and old oils hang on the walls. There are big oak tables in the restaurant, where doors open onto a terrace for alfresco summer suppers. Rooms upstairs are unmistakably smart. The small double has a beamed ceiling, the big double comes with a claw-foot bath, the suite has a sofa for kids and views over the village. All have good beds, crisp linen and piles of cushions. Passion bursts from the kitchen and the food here is popular as a result. Everything is homemade: bread, pasta, pastries, ice cream. You might get hot onion and gruyère tart, Cornish mussels with a spinach gratin, stuffed pheasant and mustard mash, bread and butter pudding with Bailey's ice cream. It's all cooked by big-hearted Bruce, who may still find time to chat.

rooms	3: 2 doubles, 1 suite.
price	£85-£105. Suite £130. Singles from £75.
meals	Lunch: main courses £8-£19. A la carte dinner from £20.
closed	Rarely.
directions	A417 west from Didcot for Wantage. Through West Hendred and Ardington signed left. In village left by bus stop and pub on left.

	Bruce & Kay Buchan
tel	01235 833254
email	info@boarsheadardington.co.uk
web	www.boarsheadardington.co.uk

Inn

Map 3 Entry 166

The Miller of Mansfield

High Street, Goring on Thames, Oxfordshire RG8 9AW

Ice-age melt water formed the Goring Gap; 14,000 years later 'cool' is back in town. The Miller, once a sedate red-brick coaching inn, has lavished a small fortune on rejuvenating itself and the results are decidedly groovy. You'll find pink suede beds, Cole & Son wallpaper, leather armchairs in the bar and silver-leaf mirrors above open fires. Beams have been sand blasted, panelling brought up from Devon to dress the bar. Expect shiny wooden floors, black suede bar stools, fairy-light chandeliers and candles flickering on the mantelpiece. Bedrooms pack a punch. The chrome four-poster has a leather bedhead, there are cow-hide rugs on white wood floors. You get plasma screens and wi-fi, bath robes and fluffy towels; flower-power colours come in pink, orange and electric green. Bathrooms tend towards the extravagant (though two have no door from the bedroom), with monsoon showers or claw-foot baths; one has a Japanese bath for two. Seriously good food, so walk by the Thames, take to the hills, then return to the Miller for a night of carousing. Bells peel at the Norman church. One for the young at heart.

rooms	14: 11 doubles, 1 twin, 2 suites.
price	£90–£140. Suites from £150.
meals	Continental breakfast included; full English £9.50. Bar meals available all day. Lunch from £7.50. Dinner from £22.
closed	Never.
directions	North from Reading on A329. In Streatley right onto B4526. Over bridge; hotel on left.

	Adam Bisset
tel	01491 872829
fax	01491 873100
email	info@millerofmansfield.com
web	www.millerofmansfield.com

Hotel

Map 3 Entry 167

The Cherry Tree Inn

Stoke Row, Henley-on-Thames, Oxfordshire RG9 5QA

A cherry orchard flourished here 400 years ago and farm workers lived in these brick and flint cottages. Five trees survive on the sprawling lawn at the front, so come in spring for the blossom. Beds of lavender lead up to the front door, inside you find ancient stone flagging and low beamed ceilings. It's a real treat, with board games in a cupboard, fairylights in the fireplace and a different colour on the walls in each room. Food is the big draw and on a Sunday in February a fanatical crowd gathered. Huge bowls of mussels flew from the kitchen, then plates of rare roast beef, finally a tarte tatin with a calvados sauce that brought sighs of ecstasy from a lucky diner. Rooms in the next-door barn are super value for money, stylish and private, with walls of colour, creamy carpets, silky red throws and leather headboards. Two have high beamed ceilings, bathrooms with slate floors are just the ticket, and each room has its own thermostat. A breakfast club for locals runs on the first Saturday of each month, so you may have company. Expect smoked kippers, scrambled eggs, the full works.

rooms	4 doubles.
price	£75–£95.
meals	Lunch from £7.50.
	A la carte dinner from £22.50.
closed	Christmas & New Year.
directions	A4070 north from Reading. After four miles, right, through Checklade, to Stoke Row. Pub in village.

Richard Coates & Paul Gilchrist

tel	01491 680430
email	info@thecherrytreeinn.com
web	www.thecherrytreeinn.com

Thamesmead House Hotel

Remenham Lane, Henley-on-Thames, Oxfordshire RG9 2LR

Patricia's eye for a news story has proved equally adept at creating a wonderful place to stay in the home of the Royal Regatta. The former arts correspondent has transformed a "seedy" 1960s Edwardian guest house into a chic getaway just a short amble from the centre of Henley-on-Thames; the walk over the famous three-arched bridge (1786) is the best introduction to this charming town. Soak up lazy, idyllic river views in both directions, then walk along towpaths or mess about in a rowing boat. Thamesmead is small but perfectly formed. Elegant bedrooms are decorated in a comfortably crisp Scandinavian style: mustard yellows, terracotta and soothing blues, big Oxford pillows to sink into, modern art on the walls, an extraordinary fossil fireplace in one, and painted wooden panelling in the bathrooms. No lounge, but the breakfast/tea room is relaxing, with Thompson furniture – spot the distinctive carved mouse motif – and French windows that let in lots of light, and maybe a gentle summer's breeze. Presiding over all is the erudite and fun-loving Patricia, a Dubliner to the core.

rooms	6: 4 doubles, 1 twin/double, 1 single.
price	£115–£145. Singles £95–£115.
meals	Afternoon tea available. Restaurants in Henley.
closed	Rarely.
directions	From M4 junc. 8/9, A404 (M) to Burchett's Green; left on A4130, for Henley (5 miles). Before bridge, right just after Little Angel pub. On left.

	Patricia Thorburn-Muirhead
tel	01491 574745
fax	01491 579944
email	thamesmead@supanet.com
web	www.thamesmeadhousehotel.co.uk

Hotel

Map 3 Entry 169

Phyllis Court Club Hotel
Marlow Road, Henley-on-Thames, Oxfordshire RG9 2HT

Classically English right down to the rose emblem, with the sort of protocol you'd expect from a private member's club, Phyllis Court is a class apart. Founded almost a century ago to create somewhere swish for bright young things from the city to zoom up to in their new motor cars, it still attracts the great and the good. It isn't hard to see why. Apart from the grandstand and its own Thames frontage with moorings – it's bang opposite the finishing line of the Royal Regatta – the house itself is a grandly self-effacing place: tweed, tennis and *The Telegraph* blend with a sense of fun. Members number some 3,000 today, and run the place with great pride – and grace. There *are* 'rules' but Muirfield it isn't! The club is named after the old English word for a red rose, 'fyllis'. Once moated, Phyllis Court was rebuilt in the 17th century, then again in the 18th and 19th. Bedrooms are easy on the eye and full of spoiling touches; the long drive sweeps past lawn and croquet courts. There are river walks, and Henley buzzes with day-trippers just as it always has. *Teas & meals for residents only.*

rooms	17: 9 doubles, 8 twins/doubles.
price	£131-£161. Singles £90-£126.
meals	Dinner, 3 courses, à la carte, around £27.50.
closed	Rarely.
directions	From Henley-on-Thames, A4155 towards Marlow. Club on right.

	Sue Gill
tel	01491 570500
fax	01491 570528
email	enquiries@phylliscourt.co.uk
web	www.phylliscourt.co.uk

Hotel

Map 3 Entry 170

Hambleton Hall

Hambleton, Oakham , Rutland LE15 8TH

A sublime country house, one of the loveliest in England. The position here is matchless. The house, a shooting box for the Earls of Rutland, stands on a tiny peninsular that juts into Rutland Water. You can sail on it or cycle round it, then come back to the undisputed wonders of Hambleton: sofas by the fire in the panelled hall, a pillared bar in red for cocktails and a Michelin star in the dining room. French windows in the sitting room (beautiful art, fresh flowers, the daily papers) open onto idyllic gardens. Expect clipped lawns and gravel paths, a formal parterre garden that bursts with summer colour and a walled swimming pool with huge views over grazing parkland down to the water. Bedrooms are the very best. Hand-stitched Italian linen, mirrored armoires, mullioned windows, marble bathrooms – and Stefa's eye for fabrics, some of which coat the walls, is faultless; the Croquet Pavilion, a suite with two bedrooms, has its own terrace. Polish the day off with a serious dinner, perhaps scallop ravioli, breast of Goosnargh duck, then poached pear with caramel ice cream. Wonderful.

rooms	17: 14 twins/doubles, 2 four-posters. Pavilion: 1 suite for 6.
price	£195-£360. Singles from £160. Pavilion £500-£600.
meals	Continental breakfast included; full English £15. Lunch from £18.50. Dinner £40-£70.
closed	Never.
directions	From A1, A606 west towards Oakham for about 8 miles, then left, signed Hambleton. In village, bear left and hotel signed right.

	Tim & Stefa Hart
tel	01572 756991
fax	01572 724721
email	hotel@hambletonhall.com
web	www.hambletonhall.com

Hotel

Map 6 Entry 171

Mr Underhill's at Dinham Weir

Dinham Bridge, Ludlow, Shropshire SY8 1EH

Chris and Judy moved Mr Underhill's from its Suffolk home after 16 years, to the foot of Ludlow Castle in 1998 – they regained their Michelin star in the first year. The setting of this restaurant with rooms is dreamy; in summer you can eat in the courtyard and watch the river Teme drift by. The dining room, too – long, light and airy, modern, warm and fun – has river views and masses of glass to draw it in. Bedrooms dazzle with natural fabrics, locally-woven carpet, cherry, maple and blond oak and big, comfy beds. Judy has designed the smaller rooms so they feel bigger; all are good and restful with stylish bathrooms. Fabulous new suites in the Miller's House have their own sitting rooms and look over the Green to Dinham Bridge, but the biggest 'wow' is saved for The Shed, a green oak building with an open-plan studio room: at the press of a button the curtains open to reveal breathtaking views up river. Good people with huge commitment – not forgetting Mungo and Toby, two British blues and heirs to Frodo's empire, after whose alias, as Tolkien fans will confirm, the restaurant is named.

rooms	9: 4 doubles, 2 twins/doubles, 3 suites.
price	£135-£170. Singles from £100. Suites £220-£260.
meals	Dinner £45. Not Tuesdays & Mondays.
closed	Occasionally.
directions	Head to castle in Ludlow centre, take 'Dinham' Road to left of castle; down hill, right at bottom before crossing river. On left, signed.

	Chris & Judy Bradley
tel	01584 874431
web	www.mr-underhills.co.uk

Restaurant with Rooms

Map 2 Entry 174

Porlock Vale House
Porlock Weir, Somerset TA24 8NY

Exmoor National Park runs into the sea here; tiny lanes ramble down into lush valleys while headlands fall to meet the waves. Sit out under the wisteria on the terrace and you can meet the locals; pheasants stroll among the daffodils and deer come to eat the garden. Across two fields, the sea; wave after wave rolls onto the beach, so pull on your boots and walk down to the shoreline, or pick up a rod and try to catch your supper. Whatever you do, you'll enjoy coming back to this relaxed country house with its comforting smells of polish, wood smoke and fresh flowers. There's a crackling fire in the hall everyday, delicious food in the oak-panelled dining room, deep sofas and sea views in the pretty sitting room, a snug bar for a night cap. Also, books, games, prints and pictures galore. Plush bedrooms are warm and comfy – big and bright with sofas if there's room; most have sea views and the biggest are huge. Make sure you see the beautiful Edwardian stables... you may find the blacksmith at work. The horses couldn't be better looked after and you will be too – owners and staff are just great.

rooms	15: 10 doubles, 4 twins, 1 single.
price	£110–£155. Suite £170. Singles £70–£100. Half-board £60–£95 p.p.
meals	Lunch from £5. Dinner £26.
closed	Mid-week in January & early February.
directions	West past Minehead on A39, then right in Porlock, for Porlock Weir. Through West Porlock, signed right.

Kim & Helen Youd

tel	01643 862338
fax	01643 863338
email	info@porlockvale.co.uk
web	www.porlockvale.co.uk

Hotel

Map 2 Entry 175

Bindon Country House Hotel

Langford Budville, Wellington, Somerset TA21 0RU

Bindon is a lovely old pile and it hides on the edge of woodland where wild flowers flourish. Once derelict, it now shines, and what strikes you most as you enter through the large glass front door is the crispness of it all: the open fires, the tiled entrance hall, the stained-glass windows, the wall tapestries, the plaster moulded ceilings, the galleried staircase, the glass-domed roof. Keep going into the snug panelled bar, past the wrought-iron candlesticks, for coffee served with piping hot milk and delicious homemade biscuits. In summer doors are flung open and you can sit by a magnificent stone balustrade that looks over rose gardens down to an old dovecote. Bright bedrooms come in different sizes: two oval rooms at the front of the house are *huge*, all dusky pink furniture, patterned wallpaper, high brass beds and Victorian baths. The rest are a good size, very comfortable; a couple are warm and cosy up in the eaves. High teas for children, gorgeous food, a small heated pool and a tennis court. In short, a treat, so come to get married or take the whole place over and cook for yourselves.

rooms	12: 10 twins/doubles, 2 four-posters.
price	£115-£215. Singles £95. Half-board from £85 p.p. (min. 2 nights). Whole house available to rent.
meals	Lunch £12.95. Dinner, 5 courses, £35.
closed	Rarely.
directions	From Wellington, B3187 for 1.5 miles; left at sharp S-bend for Langford Budville; right for Wiveliscombe; 1st right; on right.

	Lynn & Mark Jaffa
tel	01823 400070
fax	01823 400071
email	stay@bindon.com
web	www.bindon.com

Hotel

Map 2 Entry 176

Carew Arms

Crowcombe, Taunton, Somerset TA4 4AD

Supposedly retired, Reg Ambrose is back – if not behind the bar, then assisting son Simon and his wife Krystal in reviving this pub in the shadow of the Quantock Hills. It was, and still is, a mammoth task. But the outside loos have been spruced up and the old skittle alley transformed. Now it's a bar-dining room whose French windows lead to a sunny back terrace and a garden with tables and gentle woodland views, and you can still play skittles, or try your luck with boules in the new court. The front room, with its hatch bar, flagstones, plain settles, pine tables with benches and vast inglenook remains the same: delightfully unspoilt. Enjoy a pint of Exmoor Ale, engage in lively conversation and make the most of Cornish seafood casserole, grilled lamb cutlets with braised onions, locally farmed beef steaks and orange trifle. Bedrooms and bathrooms are newly decorated, quite plain, with beamed ceilings, good linen and creaking floor boards – but don't try to drop off before closing time, join in instead! There's Sunday jazz once a month and children and dogs get a proper welcome.

rooms	6: 3 doubles, 3 twins.
price	£84. Singles £55.
meals	Lunch & dinner from £15.
closed	Rarely.
directions	Off A358 between Taunton & Minehead. In centre of village.

Simon & Krystal Ambrose

tel	01984 618631
fax	01984 618428
email	info@thecarewarms.co.uk
web	www.thecarewarms.co.uk

Inn

Map 2 Entry 177

Combe House Hotel

Butterfly Combe, Holford, Bridgwater, Somerset TA5 1RZ

Amble down through the woods from the heights of the lush Quantocks (as fine a walking area as Exmoor), stroll through the village and up again to the hotel – its arms open to a scene of bucolic bliss. You are here because the setting is magical, the gardens enchanting, the food excellent (fruit and veg grown in their own organic garden, local meat and fish) and the mood exactly what you need in the Quantocks. The sign by the entrance sets the tone: here is an informal, easy-going, open-minded welcome to all, muddy-booted walkers included. The interior is surprisingly smart, with yellow carpet and a yellow theme in the big dining room; there is a modern bar with black leather armchairs and a little anteroom with a good sofa. The overall effect is one of cosy efficiency. Refurbished bedrooms are nicely colourful and come with thick fabrics, piles of pillows and spotless bathrooms. A good library, a heated indoor swimming pool, a sauna and tennis mean there's plenty to do without going out and enough chairs and tables scattered about the lawn to encourage privacy or conviviality.

rooms	15: 11 doubles, 4 singles.
price	From £110. Half-board from £65 p.p.
meals	Dinner, 3 courses, from £27.50.
closed	Never.
directions	From Bridgwater, A39 to Minehead. At Holford, left in front of Plough Inn and follow lane through village. Bear left at fork signed Holford Combe; drive near to end of road on right.

Hotel

	Andrew Ryan
tel	01278 741382
fax	01278 741322
email	enquiries@combehouse.co.uk
web	www.combehouse.co.uk

Map 2 Entry 178

Glencot House

Glencot Lane, Wells, Somerset BA5 1BH

Jacobean elegance spills from this beautiful late-Victorian mansion into its 18-acre parkland setting. Inside, it's as you would expect: find four-poster beds, carved ceilings, walnut panelling and hallways filled with antique furniture; at night candles flicker. The drawing room is the magnet of the house; you'll meet the other guests here, admiring the carved ceiling and the inglenook fireplace with open chimney flue the size of a room; in winter the flames leap six-feet high. Hard to believe it has all the mod cons — you get flat-screen TVs and wireless internet connection throughout — though there's snooker and croquet for die-hard traditionalists, too. Glencot was rescued from a state of dilapidation; long hours of toil have brought it back to life. Don't miss the garden: a magnificent terrace with stone balustrade and wide, gracious steps which sweep you down to the river Axe. And there are fountains, a waterfall and an old stone bridge to take you over to the cricket pitch where the village team plays.

rooms	14: 3 doubles, 3 twins, 5 four-posters, 3 singles.
price	From £175.
meals	Dinner, 3 courses, about £30.
closed	Rarely.
directions	From Wells, follow signs to Wookey Hole. Sharp left at finger post, 100m after pink cottage. House on right in Glencot Lane.

	Martin Miller
tel	01749 677160
fax	01749 670210
email	relax@glencothouse.co.uk
web	www.glencothouse.co.uk

Hotel

Map 2 Entry 179

Pennard Hill Farm

Stickleball Hill, East Pennard, Shepton Mallet, Somerset BA4 6UG

You're in 90 acres at the top of the hill with Mendips views, surrounded by hay meadows and wild flowers, a scattering of sheep and three donkeys. Waiting at the end of the drive are three self-catering cottages, chic boltholes deep in the country. In the Old Hayloft you sleep on a French antique bed under the rafters; downstairs, a door opens onto an indoor swimming pool and an arched window frames the view. The Lamb and the Golden Fleece have gardens for barbecues on summer nights and dreamy views from bedrooms at the front. The Lamb is snugly romantic, with faux leopard-skin throws on a sofa in front of the fire; the Golden Fleece sleeps eight in contemporary splendour and comes with a conservatory that opens onto its garden. Gingham curtains hang on whitewashed walls, you get crisp white linen and cast-iron beds. All have full kitchens, and provisions for a big breakfast waiting in the fridge – and if you don't want to cook, meals can be delivered to your door. Glastonbury and Wells are close and the walking is stupendous. *Minimum stay two nights.*

rooms	3 cottages: 2 for 2, 1 for 7-8.
price	£150 for 2; £280 for 4; 4-6, extra £70 p.p.; 6-7, extra £55 p.p.
meals	Self-catering. Meals can be delivered. Pubs & restaurants in Wells.
closed	Rarely.
directions	East from Glastonbury on A361. Through Pennard, 1st right after Apple Tree Pub. Up to top of hill and on left.

	Phil & Rosie Bailey
tel	01749 890221
fax	01749 890665
email	sales@pennardhillfarm.co.uk
web	www.pennardhillfarm.co.uk

Other Place

Map 2 Entry 180

Orchards Restaurant at Wrexon Farmhouse

Dipford Road, Angersleigh, Taunton, Somerset TA3 7PA

The axiom that some people are made for each other surely applies to the immensely likeable owners of Orchards Restaurant. Norman and Julie have known each other for ever and this charming, established restaurant in an old Somerset crofter's cottage marks a lifetime of unswerving devotion. Feel cocooned from the world in the spruce bar with brick inglenook – or spill into a courtyard full of honeysuckle and rosemary. Herbs, salads, apples, damsons and plums grow on four acres for the table. Norman is a no-frills cook, preferring classic English methods to current trends: fish from Brixham, roast duckling, homemade ice creams and a tempting dessert trolley. In the carpeted, oak-panelled restaurant, tables lit by candlelight fit cosily under old beams. One airy, vaulted bedroom awaits in Cherry Barn; sofa and armchairs, shower room, much comfort and breakfast at the time of your choosing. As for the traffic, you'll be too busy enjoying yourself to notice the hum of the nearby motorway. Thick walls insulate and the prevailing wind blows the sound in the other direction!

rooms	1 suite for 2-3.
price	£71. Singles £55.
meals	Continental breakfast £6.95. Dinner, à la carte, around £30. Restaurant closed Sun & Mon.
closed	Rarely.
directions	From Taunton centre, follow signs to Trull; right after Queen's College, into Dipford Road, for Angersleigh. 2 miles on right, just after bridge over M5.

	Norman & Julie White
tel	01823 275440
email	mail@orchardsrestaurant.co.uk
web	www.orchardsrestaurant.co.uk

Restaurant with Rooms

Map 2 Entry 181

Farmer's Inn

Slough Green, West Hatch, Taunton, Somerset TA3 5RS

You don't often trek into deepest Somerset and wash up at a deeply groovy inn, but that's what you get at the Farmer's, so brave the narrow country lanes and head to the top of the hill for colour and comfort in equal measure. All the country treats are on hand. Outside, cows in the fields, cockerels crowing and long clean views; inside, friendly natives, open fires and a timber-framed bar. It's all the result of a total renovation, and one airy room now rolls into another giving a sense of space and light. Imagine terracotta-tiled floors and beamed ceilings, yellow-painted tongue-and-groove panelling, old pine dining tables dressed with pots of rosemary and logs piled high in the alcoves. Bedrooms are the best, some big, some huge. They come with off-white walls, seagrass mats on shiny wooden floors, cast-iron beds, power showers or claw-foot baths. Some have daybeds, others have sofas, one has a private courtyard. Super food is all homemade – Welsh rarebit, pork and cider sausages, goats' cheese ravioli – and you can eat on the terrace in summer. Great walking, too: bring the boots.

rooms	5: 4 doubles, 1 twin.
price	£80–£110.
meals	Bar meals from £4.50. A la carte dinner from £25.
closed	Never.
directions	M5 junc. 25, then south on A358. Right at Nag's Head pub, up hill for two miles, following signs past RSPBA. On right.

Debbie Lush

tel	01823 480480
email	letsgostay@farmersinnwesthatch.co.uk
web	www.farmersinnwesthatch.co.uk

Inn

Map 2 Entry 182

Greyhound Inn

Staple Fitzpaine, Taunton, Somerset TA3 5SP

A classic English country pub, walls bedecked with collages of pictures and fishing memorabilia that create an atmosphere of warmth and hospitality. Let the eye wander while sitting at tables worn nicely from frequent use and decorated with vases of wild flowers. Interconnecting bars with open fires and flagstoned floors are perfect for enjoying cask marque real ales and Somerset ciders. Super food is very special; this is a 16th-century inn and head chef Paul Webber recreates the odd 16th-century dish – perhaps spring lamb with lavender or roasted fallow deer. Constantly changing menus brim with fresh local produce – it's no surprise to discover this is Somerset Dining Pub of the Year. Dine well, then "retreat in good order", as one boxing print wisely suggests, to simple rooms, clean and comfortable, more hotel than individual, with floral curtains and bed covers. Ivor and Lucy are relaxed hosts and seemingly made for the job of community landlords. All this in deepest rural Somerset with walks through forest to Castle Neroche and stunning views from the Blackdown Hills. *Children over 12 welcome.*

rooms	4: 2 doubles, 2 twins.
price	From £80. Singles from £55.
meals	Lunch from £4. Dinner, à la carte, around £20.
closed	Rarely.
directions	M5, junc. 25, A358 towards Ilminster for 4 miles, then right, for Staple Fitzpaine. Left at T-junc. Village 1.5 miles further. Inn on right at x-roads.

	Ivor & Lucy Evans
tel	01823 480227
fax	01823 481117
email	info@thegreyhoundinn.fsbusiness.co.uk

Inn

Map 2 Entry 183

Devonshire Arms Hotel

Long Sutton, Near Langport, Somerset TA10 9LP

A lively English village with a well-kept green; the old school house stands to the south, the church to the east and the post office to the west. The inn (due north) is 400 years old and was once a hunting lodge for the Dukes of Devonshire; a rather smart pillared porch survives at the front. These days open-plan interiors are warmly contemporary with high ceilings, shiny blond floorboards and fresh flowers everywhere. Hop onto white leather stools at the bar and order a pint of Crop Circle, or sink into sofas in front of the fire and crack open a bottle of wine. In summer, life spills onto the terrace at the front, the courtyard at the back and the lawned garden beyond. Super bedrooms run along at the front; all are a good size, but those at each end are huge. You get low-slung wooden beds, seagrass matting, crisp white linen and freeview TV. One has a purple claw-foot bath, some have compact showers. Delicious food is on tap in the restaurant – chargrilled scallops, slow-cooked lamb, passion fruit crème brûlée – so take to the nearby Somerset levels and walk off your indulgence in style.

rooms	9: 8 doubles, 1 twin.
price	£75-£110. Singles from £55.
meals	Lunch from £5. Dinner from £10.
closed	Rarely.
directions	A303, then north on B3165, through Martock, to Long Sutton. Pub on green in village.

Philip & Sheila Mepham

tel	01458 241271
fax	01458 241037
email	mail@thedevonshirearms.com
web	www.thedevonshirearms.com

Inn

Map 2 Entry 184

The Queen's Arms

Corton Denham, Somerset DT9 4LR

Stride across rolling fields with Dorsetshire views, feast on Corton Denham lamb, retire to a perfect room. Buried down several Dorset and Somerset-border lanes, this 18th-century stone pub has an elegant exterior – more country gentleman's house than pub. Inside, Rupert and Victoria (ex-Londoners with experience in the business) have created a calm, relaxing space. The bar, with its rug-strewn flagstones and bare boards, pew benches, deep sofas and crackling fire, has not lost its country feel. In the dining room – big mirrors on terracotta walls, new china on old tables – happy eaters dine on robust British dishes distinguished by fresh ingredients from local suppliers. Try smoked haddock and spinach tart with a glass or two of Jim Barry's Aussie shiraz, follow with pan-fried calf's liver, black spot bacon, mash and gravy; find room for a comforting crumble. The bedrooms and bathrooms are beautifully designed in gorgeous colours; a duck-egg blue wall here, dear little red and cream checked curtains there. All have lovely views and the bathrooms are immaculate. There's a garden too, small but sunny.

rooms	5: 4 doubles, 1 twin.
price	£75–£120.
meals	Lunch from £3.90.
	Dinner from £18.50.
closed	Rarely.
directions	From A303 take Chapel Crosse turning, through South Cadbury village. Next left and follow signs to Corton Denham. Pub at end of village on right.

Rupert & Victoria Reeves

tel	01963 220317
email	relax@thequeensarms.com
web	www.thequeensarms.com

Inn

Map 2 Entry 185

Bellplot House Hotel & Thomas's Restaurant
High Street, Chard, Somerset TA20 1QB

The original 1727 plot was, and still is, bell-shaped – hence the name. The listed, four-square Georgian house has had some interesting owners down the years, including a Malayan rubber planter and a clutch of spinster sisters; bedrooms Anne, Mary, Sarah and Lydia are named in their honour. Today an atmosphere of sunny bonhomie reigns, thanks to Betty, who does warm front of house, and son Thomas, who stars in the kitchen, with a little help from dad. Dennis also mans the bar, a sunny, south-facing room with an almost clubby feel (green walls, polished floors, a chesterfield). No tennis or pool, but a special arrangement enables you to stretch and pamper at the leisure club a short drive away. Then back to the elegant dining room and some seriously good food that includes the catch of the day – and the occasional dinner devoted to 'Italian Specialities', 'Champagne' or, tantalisingly, 'Puddings'. Bedrooms are uncluttered and airy: modern pine, white duvets, navy curtains, impressive showers, wireless broadband and rooftop views. A super bolthole in the centre of Chard.

rooms	7: 5 doubles, 1 family, 1 single.
price	£79.50. Single £69.50.
meals	Breakfast £5–£9.
	Dinner, 3 courses, £20–£25.
	Picnic lunch £12.
	Restaurant closed Sunday.
closed	Rarely.
directions	In centre of Chard, 500 yds from the Guildhall. Car park available.

	Betty Jones
tel	01460 62600
fax	01460 62600
email	info@bellplothouse.co.uk
web	www.bellplothouse.co.uk

Hotel

Map 2 Entry 186

Lord Poulett Arms

High Street, Hinton St George, Crewekerne, Somerset TA17 8SE

In a ravishing village, an idyllic village inn, French at heart and quietly groovy. Part pub, part country house, with walls painted in reds and greens and old rugs covering flagged floors, the Lord Poulett gives a glimpse of a 21st-century dream local, where classical design fuses with earthy rusticity. A fire burns on both sides of the chimney in the dining room; on one side you can sink into leather armchairs, on the other you can eat under beams at antique oak tables while candles flicker. Take refuge with the daily papers on the sofa in the locals' bar or head past a pile of logs at the back door and discover an informal French garden of box and bay trees, with a piste for boules and a creeper-shaded terrace. Bedrooms upstairs come in funky country-house style, with fancy flock wallpaper, perhaps crushed velvet curtains, a small chandelier or a carved-wood bed. Two rooms have slipper baths behind screens in the room; two have claw-foot baths in bathrooms one step across the landing; Roberts radios add to the fun. Delicious food includes summer barbecues, Sunday roasts and the full works at breakfast.

rooms	4: 2 doubles; 2 doubles, each with separate bath.
price	£72. Singles £48.
meals	Lunch & dinner: main courses £9–£15.
closed	Never.
directions	A303, then A356 south for Crewekerne. Right for West Chinnock. Through village and first left for Hinton St George. Pub on right in village.

	Steve & Michelle Hill
tel	01460 73149
email	steveandmichelle@lordpoulettarms.com
web	www.lordpoulettarms.com

Inn

Map 2 Entry 187

Ounce House
Northgate Street, Bury St Edmunds, Suffolk IP33 1HP

Bury St Edmunds, an ancient English town, is a dream; if you've never been, don't delay. The Romans were here, the barons hatched plans for Magna Carta within the the now-crumbled walls of its ancient monastery and its Norman abbey attracted pilgrims by the cartload. The town was made rich by the wool trade in the 1700s and highlights include the cathedral (its exquisite new tower looks hundreds of years old) and the magnificent Abbey Gardens (perfect for summer picnics). Just around the corner, Ounce House, a handsome 1870 red-brick townhouse, overflows with creature comforts, so slump into leather armchairs in front of a carved fireplace and gaze at walls of art. You'll also find a snug library, a lawned garden and homely bedrooms packed with books, mahogany furniture and fresh flowers. Princely breakfasts are served on blue-and-white Spode china at one vast table. This is B&B in a grand-ish home, and Jenny and Simon will pick you up from the station or book a table at a local restaurant. Try The Chalice (traditional English) or Maison Bleu (good seafood). Don't miss the May arts festival.

rooms	3: 2 doubles, 1 twin.
price	£90-£120. Singles £70-£85.
meals	Restaurants 5-minute walk.
closed	Rarely.
directions	A14 north, then central junction for Bury, following signs to historic centre. At 1st r'bout, left into Northgate St. On right at top of hill.

	Simon & Jenny Pott
tel	01284 761779
fax	01284 768315
email	pott@globalnet.co.uk
web	www.ouncehouse.co.uk

B&B

Map 4 Entry 188

The Great House
Market Place, Lavenham, Suffolk CO10 9QZ

Lavenham is a Suffolk gem, a medieval town made prosperous by 14th-century wool merchants, hence the timber-framed houses that jut out over narrow streets at impossible angles. The Great House stands across the market place from the Guildhall, its 18th-century façade giving way to a 15th-century interior of timber frames, varnished wood floors, beamed ceilings and a carved bressumar beam that straddles the inglenook and which dates to 1550. The poet Stephen Spender once lived here and the house became a meeting places for artists, but these days it's the irresistible allure of French cooking that draws the crowd. You might get fois gras, local lamb, crème brûlée, but whatever you do, don't miss the cheese board: it's a work of art. Super-comfy bedrooms at the top of a creaky wooden staircase have antique dressers, fresh flowers, bowls of fruit, a decanter of sherry and sparkly marble bathrooms. One room has a Jacobean four-poster: an island in a sea of rugs; another, in the roof, has huge beamed timbers. Four rooms have their own sitting area and those at the front overlook the square.

rooms	5: 1 double, 4 suites.
price	£96–£150. Singles from £70. Half-board from £75 p.p.
meals	Continental breakfast £6.50; full English £9.50. Lunch from £11. Dinner from £24.95. Not Sunday nights & Mondays.
closed	First 3 weeks in January.
directions	A1141 to Lavenham. At High Street, 1st right after The Swan or up Lady Street into Market Place.

	Régis & Martine Crépy
tel	01787 247431
fax	01787 248007
email	info@greathouse.co.uk
web	www.greathouse.co.uk

Hotel

Map 4 Entry 189

The Bildeston Crown
Bildeston, Suffolk IP7 7ED

There are flagstones in the locals' bar, warm reds on the walls and sweet-smelling logs smouldering in open fires. The inn dates from 1529, the interior design from 2005. Not that the feel is overly contemporary; ancient beams have been reclaimed from under a thick coat of black paint and varnished wood floors shine like honey. There are gilded mirrors and oils on the walls, candles in the fireplace, happy locals at the bar. An airy open-plan feel runs throughout, with lots of space in the dining room and smart leather chairs tucked under hand-made oak tables. You'll also find flowers in the courtyard, old radiators and high-backed settles in the front bar and local Suffolk beers to quench your thirst. Bedrooms come in different sizes, but all are stuffed with luxury. Imagine regal reds and golds, faux fur blankets, silk curtains, perhaps a bust in a gorgeous bathroom. A hi-tech music system holds 1,000 albums (listen as you soak); and there are flat-screen TVs. Hire bikes from the shop next door and dive into the country, or come for the beer festival in the last week of May.

rooms	10: 6 doubles, 3 twins, 1 single.
price	£100–£150. Singles £45–£75.
meals	Bar meals from £5. A la carte dinner from £25; 8-course tasting menu £50.
closed	Never.
directions	A12 junc. 31, then B1070 to Hadleigh. A1141 north, then B1115 into village. Pub on right.

Hayley Robertson
tel   01449 740510
fax   01449 741843
email   info@thebildestoncrown.co.uk
web   www.thecrownbildeston.com

Inn

Map 4 Entry 190

The White Hart Inn

High Street, Nayland, Colchester, Suffolk CO6 4JF

Michel Roux's other place is exquisite on all counts and the way things are done here is second to none. Locals love it and flock in for coffee, lunch and dinner, even a pint at the bar. The inn, beamed and timber-framed, dates from the 15th century. You get open fires, flagstones and stripped floorboards, but the hallmark is a rural French elegance, with light and airy rooms, very friendly staff and impeccable service. You feast on "scrumptious food", to quote an enraptured guest, and sup from a vast collection of New World wines; "people like to travel when they drink," says Michel. Bedrooms, which vary in size, have a warm country style: yellow walls and checked fabrics, crisp linen and thick blankets, sofas or armchairs and wonderful art; some have wildly sloping floors, two have vaulted ceilings, one has original murals that may be the work of Constable's brother. Breakfast on duck eggs, freshly-baked croissants, Suffolk bacon, even fried bread. There are barbecues in summer, pizzas on Sunday nights. The village is gorgeous. Don't miss the 14th-century tower or the old post office next door.

rooms	6: 5 doubles, 1 twin.
price	£85–£110. Singles £69–£87.
meals	Lunch from £11.50. Dinner around £24. Not Mondays (Mondays: continental breakfast only).
closed	27 December–9 January.
directions	Nayland signed right 6 miles north of Colchester on the A134 (no access from A12). In village centre.

	Michel Roux
tel	01206 263382
fax	01206 263638
email	nayhart@aol.com
web	www.whitehart-nayland.co.uk

Restaurant with Rooms

Map 4 Entry 191

Salthouse Harbour Hotel
1 Neptune Quay, Ipswich, Suffolk IP4 1AS

A converted Victorian dockside warehouse, with fine arched windows on the ground floor and watery views across the marina to a working dock beyond. Step in off the quay and you find sand-blasted red bricks, old cast-iron pillars and a warm contemporary design in a comfortably funky bar/restaurant. Big splashy oils hang on the walls, light floods in through fine arched windows, and the odd sailor pops in for a drink. Uncluttered lofthouse-style bedrooms come in neutral colours with crisply clad beds, low ceilings and flat-screen TVs; you get slate floors and bathrobes in spotless bathrooms. Several rooms have small balconies, those at the front have views of the marina and the penthouse suites have walls of glass. If you want to lounge around downstairs, there's a big sitting room for leather sofas, wicker armchairs and the daily papers, but life tends to gather in the airy restaurant at the front for espressos and beers and good brasserie-style food. Cardinal Wolsey's house is close for a collection of Constables and Gainsboroughs or you can head to the football at Portman Road.

rooms	43: 41 twins/doubles, 2 suites.
price	£130-£140. Suites £190-£200.
meals	Lunch from £10. Dinner from £20.
closed	Never.
directions	A14 junc. 56 for Ipswich. At 5th roundabout (by Novotel) right onto one-way system. Keep right down Grimwade St, then double back on yourself and keep left. Left for marina; left along quay; hotel on right.

	Robert Gough
tel	01473 226789
fax	01473 226927
email	staying@salthouseharbour.co.uk
web	www.salthouseharbour.co.uk

Hotel

Map 4 Entry 192

Chequers

220 High Street, Wickham Market, Woodbridge, Suffolk IP13 0RF

It's not just the fine butcher's shop, nor even the famous underwear shop, that makes a trip to Wickham Market a must – now there is Chequers too. Once an old pub, it had been boarded up for years before Katie and Mark got their clever hands on it. The three 'rooms' all have their own access and places to sit; the problem will be in choosing which one. The Garden Room has cottage windows, open beams and seagrass flooring and the Coach House an oriental twist and an iron bed with a fur throw; the Hay Loft is a love nest with mood lighting and a leather bed. All have state-of-the-art bathrooms, huge beds with clouds of white linen and extras like full room service. Sit in your own little gravelled garden and order champagne, beer or wine (you can BYO too, for corkage); breakfast (full local and organic blow-out or something lighter) is delivered and there's really no reason to leave. Except you're in striking distance of Southwold and Aldeburgh and only minutes from Snape Maltings Concert Hall. Sheer indulgence.

rooms	3 doubles.
price	£75–£130. Singles from £60.
meals	Pubs nearby.
closed	Rarely.
directions	Take A12 turn off to Wickham Market, north of Ipswich, past Woodbridge. Through Market Square, down lane opposite Spring Lane.

	Katie & Mark Casey
tel	01728 746284
fax	01728 746284
email	katie@kckc.co.uk
web	www.chequerssuffolk.co.uk

B&B

Map 4 Entry 193

The Old Rectory

Campsea Ashe, Woodbridge, Suffolk IP13 0PU

An old country rectory with contemporary interiors; what would the rector think? You get stripped floors in the dining room, fairylights in the conservatory and a 21st-century orange chaise longue by the honesty bar. Michael and Sally swapped Hong Kong for Suffolk and the odd souvenir came with them: wood carvings from the Orient and framed Burmese chanting bibles. In winter, a fire smoulders at breakfast; in summer, you feast in a huge stone-flagged conservatory where doors open onto two acres of orchard and lawns. A warm country-house informality flows within, so help yourself to a drink, sink into a sofa or spin onto the terrace in search of sun and birdsong. Smart bedrooms are warmly decorated; one is up in the eaves, one overlooks the church, another has a claw-foot bath. Delicious food includes organic sausages and homemade jams at breakfast, perhaps parsnip soup and roast rack of Suffolk lamb at dinner, then almond and lemon tart. Sutton Hoo is close as is Snape Maltings (performing opera singers occasionally stay and warm up for work in the bedrooms). A happy house.

rooms	7: 3 doubles, 2 twins, 2 four-posters.
price	£85–£120. Singles from £65.
meals	Dinner, 3 courses, £25. Not Saturday or Sunday.
closed	Occasionally.
directions	North from Ipswich on A12 for 15 miles, then right onto B1078. In village, over railway line; house on right just before church.

	Michael & Sally Ball
tel	01728 746524
email	mail@theoldrectorysuffolk.com
web	www.theoldrectorysuffolk.com

Hotel

Map 4 Entry 194

Wentworth Hotel

Wentworth Road, Aldeburgh, Suffolk IP15 5BD

Come for a little time travel; this stretch of the Suffolk coast will sweep you back to sleepy England at its loveliest: fishing boats on shingle beaches, an estuary for super walks and a music festival in summer. The Wentworth matches the mood perfectly; it's warmly old-fashioned, quietly grand, full of its own traditions. Michael's family have been here since 1920, when scores of fishermen worked the shore; the few that remain haul their boats up onto the beach across from the hotel terrace. Inside you find a warm seaside elegance, nothing too racy; instead, sunshine colours, fresh flowers, flickering coal fires, oils on the walls and shelves of books. Also: delightful sitting rooms, a bar for all seasons, and part of the hotel resembles a grand ocean liner. The restaurant looks out to sea, comes in Georgian red and spills onto the sunken lawn in summer for views of passing boats. Bedrooms (many with sea views) are plush: Zoffany wallpaper, reds and golds, French armoires, comfortable beds. Joyce Grenfell used to stay for the Aldeburgh Festival and has a room named after her.

rooms	34: 24 twins/doubles, 4 singles. Darfield House: 6 doubles.
price	£105–£210. Singles from £61. Half-board £56–£115 p.p.
meals	Lunch from £7.50. Dinner from £15.
closed	Never.
directions	A12 north from Ipswich, then A1094 for Aldeburgh. Past church, down hill, left at x-roads; hotel on right.

	Michael Pritt
tel	01728 452312
fax	01728 454343
email	stay@wentworth-aldeburgh.co.uk
web	www.wentworth-aldeburgh.com

Hotel

Map 4 Entry 195

The Crown and Castle
Orford, Suffolk IP12 2LJ

The road runs out at sleepy Orford, so saddle up and follow cycle tracks or bridal paths into the forest. You can also hop on a boat and chug over to Orfordness, the biggest vegetated shingle spit in the world. In WWII it housed a military research base where Barnes Wallace (bouncing bomb) and Robert Watson-Watt (radar) toiled all day, returning at night to the splendour of the Crown, a Victorian redbrick inn that stands close to a 12th-century castle. Today the feel is light and airy, very comfortable, with stripped wood floors, open fires and eclectic art. A mouthwatering menu (half a pint of Orford prawns, Cornish crab, roasted Suffolk pheasant) caused indecision, but the warm duck salad with spiced pear was exceptional. Rooms in the main house come in pastels, those at the back have long watery views. Garden rooms (dull on the outside, lovely within) are big and airy, with padded headboards, seagrass matting, spotless bathrooms and doors onto a communal garden. All have crisp white linen, TVs and videos. Wellington boots wait at the back door, so pull on a pair and discover Suffolk.

rooms	18: 16 doubles, 2 twins.
price	£90–£145. Singles from £72. Half-board from £75 p.p.
meals	Lunch from £9.50. A la carte dinner from £24.50.
closed	Never.
directions	A12 north from Ipswich to A1152 east of Woodbridge, then B1084 into Orford. Hotel on market square.

	David & Ruth Watson
tel	01394 450205
email	info@crownandcastle.co.uk
web	www.crownandcastle.co.uk

Inn

Map 4 Entry 196

York House Rooms

York House, Easebourne Street, Easebourne, Midhurst, Sussex GU29 0AL

A great deal of privacy and a huge amount of luxury go hand-in-hand at this rather posh house – a sanctuary after the rigours of Goodwood or Cowdray. A local stone house with an 1800s façade (the B&B wing is in a restored separate building) it also lives next to the South Downs so is a bonus for weary walkers. You have your own front door, a sitting room with a flat-screen TV, glossy magazines, bedrooms with French linen and wool blankets, and bathrooms that blast and cosset. These are tranquil, well thought-out interiors (Felicity designs) that hum with good taste: a simple lily here, a French chair there, goose down pillows on toile de Jouy-ed beds. Fabrics and textiles are expensive and in the most respectable colours: aubergines, mushrooms, deep blues and greys. And there's a tickety-boo walled garden, where you can have organic breakfast and admire raised beds with topiary and box hedging. If flowers are your thing, John Brookes's garden is near – or head to Petworth and do some antique bargain hunting.

rooms	2 suites.
price	£90–£180. Singles £70–£100.
meals	Pubs/restaurants nearby.
closed	Christmas.
directions	From London A3 to Hindhead to Midhurst. Just before Midhurst left to Easebourne. At T-junc. left, immed. left again into Easebourne St. 150 yds on left.

	Felicity & Ian Lock
tel	01730 814090
email	felicity@yorkhouserooms.co.uk
web	www.yorkhouserooms.co.uk

B&B

Map 3 Entry 197

The Foresters

Graffham, GU28 0QA

Nick is a cook, one with a history. He worked for Le Caprice and set up Daphne's in Barbados; in short, he's a bit of a name. Did he see fit to mention this when we popped in? Not for a milli-second. Luckily we have contacts prepared to spill the beans... and all the other fabulous ingredients that are whisked up for your plate. Start with duck-liver parfait and a pear chutney, move onto shepherd's pie with buttered cabbage, finish with bread and butter pudding. Everything is homemade and none of it costs a bomb. Nick and Serena are young and easy-going, happy to be out of the city doing their own thing. Their pub dates back to the 17th century, has open fires, beamed ceilings, an exposed stone wall and cider flagons in a fireplace. Bedrooms are small and simple with good linen, trim carpets and driftwood beds. As for Graffham, it's a cul-de-sac village, wonderfully English; locals get about on horseback. Paths lead into the South Downs, so come to walk or ride your bike. There are Sunday roasts, wine tastings, curry nights, quiz nights. Dogs (pub only) and kids are welcome. All this an hour from London.

rooms	2 doubles.
price	From £65.
meals	Continental breakfast. Lunch & dinner from £9.50 (not Mondays).
closed	Rarely.
directions	From Midhurst, 2 miles south on A286, then left for Heyshott and Graffham. Straight ahead, left at T-junc. in village; pub on right.

Nick Bell & Serena Aykroyd

tel	01798 867202
fax	01798 867202
email	info@foresters-arms.com
web	www.foresters-arms.com

Inn

Map 3 Entry 198

West Stoke House

West Stoke, Chichester, Sussex PO18 9BN

A long drive through gorgeous countryside brings you to a pale stone, perfectly proportioned house with huge high-ceilinged rooms and large light windows; a Georgian pile with all the trimmings. But the feel is more restaurant with rooms than hotel, and you eat well here; there's a French twist to the fresh local fish and meat, tables are neatly laid with fresh flowers and large windows pull in the light. To the gorgeous French antiques and stunning oak floors are added abstract impressionistic paintings by local artists, modern lighting and pale, contemporary colours. If all is serene and comfortable downstairs, upstairs is no less so, with clever use of textures and colours from papal purple to palest rose pink, pristine linen, cashmere bed throws and flat-screen TVs. Bathrooms are bang up to date with a minimalist look — free-standing baths and excellent lighting. Explore three acres of gardens with a croquet lawn and large cedar woods; there are old benches and wicker seats to lounge in and sculpture to admire. Chichester and its good theatre are a short drive.

rooms	5 twin/doubles.
price	£130–£150. Singles from £75.
meals	Lunch £17.50. Dinner £35.
closed	Christmas Day & Boxing Day.
directions	A3 south to Milford, A286 to Lavant. Turn right in Lavant for West Stoke.

	Rowland Leach
tel	01243 575226
fax	01243 574655
email	info@weststokehouse.co.uk
web	www.weststokehouse.co.uk

Restaurant with Rooms

Map 3 Entry 199

The Royal Oak Inn

Pook Lane, East Lavant, Chichester, Sussex PO18 0AX

There's a cheery wine-bar feel to the Royal Oak; locals and young professionals come with their children and it's all as rural as can be. Inside, a modern-rustic look with traditional touches prevails: stripped floors, exposed brickwork, dark leather sofas, open fires, racing pictures on the walls – the inn was once part of the Goodwood estate. The dining area is big, light and airy, with a conservatory; you can spill out onto the front patio that's warmed by outdoor lamps on summer nights (you face a road, but this one goes nowhere). Five chefs conjure up delicious salmon and chorizo fishcakes, honey and clove roasted ham, fillet steak. Bedrooms have a contemporary feel. Some are in converted buildings, the rest are at the back of the pub, up the stairs; ask for one with a view. All have CD players, plasma screens, a DVD library and top toiletries – the best of modern – along with excellent lighting, brown leather chairs and big comfy beds. Staff are attentive, breakfasts are good and fresh, a secret garden looks over the South Downs, and you're well-placed for Chichester Theatre and Goodwood.

rooms	6 + 2: 4 doubles, 1 twin, 1 cottage for 2. 2 self-catering cottages: 1 for 3, 1 for 4.
price	£90–£130. Singles £65–£75.
meals	Lunch & dinner, à la carte, £12.50–£25.
closed	Christmas Day & Boxing Day.
directions	From Chichester A286 for Midhurst. First right at first mini roundabout into E. Lavant. Down hill, pass village green, over bridge, pub 200 yds on left. Car park opposite.

Nick & Lisa Sutherland
tel   01243 527434
fax   01243 775062
email   nickroyaloak@aol.com
web   www.thesussexpub.co.uk

Inn

Map 3 Entry 200

Arundel House

11 High Street, Arundel, Sussex BN18 9AD

Arundel is a dream, old England at the foot of a Norman castle. Below, the Arun runs off to sea; above, a cathedral soars towards heaven. Arundel House – a listed Georgian merchant's house close to the quay – stands on the tiny high street, opposite the Tudor post office, around the corner from the market place, where castle turrets rise above rippling red roofs. Inside, warm contemporary interiors have light wood floors, clean white walls and raspberry dining chairs to match the house speciality: kir royale mixed with crème de framboise. Spotless bedrooms have the lot: wooden beds, crisp white linen, smart red throws, plasma screen TVs, swanky bathrooms. Head down for cocktails and canapés, then feast on Luke's delicious food, maybe crab and smoked haddock fishcakes, pink lamb with a rosemary jus, caramelised banana parfait with a bitter chocolate sorbet. Breakfast (fresh OJ, the full works) is equally sinful and will set you up for the day. Come by train, bring your boots, follow the river, take to the hills. There's an August arts festival and the castle opens April to November.

rooms	5 doubles.
price	£60–£160.
meals	Lunch (Sat only) & dinner (not Sun evenings) £20–£38.
closed	Rarely.
directions	A27 to Arundel, then one-way system into town. Through market square (castle on left) and opp. post office. Parking vouchers for car park at reception.

Billy Lewis-Bowker & Luke Hackman

tel	01903 882136
email	mail@arundelhouseonline.com
web	www.arundelhouseonline.com

Restaurant with Rooms

Map 3 Entry 201

The Griffin Inn

Fletching, Sussex TN22 3SS

A proper inn, one of the best, a community local that draws a well-heeled and devoted crowd. The occasional touch of scruffiness makes it almost perfect; fancy designers need not apply. The Pullan family run it with huge passion. You get open fires, 400-year-old beams, oak panelling, settles, red carpets, prints on the walls... this inn has aged beautifully. There's a lively bar, a small club room for racing on Saturdays and two cricket teams play in summer. Bedrooms are tremendous value for money and full of uncluttered country-inn elegance: uneven floors, lovely old furniture, soft coloured walls, free-standing Victorian baths, huge shower heads, crisp linen, fluffy bathrobes, handmade soaps. Rooms in the coach house are quieter, those in next-door Patcham House quieter still. Seasonal menus include fresh fish from Rye and Fletching lamb. On Sundays in summer they lay on a spit-roast barbecue in the garden, with ten-mile views stretching across Pooh Bear's Ashdown Forest to Sheffield Park. Not to be missed. *Minimum stay two nights on bank holiday weekends.*

rooms	13: 6 doubles, 7 four-posters.
price	£80-£140. Singles £60-£80 (Sun-Thur).
meals	Bar lunch & dinner £10-£20. Restaurant £22-£30.
closed	Christmas Day.
directions	From East Grinstead, A22 south, right at Nutley for Fletching. On for 2 miles into village.

	Bridget, Nigel & James Pullan
tel	01825 722890
fax	01825 722810
email	info@thegriffininn.co.uk
web	www.thegriffininn.co.uk

Inn

Map 4 Entry 202

Newick Park Hotel

Newick, Sussex BN8 4SB

A classic Georgian house in 255 acres overlooking the South Downs with a lake, fishing, tennis, swimming, old-fashioned service and the cry of peacocks. Inside, ornate picture frames, chandeliers, heavy curtains and a large, light, creamy sitting room with sofas, books and a roaring fire. Food is English with a French influence, game is from the estate, some vegetables and soft fruits are grown in the walled garden (the gardener works closely with the chef) and there's home-buzzed honey, too. Bedrooms vary in size and most are traditional and chintzy; some have little window seats and sofas, all have supremely comfortable beds, fresh flowers, stunning views and some fine antiques. Recently renovated rooms outside the house have a more contemporary feel. Come to relax and to be pampered – and don't miss the Victorian dell garden with its rare collection of very old royal ferns, camellias, azaleas and rhododendrons, with masses of bulbs in spring and a lake walk. Or pop into Brighton (only 20 minutes away) for antique hunting and funky shops.

rooms	16 twins/doubles.
price	£165-£285. Singles from £125.
meals	Lunch from £14.50. Dinner around £40.
closed	31 December-5 January.
directions	From Newick Village turn off the green and follow signs to Newick Park for 1 mile until T-junction. Turn left; after 300 yds, entrance on right.

	Michael & Virginia Childs
tel	01825 723633
email	bookings@newickpark.co.uk
web	www.newickpark.co.uk

Hotel

Map 4 Entry 203

Stone House
Rushlake Green, Heathfield, Sussex TN21 9QJ

One of the bedrooms has a bathroom with enough room for a sofa and two chairs around the marble bath – but does that make it a suite? Jane thought not. The bedroom is big, too, has a beautiful four-poster, floods with light and, like all the rooms, has sumptuous furniture and seemingly ancient fabrics. All this is typical of the generosity of both house and owners. Stone House has been in the Dunn family for a mere 500 years and Peter and Jane have kept the feel of home. Downstairs, amid the splendour of the drawing room, there's still room for lots of old family photos; across the hall in the library, logs piled high wait to be tossed on the fire. Weave down a corridor to ancient oak panelling in the dining room for Jane's cooking; she's a Master Chef with her own (stunning) kitchen garden, and regularly runs cookery courses. Having eaten, walk out to the superb, half-acre walled kitchen garden and see where it's all grown – they're 99% self-sufficient in summer. There are 1,000 acres to explore and you can fish for carp. Indulgent picnic hampers for Glyndebourne, including chairs and tables, can be arranged.

rooms	6: 3 twins/doubles, 2 four-posters, 1 suite.
price	£125–£245. Singles £80–£115.
meals	Lunch £24.95, by arrangement. Dinner £24.95.
closed	Christmas & New Year.
directions	From Heathfield, B2096, then 4th turning on right, signed Rushlake Green. 1st left by village green to crossroads and house on far left, signed.

	Peter & Jane Dunn
tel	01435 830553
fax	01435 830726
web	www.stonehousesussex.co.uk

B&B

Map 4 Entry 204

Little Hemingfold Hotel
Telham, Battle, Sussex TN33 0TT

The south-east of England is much underrated in terms of rural beauty. Those who want to get away to the simplicity of deep country will like it here; drive up the bumpy dirt track and you could be miles from the middle of nowhere. It is pretty rustic, a little like renting a remote country cottage without having to cook or clean; open fires, old sofas and armchairs, books and games, lots of flowers, floods of light. Breakfast in the yellow dining room is under a sloping glass roof; at night, the candles come out for delicious home-cooked dinners with vegetables from their own organic patch. The bedrooms are plain, clean and simple, some in the main house, others across the small, pretty courtyard. They are fairly earthy, four having woodburning stoves – again that feel of deep country – with the odd four-poster, maybe a sofa, glazed-brick walls and bathrooms with good towels. Outside, a two-acre lake to row and fish or swim in, a grass tennis court (the moles got the better of the croquet lawn), woodland to walk in and lots of peace and quiet. Bring the dogs!

rooms	12: 10 twins/doubles; 2 family rooms each with separate bath.
price	£98. Singles £59-£69. Half-board £70-£77.50 p.p.
meals	Dinner, 4 courses, £28.50.
closed	27 Dec 2006-28 Feb 2007.
directions	From Battle, A2100 for Hastings for 1.5 miles. Hotel signed left by 'Reduce Speed Now' road sign; 0.5 miles up bumpy farm track.

	Allison & Paul Slater
tel	01424 774338
fax	01424 775351
email	info@littlehemingfoldhotel.co.uk
web	www.littlehemingfoldhotel.co.uk

Hotel

Map 4 Entry 205

Jeake's House
Mermaid Street, Rye, Sussex TN31 7ET

Rye, one of the Cinque Ports, is a perfect town for whiling away an afternoon; wander and discover the tidal river, old fishing boats, arts and crafts shops and galleries. Jeake's House, on a steep and cobbled street in the heart of it all, has a colourful past as wool store, school and home of American poet Conrad Potter Aiken. Carpeted corridors weave upstairs and down; bedrooms, cosy with beams and timber frames, are generously furnished and excellent value. Some have stunning old chandeliers, others four-posters, cosy bathrooms have Bronnley soaps, and there's a mind-your-head stairway up to a generous attic room with views over roof tops and chimneys. The galleried dining room – once an old Baptist chapel, now painted deep red – is full of busts, books, clocks, mirrors and fabric flowers: a handsome setting for a full English breakfast. A cosy honesty bar with armchairs, books and papers is a convivial spot for a nightcap, the hearth is lit in winter and musicians will swoon at the working square piano. Jenny, efficient and friendly, has created a lovely atmosphere. *Children over eight welcome.*

rooms	11: 8 twins/doubles, 3 four-poster suites.
price	£88–£120. Singles £79.
meals	Restaurants in Rye.
closed	Never.
directions	From centre of Rye on A268, left off High St onto West St, then 1st right into Mermaid St. House on left. Private car park, £3 a day for guests.

	Jenny Hadfield
tel	01797 222828
fax	01797 222623
email	stay@jeakeshouse.com
web	www.jeakeshouse.com

Hotel

Map 4 Entry 206

The Hare on the Hill

37 Coventry Road, Warwick, Warwickshire CV34 5HW

Come for organic food, flamboyant art, eccentricity and colour. And Prue, who ensures you're well fed and watered, can plan your trips and gives you breakfast when you like it. She has moved from a smaller Special Place to take on The Hare, a one-time nurses' home on the Coventry Road; the woodchip has gone, and eco-friendly paints have taken its place. In the hall, an Edwardian Minton-tiled floor, Shakespearean carvings and stained glass; in the sitting room – large, light and cosy – fine watercolours and a deep gilded frieze. Bedrooms vary in size from huge to rather small; all are one-offs. You might have lilac doors and skirting, or a bright pink ceiling; an Australian dream painting or an English landscape; a stripy sofa, a four-poster made from sustainable wood, an organic mattress or a fluffy bedspread. Breakfasts stand out and there's something different every day: haloumi pancakes, crunchy stuffed mushrooms, fruit platters. Great for carnivores too: sausages come from rare breed butchers, served with free-range eggs and spicy beans. Warwick Castle is a ten-minute stroll, Stratford not much further.

rooms	7: 5 doubles, 2 twins.
price	£80–£95. Singles £65.
meals	Supper £20. Dinner £30. By arrangement.
closed	Christmas & New Year.
directions	2-minute walk from Warwick train station.

Prue Hardwick

tel	01926 491366
email	prue@thehareonthepark.co.uk
web	www.thehareonthepark.co.uk

B&B

Map 3 Entry 207

The Howard Arms

Lower Green, Ilmington, Stratford-upon-Avon, Warwickshire CV36 4LT

The Howard buzzes with good-humoured babble as well-kept beer flows from the flagstoned bar. Logs crackle contentedly in a vast open fire; a blackboard menu scales the wall above; a dining room at the far end has unexpected elegance, with great swathes of bold colour and some noble paintings; and everywhere is a smoke-free zone. Gorgeous bedrooms are set discreetly apart from the joyful throng, mixing period style and modern luxury beautifully: the double oozes olde worlde charm, the twin is more folksy (American art, patchwork quilts) and the half-tester is almost a suite, full of antiques. All are individual, all huge by pub standards. The village is a surprise, too, literally tucked under a lone hill, with an unusual church surrounded by orchards and an extended village green. Round off an idyllic walk amid buzzing bees and fragrant wild flowers with a meal at the inn, perhaps seared scallops with a sweet chilli sauce and crème fraîche, then beef, ale and mustard pie, finally spiced pear and apple flapjack crumble. Stratford and the theatre are close.

Green evolution is in full swing at the Howard: Ecotricity and Calor LPG provide the energy, state-of-the-art boilers are super-efficient, low-energy bulbs are used throughout. Glass and plastics are recycled, garden waste is composted, additive-free rapeseed oil is used in the kitchen, then turned into bio-diesel. As for the produce, it's sourced locally and seasonally wherever possible to reduce food miles, fish comes from sustainable species, and a list of growers and farmers is detailed on their web site. "There's more to do," says Robert, already hatching plans; look out for fine-spray taps in the loos soon.

rooms	3: 2 doubles, 1 twin.
price	£105-120. Singles from £80.
meals	Lunch & dinner £9.50-£24.
closed	Christmas Day.
directions	From Stratford, south on A3400 for 4 miles, right to Wimpstone & Ilmington. Pub in village centre.

Robert & Gill Greenstock
tel	01608 682226
fax	01608 682226
email	info@howardarms.com
web	www.howardarms.com

SPECIAL GREEN ENTRY see page 7

Inn

Map 3 Entry 208

Fulready Manor

Ettington, Stratford-upon-Avon, Warwickshire CV37 7PE

A manor in 125 acres. From afar it's a 16th-century castle; close up, a brand-new luxury home with all the character and none of the draughts. "Our slice of heaven," say the Spencers, who've been in the hospitality business for years and have come home to roost. Enter a stone-fireplaced hall, with floor-to-ceiling front window and Cretan chandelier. In the drawing room, paintings of children and pets, navy sofas piled high with matching cushions, hunting prints too (though the Spencers "hunt the clean boot", choosing to chase men not animals). The sense of fun extends to the bedrooms, 'themed' by daughter Verity and furnished with some magnificent antique pieces. One has midnight-blue fabric walls and faux wood panelling, a four-poster with gold-embroidered muslin and a shower for two; a second, a leather sleigh bed strewn with cushions and a bathroom in red; the third, a four-poster with lush, creamy hangings and a velvet chaise longue in palest pink. Old-fashioned comfort, soft bathrobes, no TV. Breakfasts are a feast, served on the patio on balmy mornings, surrounded by fields.

rooms	3: 1 double, 2 four-posters.
price	£105–£130.
meals	Dinner £25, by arrangement.
closed	Christmas.
directions	M40 junc. 11 towards Stratford. A422 to Wroxton, B4451 for 0.25 miles; Fulready first driveway on left.

Michael & Mauveen Spencer
tel	01789 740152
fax	01789 740247
email	stay@fulreadymanor.co.uk
web	www.fulreadymanor.co.uk

B&B

Map 3 Entry 209

The Red Lion

High Street, Lacock, Wiltshire SN15 2LQ

A comforting place – the sort you long to find after a hard morning riding or walking – and managers Paul and Sarah brim with enthusiasm and charm. The Red Lion dates from the early 1700s, and may well have been known to the impressionable Jane Austen; big open fires, tankards hanging above the bar, rugs on flagstones, bare wooden floors – not a lot has changed. Order a drink and sit down to fine home-cooked food – Joe is the chef – amid timber frames, old settles and a row of branding irons. Climb the shallow tread of the stairs to small but smart bedrooms in a Georgian style; old oak dressers, half-testers, crowns above beds, good antique furniture, a beam or two and window seats for watching the village at the front. In summer, eat outside in the atmospheric courtyard garden, with country views. This celebrated National Trust village was built around the 13th-century Abbey and on the old cloth route between London and Bristol. Fabulous walks from the pub, Lacock Abbey (home to the famous 'Harry Potter' cloisters) and the Fox Talbot Museum of Photography just down the road.

rooms	5 doubles.
price	£80. Singles from £55.
meals	Lunch from £6. Dinner around £15.
closed	Rarely.
directions	Lacock off A350 between Chippenham & Melksham. Inn on High Street.

	Sarah & Paul Haynes
tel	01249 730456
fax	01249 730766
email	redlionlacock@wadworth.co.uk
web	www.redlionlacock.2day.ws

Inn

Map 3 Entry 210

Queenwood Lodge

Bowood Golf & Country Club, Derry Hill, Calne, Wiltshire SN11 9PQ

If you like golf, you'll love Queenwood, a Georgian manor house tucked up in the trees of Bowood's championship golf course. The idea here is that you gather a group of friends (Queenwood is for one party only), skip down for a round of golf, then come home to this wonderful country house on the seventh fairway, where you dig into a cream tea, soak in the bath, enjoy drinks out on the terrace, then feast like a king at your very own dinner party. Queenwood is part of the Bowood estate, seat of the Marquis of Lansdowne; you're wrapped in 4,000 acres of silence and rich interiors come courtesy of Lady Lansdowne's indulging eye. Climb up to country-house bedrooms (fresh flowers, mahogany furniture, cushioned armchairs) for a well-earned sleep, then down for a full cooked breakfast before hitting the fairways the following morning. Expect the best: exemplary service, soaring chimney pots, a verdant garden (deer come to eat the roses), an honesty bar, open fires, a couple of sitting rooms. Prices start from £150 per person (an absoulte steal), so fish out the sticks and start practising.

rooms	4: 1 twin/double, 3 twins.
price	Half-board £980-£1,475 for 8 (same-party bookings only). Includes 2 rounds of golf per person.
meals	Half-board only.
closed	3 weeks in January.
directions	M4 junc 17, A350 south, A4 west from Chippenham, then A342 south. Up hill and through ornate gates opposite Lansdowne Arms.

	Lisa Smith
tel	01249 822228
fax	01249 822218
email	queenwood@bowood.org
web	www.bowood.org

Other Place

Map 3 Entry 211

The Pear Tree Inn

Top Lane, Whitley, Melksham, Wiltshire SN12 8QX

A cool rustic chic flows effortlessly through the Pear Tree; miss it at your peril. This is a dreamy blend of French inspiration and English whimsy, a sweep of warm airy interiors that make you feel that you've washed up in dining-pub heaven. Step in under the beams, glide across the flagged floors, dive into an armchair and roast away in front of the fire. Keep going and you come to high-ceiling'd dining rooms, where stripped floors are dressed in smart old rugs, with wooden scythes, shovels and ladders hanging from the walls. French windows flood the place with light and open up in summer for alfresco suppers (there's a boules piste out there, too). Exquisite bedrooms (up in the eaves or out in the old barn) come in Farrow & Ball lime white and have suede bedheads, wonderfully upholstered armchairs, Bang & Olufsen TVs and funky rugs for colour; bathrooms too, with robes and creamy tiles, are spoiling. As for the food, don't miss that either – particularly the warm pear and almond tart with rosemary ice cream. Locals flock in, so no surprise to discover that Martin and Debbie are opening a farm shop nearby.

rooms	8: 6 doubles, 2 family.
price	£105. Family £140. Singles £75.
meals	Lunch from £13.50. A la carte dinner from £25.
closed	Christmas & New Year.
directions	West from Melksham on A365, then right onto B3353 for Whitley. Through village, then left, signed Purlpit. Pub on right after 400 yards.

	Martin & Debbie Still
tel	01225 709131
fax	01225 702276
email	enquiries@thepeartreeinn.com
web	www.thepeartreeinn.com

Inn

Map 3 Entry 212

The Bath Arms

Longleat Estate, Horningsham, Warminster, Wiltshire BA12 7LY

A 17th-century coaching inn on the Longleat estate in a gorgeous village lost in the country; geese swim in the river, cows laze in the fields and lush woodland wraps around you. At the front, the 12 apostles – a dozen pollarded lime trees – shade a gravelled garden, while at the back, two large stone terraces, separated by beds of lavender, soak up the sun (you can eat out here in good weather). Inside are the best of old and new: flagstones and boarded floors mix with a stainless steel bar and Farrow & Ball paints. The feel is smart and airy, with a skittle alley that doubles as a sitting room (they show movies here too) and shimmering Cole & Son wallpaper in the dining room. Stop for caramelised onion tart, bavette steak with Lyonnaise potatoes, then Pimms granita. Bedrooms are a real treat, some in the main house, others in a converted barn. Expect lots of colour, big wallpapers, beds dressed in Eygptian cotton, DVD and CD players; bathrooms come in black slate, some with free-standing baths, others with deluge showers. Longleat is at the bottom of the hill – the walk down is majestic.

rooms	14: 10 doubles, 2 twins, 2 singles.
price	£80–£145. Singles from £60.
meals	Lunch & dinner £5–£30.
closed	Never.
directions	A303, then A350 north to Longbridge Deverill. Left for Maiden Bradley, then right for Horningsham. Through village, on right.

	Christoph Brooke
tel	01985 844308
fax	01985 844157
email	enquiries@batharms.co.uk
web	www.batharms.co.uk

Hotel

Map 2 Entry 213

Spread Eagle Inn

Stourton, Warminster, Wiltshire BA12 6QE

While Stourhead Gardens "echo with references to the heroes and gods of ancient Rome", this proper inn with rooms makes more than a passing nod to Bacchus. Mellow and old-fashioned it may appear but peep inside and you see slate or coir floors, Farrow & Ball colours and understated jugs of garden flowers on old pine tables. In the bar a woodburning stove is merry and the seats are comfy; you can eat here or in the restaurant that doubles as a sitting room. Red walls, large modern paintings and old prints create a mood that is cosy and warm. The higgledy-piggledy stairs are great if you're nimble and the bedrooms peaceful – expect muted colours, white linen, original fireplaces and delightful views. Bathrooms are not state-of-the-art but perfectly plain – and spotless. Food is English and locally supplied: Wiltshire ham with sweet mustard, west country fish soup, griddled organic salmon salad with anchovy mayonnaise. The village is charming – and you can pretend that this stupendous example of a landscape garden with its lake and follies is yours when the hoards have gone home.

rooms	5: 2 doubles, 3 twins/doubles.
price	£98. Singles £70.
meals	Lunch from £6.95. Dinner from £10.50.
closed	Christmas Day.
directions	Turn off B3092 signed Stourhead Gardens. Spread Eagle is below main car park on left at entrance to garden. Private car park for Inn.

	Tom Bridgeman
tel	01747 840587
email	enquiries@s-eagle.co.uk
web	www.spreadeagleinn.com

Inn

Map 2 Entry 214

The Compasses Inn

Lower Chicksgrove, Tisbury, Wiltshire SP3 6NB

Set between ancient villages on a lane to nowhere and back, the Compasses is the quintessential English inn, so content with its lot it could almost be a figment of your imagination. Modest, ineffably pretty, perfect inside and out, it's been here since 1368, a low thatched refuge for drovers and smugglers. Duck instinctively into the sudden darkness of the bar and experience a wave of nostalgia as your eyes adjust to a long wooden room with flagstones, oak beams from a galleon, crackling logs and cosy booths divided by farmyard salvage: a cartwheel here, some horse tack there and a piano at one end. The pub glows warmly with Alan and Susie's enthusiasm and the daily-changing blackboard proclaims fresh and inventive cooking from two chefs who sometimes pop out for a chat with the guests. Bedrooms are at the top of some stone stairs outside the front door (so there's not too far to stagger) and have the same effortless charm; walls are thick, windows are wonky, bathrooms are new and the sweet serenity of Wiltshire lies just down the lane. The wonderful welcome extends to children and dogs.

rooms	4 + 1: 2 doubles, 2 twins/doubles. 1 self-catering cottage for 2.
price	From £75. Singles £55.
meals	Lunch from £5. A la carte dinner, around £20.
closed	Mondays except bank holidays, then closed Tuesdays.
directions	From Salisbury, A30 west, 3rd right after Fovant, signed Lower Chicksgrove, then 1st left down single track lane to village.

Alan & Susie Stoneham

tel	01722 714318
fax	01722 714318
email	thecompasses@aol.com
web	www.thecompassesinn.com

Inn

Map 3 Entry 217

Colwall Park

Colwall, Malvern, Worcestershire WR13 6QG

Actors stay here when treading the boards at the Malvern theatre down the road – rather famous ones, judging by the signed photos on the wall. The house is handsome Edwardian and its interiors match – but unintimidatingly so. Past the potted bay trees, beneath the flowered basket into green-carpeted reception, nicely kitted out with hunting photos, lilies and a ledger from 1907. Then up the stairs to coordinated wallpapers and bedspreads, white and chrome bathrooms, zappy showers, garden views and every extra, from baby listeners to satellite TV. Just-marrieds have a peach canopied bed with sofas to match and acres of space. The lounge has glass-topped tables and thick drapes, the bar real ales and cheery meals, and the dining room is the hub of the place: all oak panelling, white napery and sparkling glass, a sophisticated setting for some seriously good food. Iain and Sarah have been here five years and word has spread about the comfort and the smiles, the walks to the Malvern Hills – and the heavenly chocolate and amaretto crème brûlée with almond biscotti.

rooms	22: 17 twins/doubles, 3 singles, 1 suite, 1 family suite.
price	£89–£140. Singles £79. Suites £150.
meals	Lunch £15.95–£19.95. Dinner £24.95; à la carte about £30.
closed	Rarely.
directions	M5 junc. 7 or M50 junc. 2. Colwall halfway between Ledbury & Malvern. Colwall Park in centre of village.

	Iain Nesbitt
tel	01684 540000
fax	01684 540847
email	hotel@colwall.com
web	www.colwall.com

Hotel

Map 2 Entry 218

The Cottage in the Wood
Holywell Road, Malvern Wells, Worcestershire WR14 4LG

Walk along a path through the woods, dappled with light, and emerge in a clearing in this English jungle. There, the Cottage gazes across the wide, flat Severn Valley to the distant Cotswolds – a heart-stopping view. It is enough just to be here, near the breezy top of the Malvern Hills, but to find such an endearingly friendly, book-lined and log-fired country-house hotel is a treat. The décor is polished, swagged, patterned and lined – distinctly pre-modern – with a choice antique round every corner. Many of the bedrooms are in a new building and have wonderfully luxurious bathrooms. Service is courteous and charming, the sort you only get when a large and talented family is at the helm, and Dominic's cooking is as exemplary as his father's hotel-keeping. Local produce is used in an imaginative way and portions are generous: risotto comes with rosemary and borlotti beans, partridge with baby onions and chestnuts, salmon with langoustine ravioli and lemon grass velouté. Relax, drink in the views and your host's well-chosen wines, play basketball from your bath. A civilised retreat.

rooms	30: 21 doubles, 8 twins/doubles, 1 four-poster.
price	£99–£185. Singles £79–£110. Half-board (min. 2 nights) £73–£125 p.p.
meals	Lunch from £4.95. Dinner, à la carte, £35. Packed lunch £8.50.
closed	Rarely.
directions	M5 junc. 7; A449 through Gt Malvern. In Malvern Wells, 3rd right after Railway Pub. Signed.

John & Sue Pattin
tel	01684 575859
fax	01684 560662
email	reception@cottageinthewood.co.uk
web	www.cottageinthewood.co.uk

Hotel

Map 2 Entry 219

Russell's

The Green, 20 High Street, Broadway, Worcestershire WR12 7DT

Set back from the High Street in this chocolate-box-pretty village – all tourist temptations and chi-chi shops – is an 18th-century former office to a long-gone factory. Walk in to blasted beams, new pale stone floors, sleek lighting and mellow walls, wooden tables set with slate mats, and glass doors at the back that open to a flagstoned terrace. Food is modern, English and extremely good value; try ham hock with homemade piccalilli or grilled Cornish plaice with rosemary and new potatoes. The global wine list is short but intelligently chosen by Barry, an easy, charming and friendly host. Once dinner is over there's a quiet little sitting room with an honesty bar upstairs, or you could sprawl in a very comfortable chair in your super-crisp bedroom (the suite is spectacular). Beds are large and plump with pure wool throws and clouds of pillows, bathrooms are state-of-the-art with shiny chrome accessories, stone floors, thick towels and nurturing bubbles and creams. Whether you plan to explore the shops or stride the Cotswolds, breakfast (whatever you want really) will set you up beautifully.

rooms	7: 3 doubles, 1 twin/double, 2 family, 1 suite.
price	£115–£180. Suite £245–£295.
meals	Lunch, 2 courses, from £14.95. Dinner, 3 courses, from £16.95.
closed	Rarely.
directions	A44 from Oxford & Evesham; B4632 from Cheltenham; in centre of Broadway on High Street.

	Barry Hancox
tel	01386 853555
fax	01386 853964
email	info@russellsofbroadway.com
web	www.russellsofbroadway.com

Restaurant with Rooms

Map 3 Entry 220

Simonstone Hall

Hawes, Yorkshire DL8 3LY

The view from the terrace is magnificent, a five-mile drift through Wensleydale to the summit of Dodd Fell, and in summer you can breakfast here under the shade of beech trees. This is the 1773 shooting lodge of the Earls of Wharncliffe. Stag Fell rises behind. Inside you find a quirky mix of old and new: trophies and oils jostle with wicker armchairs and thick blue carpet. Painted panelling soaks up the light in the drawing room and dining room, there are stripped wood floors in the Orangerie and a pitch-pine snug that's warmed by its own wood-burner in the bar. Bedrooms come in different shapes and sizes. Those at the front are big and grand and have the view; those at the back are simpler altogether. Expect a country-house feel: mahogany dressers, ornate fireplaces, shelves of books, perhaps mullioned windows, a four-poster bed or a claw-foot bath. You can eat (very well) all over the place, three courses in the dining room, soup or a steak in the Orangerie and bar. All around you is some of the loveliest walking in the land, and don't forget the Champagne picnic.

rooms	18: 9 doubles, 2 twins/doubles, 5 four-posters, 2 suites.
price	£110–£180. Singles from £75.
meals	Lunch from £5. Dinner around £30. Champagne picnic from £25 for two.
closed	Rarely.
directions	From Hawes, north for Muker for about 2 miles. Hotel on left, at foot of Buttertubs Pass.

	Mark Glendinning
tel	01969 667255
fax	01969 667741
email	e-mail@simonstonehall.demon.co.uk
web	www.simonstonehall.com

Hotel

Map 6 Entry 221

Waterford House

19 Kirkgate, Middleham, Yorkshire DL8 4PG

In a lively village dominated by Middleham Castle – northern stronghold of Richard III – is this very pretty Georgian house, now a small hotel. Martin and Anne are exceptional hosts, easy and delightful, their house full of beautiful things. Settle into sofas for drinks and canapés in the cosiest drawing room, then amble across to the red dining room for a memorable meal and ambrosial wines. On summer evenings dine alfresco in the small garden with its summer house and trickling stream. Bedrooms, up narrow – in parts steep – stairs, have bags of old-fashioned comfort: wrought-iron beds, William Morris wallpaper, pictures, books, sherry, homemade cakes. The panelled four-poster with blue bedspread and bolsters is a treat. Middleham is a racing village and has 14 stable yards; horses clop by in the morning on their way to the gallops. Breakfast, served on white linen, is a feast of local produce. Linger as long as you like – it's that sort of place – then grab a rod and fish the Ure or pull on your hiking boots and unravel the Dales. Leyburn, for the biggest auction house in the north, is close.

rooms	5: 2 doubles, 1 twin/double, 2 four-posters.
price	£85–£115. Singles £65–£75.
meals	Dinner, 3 courses, £31 (not Sunday).
closed	Rarely.
directions	Southbound from A1 at Scotch Corner via Richmond & Leyburn. Northbound from A1 on B6267 via Masham. House in northern corner of square.

Martin Cade & Anne Parkinson Cade

tel	01969 622090
fax	01969 624020
email	info@waterfordhousehotel.co.uk
web	www.waterfordhousehotel.co.uk

Hotel

Map 6 Entry 222

The Austwick Traddock

Austwick, Settle, Yorkshire LA2 8BY

Friendly, unpretentious and full of traditional comforts, this family-run hotel is a terrific base for walkers – the Three Peaks are at the door. The house is Georgian with Victorian additions and its name originates from the horse sales that once took place in next door's paddock. Open fires smoulder on winter days, deckchairs dot the garden in summer. Country-house bedrooms have bags of charm: antique dressing tables, quilted beds, perhaps a bergère bedhead or a claw-foot bath. Those on the second floor have a cosy attic feel, all have fresh flowers, flat-screen TVs, decanters of sherry and Dales views. As for the restaurant, it's the first in the north of England to be certified 100% organic by the Soil Association; dig into delicious seared scallops, wild venison, lemon soufflé with a Yorkshire curd sorbet. There's a cheerful William Morris feel to it all – polished brass in front of the fire, a panelled breakfast room, beds of lavender in the garden – and the village, with two clapper bridges, is a gem. Don't miss the amazing caves at Ingleborough, or Settle for antiques. *Minimum two nights at weekends.*

It's good news indeed when a hotelier in the north can serve nothing but organic food, and source most of it from local farms. Game comes from nearby estates, lambs are reared in neighbouring fields, vegetables are grown in the next-door village, even the milk comes from county cows. If Bruce can't find it locally, he'll look further afield, to Wales for the black pudding (the only organic pudding available in the country), or to France for the champagne. Which proves a point: you don't just eat organic at Austwick, you can drink 'green' too; wines, ales and ciders are all certified.

rooms	10: 7 doubles, 1 twin/double, 1 family, 1 single.
price	£130–£160. Singles £70–£90. Half-board from £75 p.p.
meals	Lunch £14–£18 Dinner £22.50–£27.50.
closed	Rarely.
directions	0.75 miles off the A65, midway between Kirkby Lonsdale & Skipton.

	Bruce Reynolds
tel	01524 251224
fax	01524 251796
email	info@austwicktraddock.co.uk
web	www.austwicktraddock.co.uk

SPECIAL GREEN ENTRY
see page 21

Hotel

Map 6 Entry 223

The Yorke Arms
Ramsgill-in-Nidderdale, Harrogate, Yorkshire HG3 5RL

It takes a lot of nous to establish one of the best restaurants in Britain, let alone one up a small country lane in the middle of the Yorkshire Dales. The Yorke Arms is near perfection; exquisite food, excellent rooms and beautiful countryside make it irresistible. The oldest part was built by monks in the 11th century, the rest added in 1750 when it became a coaching inn. The interior is charming, with polished flagstone floors, low oak beams, comfy armchairs, open fires and antique tables; in summer, eat under a pergola near a burbling beck. Newly-decorated bedrooms are just-so; attention to detail is guaranteed. Bill, affable and considerate, is a natural host, while Frances scintillates the palette in the kitchen, using fish from the east and west coasts and meat and game from the Dales. Lunch is terrific value. Wander from Ramsgill to nearby Gouthwaite reservoir – formed during the Industrial Revolution to supply the city of Bradford with water – or work up an appetite visiting Brimham Rocks or Stump Cross Caverns.

rooms	14: 7 doubles, 3 twins/doubles, 3 singles.
price	£150-£240. Singles from £100.
meals	Lunch, 3 courses, £21. Dinner £35-£40 (not Sunday evenings).
closed	Rarely.
directions	From Ripley, B6165 to Pateley Bridge. Over bridge at bottom of High St; 1st right into Low Wath Road to Ramsgill (4 miles).

Bill & Frances Atkins

tel	01423 755243
fax	01423 755330
email	enquiries@yorke-arms.co.uk
web	www.yorke-arms.co.uk

Inn

Map 6 Entry 224

The Red Lion

By the Bridge at Burnsall, Skipton, Yorkshire BD23 6BU

A very pretty village in the middle of the Dales; fells rise all around, there's cricket on the green in summer and the river Wharfe flows past the hotel garden. Family-run and family-friendly, The Red Lion is an inn for all ages, full of old-world charm. Elizabeth still keeps a matriarchal eye on things but her daughters have taken the helm, their husbands by their sides; Robert farms, providing much for the kitchen, Jim and Olivier cook seriously good food. The net result is a cosy, happy, comfortable inn that hums with contented locals. Expect coal fires, books in the sitting room, a good supply of well-kept ales and pink roses rambling across the mellow stone exterior. Bedrooms above aren't huge but have bags of character: low beamed ceilings, big brass beds, fancy compact bathrooms, fluffy white robes. Rooms in the next-door courtyard barn are larger and two have open fires. Eat under pear blossom on the terrace while walkers pass, following the Dales Way along the river. August's Fell Race – eight minutes up, four minutes down – starts from the front door. *Minimum two nights at weekends.*

rooms	14: 7 doubles, 5 twins/doubles, 1 family, 1 single.
price	£125–£145. Singles from £62.50.
meals	Brasserie lunch & dinner from £7.50. Dinner in restaurant about £30.
closed	Never.
directions	From Harrogate, A59 west to Bolton Bridge; B6160 to Burnsall. Hotel next to bridge.

Elizabeth & Andrew Grayshon

tel	01756 720204
fax	01756 720292
email	redlion@daelnet.co.uk
web	www.redlion.co.uk

Inn

Map 6 Entry 227

The Boar's Head Hotel

Ripley Castle Estate, Harrogate, Yorkshire HG3 3AY

The Boar's Head sits four-square in this peaceful, pretty Model Estate village. Across the street are Birchwood House and the Courtyard, with a further six rooms. Expect firm, generous beds, floral bedheads, an armchair or sofa and rag-rolled bathrooms; those in the Courtyard have the odd beam and pretty pine panelling. The sitting rooms are carpeted and draped: pink and green sofas, button-back armchairs, glass-topped tables, ancestor oils with brass lights over, an evening fire. There are games to play, newspapers, menus to drool over and a parasoled garden where you are served long summer drinks by delightful staff. The restaurant is warm crimson, candlelit at night; you drink from blue glass and the food is rich and generous 'modern English', employing Yorkshire beef, guinea fowl and Nidderdale lamb. Up the pretty staircase, past more ancestors, to comfy bedrooms, with sherry and fresh flowers in the best. Visit the castle gardens and the National Hyacinth Collection as a guest of the hotel; umbrellas and wellies are put out on rainy days.

rooms	25: 4 doubles, 21 twins/doubles.
price	£125–£150. Singles £105–£125. Half-board from £80 p.p. (min. 2 nights).
meals	Dinner, 3 courses, from £30. Bistro lunch & dinner, dishes from £9.95.
closed	Rarely.
directions	From Harrogate, A61 north for 3 miles, then left at r'bout, signed to Ripley & castle.

	Sir Thomas & Lady Emma Ingilby
tel	01423 771888
fax	01423 771509
email	reservations@boarsheadripley.co.uk
web	www.boarsheadripley.co.uk

Inn

Map 6 Entry 228

Gallon House

47 Kirkgate, Knaresborough, Yorkshire HG5 8BZ

Ancient stone steps wind around the house and then down to the beautiful Nidd Gorge. As you sit on the south-facing veranda and pop another smoked salmon parcel into your mouth you will relish that spectacular view – rain or shine. Rick and Sue, who had another Special Place in Harrogate, fell in love with the eccentricities of this house and created an intimate hotel – and their natural enthusiasm for getting things right shows. The charming dining room gives a sense of eating en famille: soup is brought to the shared table in a tureen, vegetables arrive in one bowl, and breakfasts are better than anything you'd get at home: local duck eggs, Rick's breads and preserves, poached fruits, black pudding. A comfortable sitting room has damask sofas and French windows; small, pretty bedrooms – Castle View, River View, Station View – have deep mattresses, baskets of magazines, CDs, videos, Black Sheep ale; two have breathtaking views over the the gorge. Loos are en suite, showers tucked into a corner, towels freshly white. Lovely. *Private dining for special occasions.*

rooms	3: 2 doubles, 1 twin.
price	£90. Singles £70.
meals	Lunch £12. Dinner, 3 courses, £22.50, by arrangement.
closed	Rarely.
directions	3 miles from A1, in town centre, by railway station.

Sue & Rick Hodgson

tel	01423 862102
email	gallon-house@ntlworld.com
web	www.gallon-house.co.uk

Hotel

Map 6 Entry 229

The Weavers Shed Restaurant with Rooms

88 Knowl Road, Golcar, Huddersfield, Yorkshire HD7 4AN

Sublime simplicity at the top of the hill; the welcome is second to none, the food is some of the best in Yorkshire, and those who make the detour find unbeatable value for money. Wander around outside for a well-kept garden and cobbles in the courtyard, then step inside and discover whitewashed walls, thick stone arches and terracotta-tiled floors. All is bright and breezy – Provence in the Colne Valley! – with menus from around the world framed on the walls. As for the food, Stephen's passion stretches as far as tending a one-acre kitchen garden which supplies most of his needs. You may get duck cooked four ways, calf's liver with a red-onion marmalade, then soufflé of Yorkshire rhubarb with crumble ice cream. Retire to super bedrooms for warm colours, comfy beds, fluffy bath robes – and pop back down in the morning for a fabulous breakfast: flagons of freshly-squeezed orange juice, delicious sausages, homemade marmalades and jams. Take to the glorious Pennines and work off your indulgence or simply climb the hill – *Last of the Summer Wine* is filmed on these streets. Brilliant.

Is Stephen obsessed by food? Very probably. When he's not in the kitchen cooking the stuff, he's at his parents' place growing it. His one-acre plot is home to a couple of big greenhouses, a 40-foot polytunnel and an orchard – supplying most of the needs of his restaurant. Planting is planned well in advance to ensure native and exotic foods are available all year round. In a cycle of wonderful simplicity, menus are hatched, the produce grown, cooked and eaten. Plates brim with the day's harvest – soft fruits, Jerusalem artichokes, English asparagus. They also keep free-range chickens and ducks for eggs at breakfast.

rooms	5: 3 doubles, 1 twin/double, 1 four-poster.
price	£90–£95. Singles from £70.
meals	Lunch from £14.95. Dinner, 3 courses, around £40. Restaurant closed Sun/Mon; no lunch Sat.
closed	Christmas & New Year.
directions	From Huddersfield A62 west for 2 miles, then right for Milnsbridge & Golcar. Left at Somerfield; signed on right at top of hill.

	Stephen & Tracy Jackson
tel	01484 654284
fax	01484 650980
email	info@weaversshed.co.uk
web	www.weaversshed.co.uk

SPECIAL
GREEN ENTRY
see page 21

Restaurant with Rooms

Map 6 Entry 230

The Grange Hotel

1 Clifton, York, Yorkshire YO30 6AA

Half a mile from the city wall where the ancient Minster stands, a Regency townhouse once occupied by the merchants of York. It is handome, elegant and sumptuously grand. Jeremy and Vivien rescued the Georgian building from years of municipal neglect and an effortless style runs throughout; imagine stone floors, Doric columns and an urn erupting with orchids in the hall. You get deep comfy sofas in the morning room, a vaulted red-brick ceiling in the cellar bar, and unpretentious modern British food in the the bright and airy brasserie, which gets lively during the Races when punters, journalists and famous trainers meet up. The horse racing link is a propos: York's course is considered one of the most exciting in Britain. More racing touches in the bedrooms, and perfect mattresses on good high beds. The quietest are at the back. Expect bold greens and reds, a silky purple four-poster, writing paper on the desks and rich fabrics. A particular treat for Americans, single women, traditionalists and trenchermen – and race-goers, naturally.

rooms	30: 8 doubles, 16 twins/doubles, 2 four-posters, 3 singles, 1 suite.
price	£150-£215. Singles £115-£180. Suite £260.
meals	Lunch from £12.50. Dinner, 2 courses, from £20.
closed	Never.
directions	From York ring road, A19 south into city centre. Hotel on right after 2 miles, 400 yds from city walls. Parking.

Amie Postings

tel	01904 644744
fax	01904 612453
email	info@grangehotel.co.uk
web	www.grangehotel.co.uk

Hotel

Map 6 Entry 231

The Abbey Inn
Byland Abbey, Coxwold, Yorkshire YO61 4BD

The monks of Ampleforth who built this farmhouse would surely approve of its current devotion to good food; whether they'd be as accepting of its devotion to luxury is another matter. But one monk's frown is another man's path to righteousness. The Abbey Inn is a delightful oasis next to a ruined 12th-century abbey – lit up at night – that indulges the senses. They measure success in smiles up here; Jane loves to see the look on people's faces as they enter the Piggery restaurant, a big flagstoned space, lit by a skylight, full of Jacobean-style chairs and antique tables, that demands your joyful attention. Bedrooms are jaw-dropping, too. Abbot's Retreat has a huge four-poster while a bust of Julius Caesar in the gorgeous black and white tiled bathroom strikes a nice, decadent note – order a bottle of bubbly and jump in the double-ended bath. Priors Lynn has the best view – right down the aisle of the abbey; all have bathrobes, aromatherapy oils, fruit, homemade biscuits and a 'treasure chest' of wine. Come to revel in it all.

rooms	3 suites.
price	£95–£155.
meals	Lunch & dinner: main courses £7–£16.50. Not Sunday evenings or Monday lunchtimes.
closed	Rarely.
directions	From A1 junc. 49, A168 for Thirsk for 10 miles, A19 for York at r'bout. Left after 2 miles, for Coxwold. There left for Byland Abbey. Opposite abbey.

Jane Nordli

tel	01347 868204
fax	01347 868678
email	jane@nordli.freeserve.co.uk
web	www.bylandabbeyinn.com

Inn

Map 6 Entry 232

The White Swan Inn
Market Place, Pickering, Yorkshire YO18 7AA

Victor swapped the City for the North Yorkshire Moors and this old coaching inn; the place oozes comfort and style. Duck in through the front door to find a snug bar, smart country furniture, fine French wines and eager young staff. Best of all is the dining room; food matters here and you'll find heaven on a plate when you dig into supper. Try seared pigeon breast with pea tart, Levisham mutton with Irish cabbage, poached rhubarb on toasted brioche with rhubarb ice cream. Menus change monthly and 80% of the ingredients are locally sourced, with meat coming from local 'Ginger Pig', who also supply London's River Café. Breakfast is just as good, and inspired one traveller to write a poem, now framed. Bedrooms – some cool and chic, others warmly traditional – come with pleasing colours, elegant fabrics, antique beds, maybe an armchair and a view of the pretty courtyard. Don't miss the beamed club room for roaring fire, board games and an honesty bar. Castle Howard is nearby, the moors are wild and the steam railway a treat. *Pet surcharge, £12.50 per pet.*

rooms	21: 14 doubles, 4 twins/doubles, 3 suites.
price	£129-£169. Singles from £79. Suites £169-£229.
meals	Lunch about £15. Dinner about £25.
closed	Rarely.
directions	From North, A170 to Pickering. Entering town, left at traffic lights, then 1st right, Market Place. On left.

Victor & Marion Buchanan

tel	01751 472288
fax	01751 475554
email	welcome@white-swan.co.uk
web	www.white-swan.co.uk

Inn

Map 6 Entry 233

Grinkle Lodge
Snipe Lane, Grinkle, Whitby, Yorkshire TS13 4UD

If you appreciate the gradual discovery of unannounced treats (homemade biscuits, good books, bowls of fruit, drinks to hand) then you will love Grinkle Lodge. It is also a temple to Tim and Janette's passion for all things Victorian. Swags and tails abound, hand-painted murals delight, trompe l'oeil entertains and the touch is soft and pretty. Oodles of seductive fabric in the bedrooms, which are deeply comfortable, and bathrooms that sparkle with snowy white towels, robes and plentiful mirrors. A super-warm and restful sitting room, framed by acres of curtain, has a sink-into sofa, a roaring fire and big views over the garden. There's a well-stocked games chest for quiet moments, accompanied – why not? – by a pre-prandial glass of red wine while ex-restaurateur Tim rustles up roast rack of lamb with wild blackberry and mint sauce. You dine at your own polished antique table in a carpeted dining room where the produce is the best. Expect high quality at every turn, from Grinkle eggs at breakfast and homemade scones at tea to Janette's remarkable oil paintings gracing several finely patterned walls.

rooms	3: 2 doubles, 1 twin.
price	£70–£82.
meals	Dinner £20. Packed lunch £7.50.
closed	Occasionally.
directions	From A171 Whitby to Guisborough road travelling north, take right turn to Grinkle and Easington. After 2 miles take right turn. Signed.

Tim & Janette Boskett

tel	01287 644701
email	grinklelodge@yahoo.co.uk
web	www.grinklelodge.co.uk

B&B

Map 6 Entry 234

White House Hotel
Herm, Channel Islands GY1 3HR

A coastal path rings idyllic Herm; you'll find high cliffs to the south, sandy beaches to the north and cattle grazing in the hills between. You get fabulous views at every turn – shimmering islands, pristine waters, yachts and ferries zipping about – while the pace of life is wonderfully lazy, so stop at the grocery store, gather a picnic, find a meadow and bask in the sun. There are beach cafés, succulent gardens, an ancient church, even a tavern. Herm's owners are eminently benign; Pennie was born here, Adrian migrated from Guernsey, together they've kept things blissfully simple: no cars, no TVs, just an old-fashioned England that kids love (the self-catering cottages are extremely popular with families). As for the hotel, it's exceptionally comfortable with one toe lingering in an elegant past; come for open fires, delicious food, a tennis court with watery views and a pool to keep you cool. Bedrooms are scattered around, some in the village's colour-washed cottages, others with balconies in the hotel. Expect warm colours, padded headboards, and spotless bathrooms.

rooms	40: 12 twins/doubles, 5 family rooms. Cottages: 16 twins/doubles, 5 family rooms, 2 singles.
price	Half-board £73–£110 p.p.
meals	Half-board only. Lunch from £7. Dinner, 4 courses, included; non-residents £23.50.
closed	14 October–31 March.
directions	Via Guernsey. Trident ferries leave from the harbour at St Peter Port 8 times a day in summer (£8.50 return).

	Adrian & Pennie Heyworth
tel	01481 722159
fax	01481 710066
email	hotel@herm-island.com
web	www.herm-island.com

Hotel

Map 3 Entry 236

La Sablonnerie
Little Sark, Channel Islands GY9 0SD

If you tell Elizabeth which ferry you're arriving on, she'll send down her horse and carriage to meet you. "Small, sweet world of wave-encompassed wonder," wrote Swinburne of Sark. The tiny community of 500 people lives under a spell, governed feudally and sharing this magic island with horses, sheep, cattle, carpets of wild flowers and birds. There are wild cliff walks, thick woodland, sandy coves, wonderful deep rock pools, aquamarine seas. On the island, no cars, only bikes, horse and carriage and the odd tractor. In the hotel – a 400-year-old farmhouse – no TV, no radio, no trouser press... just a dreamy peace, kindness, starched cotton sheets, woollen blankets and food to die for. Eat in the lovely dining room or in the prettiest of well-tended gardens with gorgeous colourful borders. The Perrées still farm and, as a result, the hotel is almost self-sufficient; you also get home-baked bread and lobsters straight from the sea. Elizabeth is Sercquaise – her mother's family were part of the 1565 colonisation – and she knows her land well. Let her point you to the island's secrets.

rooms	24: 5 doubles, 6 twins, 6 family, 1 suite; 2 doubles, 2 twins, sharing 2 baths.
price	£95-£155. Half-board £59.50-£95 p.p.
meals	Dinner, 5 courses, £30.
closed	2nd Monday in October-Wednesday before Easter.
directions	Take ferry to Sark & ask!

	Elizabeth Perrée
tel	01481 832061
fax	01481 832408

Hotel

Map 3 Entry 237

Scottish Counties

We've combined some of the counties in Scotland to make it easier to find the area you're looking for in the book:

Aberdeenshire = Aberdeen city & Aberdeenshire
Ayrshire = East, North & South Ayrshire
Dunbartonshire = East & West Dunbartonshire
Edinburgh & the Lothians = Edinburgh, Midlothian, East & West Lothian
Lanarkshire = North & South Lanarkshire
Renfrewshire = East Renfrewshire and Renfrewshire

Below you'll find a complete list of the Scottish counties and a map to help you locate the area you're interested in:

Aberdeen City
Aberdeenshire
Angus
Argyll & Bute
Clackmannanshire
Dumfries & Galloway
Dundee City
East Ayrshire
East Dunbartonshire
East Lothian
East Renfrewshire
Edinburgh City
Falkirk
Fife
Glasgow City
Highlands
Inverclyde
Midlothian
Moray
North Ayrshire
North Lanarkshire
Orkney Islands
Perth & Kinross
Renfrewshire
Scottish Borders
Shetland Islands
South Ayrshire
South Lanarkshire
Stirling
West Dunbartonshire
Western Isles (Eilean Siar)
West Lothian

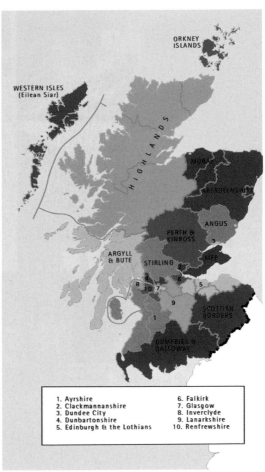

1. Ayrshire
2. Clackmannanshire
3. Dundee City
4. Dunbartonshire
5. Edinburgh & the Lothians
6. Falkirk
7. Glasgow
8. Inverclyde
9. Lanarkshire
10. Renfrewshire

Darroch Learg
Braemar Road, Ballater, Aberdeenshire AB35 5UX

The Royal Family escapes to the fir district of Deeside in summer; the Franks family stays all year, welcoming those in search of genuine Scottish hospitality. They have been here 40 years and know how to run a good hotel; nothing is too much trouble. Darroch Learg is Gaelic for 'an oak copse on a sunny hillside' and this turreted 1888 granite building is in a raised position on the outskirts of the pretty village of Ballater. Views stretch across the Dee Valley to Lochnagar, snow-capped for much of the year. The main part of the hotel is a baronial Victorian manor house, with a twist of Scottish grandeur thrown in for good measure. Regency-style bedrooms are split between here and a next-door annexe: all are subtly different, with warm colours, local watercolours, fresh flowers, thick curtains and modern bathrooms with spoiling touches; most rooms have the view. An intimate conservatory-style dining room, with lamps at each table, draws in the view as well. Chef David Mutter's modern Scottish cooking has won various awards, supported by a good wine list. You'll feel good staying here.

rooms	12: 10 twins/doubles, 2 four-posters.
price	£140–£180. Half-board (May–September) £95–£120 p.p.
meals	Sunday lunch £22. Dinner £40–£45.
closed	Christmas week & last 3 weeks in January.
directions	From Perth, A93 north to Ballater. Entering village, hotel 1st building on left above road.

	Nigel & Fiona Franks
tel	01339 755443
fax	01339 755252
email	info@darrochlearg.co.uk
web	www.darrochlearg.co.uk

Hotel

Map 9 Entry 238

Glebe House

Gott Bay, Isle of Tiree, Argyll & Bute PA77 6TN

Beaches everywhere; Tiree is ringed by them, each one a highway of pure white sand. If the temperature were 20 degrees higher, this would be some of the most expensive real estate in the world. Because it's not, you get the place to yourself. Follow coastal paths past neolithic brochs and ancient sites of worship, scan the high seas for seals, dolphins, sharks, even whales, then picnic amid the wild flowers of the machair. As for Glebe House, it stands 100 yards from the beach with imperious views across the sea to Mull (day trips to Fingal's Cave are easily arranged). It's a supremely comfortable island base, pristine from top to toe. Impeccable bedrooms come with pretty linen and island art, while fabulous bathrooms have fluffy robes and two have showers that look out to sea. Downstairs are books and maps in the sitting room. Step into the garden to find an extremely productive vegetable garden which underpins Eileen's delicious dinners (cream of leek soup, Tiree lamb casserole, lemon cheese cake). Night skies are spectacular, as is the Glebe House.

rooms	5: 3 doubles, 2 twins/doubles.
price	£70-£100. Singles from £55.
meals	Dinner, 3 courses, £24 (not Sunday or Tuesday).
closed	Rarely.
directions	Oban ferry to Tiree. On island, off boat, right at T-junction after 0.5 miles, and 1st house on right, signed.

	Ian & Eileen Tainsh
tel	01879 220758
fax	01879 220091
email	enquiries@glebehousetiree.co.uk
web	www.glebehousetiree.co.uk

B&B

Map 10 Entry 239

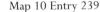

Highland Cottage
Breadalbane Street, Tobermory, Isle of Mull PA75 6PD

A restored cottage high above this pretty, sheltered port in the capital of wild Mull. This is clearly a great place to eat; locals flock here for Croig crab cakes, Ardnamurchan venison or Tobermory smoked salmon parcels. And the puddings don't disappoint; try chocolate nemesis or burnt honey ice cream. Bedrooms aren't enormous but they are comfortable with beautifully ironed sheets and proper blankets, crushed-velvet cushions, silk bedspreads, tartan tiles in the bathrooms, Cadell prints, huge porcelain lamps, a French sleigh bed, even the odd sea view. In the upstairs sitting room there's an honesty bar, CDs wait to be played and pot-boilers (or *Kidnapped* – it's set on the island) wait to be read. If you can rouse yourself, head to Iona, Fingal's Cave, the white sands of Calgary bay. Or just wander around Tobermory, the prettiest town in the Western Isles, with its Highland games, art festivals, yachting regattas, and the daily to and fro of islanders stocking up on supplies. Marvellous. *Children over ten welcome.*

rooms	6: 2 doubles, 2 twins, 2 four-posters.
price	£125–£160. Singles from £100.
meals	Dinner, 4 courses, £37.50.
closed	November–February.
directions	From ferry, A848 to Tobermory. Across bridge at mini-r'bout, immed. right into Breadalbane St. On right opp. fire station.

David & Jo Currie

tel	01688 302030
email	davidandjo@highlandcottage.co.uk
web	www.highlandcottage.co.uk

Restaurant with Rooms

Map 8, 10 Entry 240

Tiroran House
Isle of Mull, Argyll & Bute PA69 6ES

A stunning country house in a wild and rugged landscape; Mull is an island of moors, peaks and spectacular beaches. See dolphins, otters, golden eagles and thousands of red deer; try whale spotting or a trip to Staffa or Iona. Return to pre-dinner drinks in one of the two drawing rooms (deep sofas, log fires, long views), then sit down to Katie's delicious Cordon Bleu cooking, perhaps Loch Linnhie langoustine, roast lamb with rosemary and garlic, then fresh strawberries with gin and tonic syllabub. Big bedrooms are wonderfully comfy and have great views, fresh flowers, smart linen, big beds and an understated elegance. They're also blissfully quiet – you'll hear nothing at night except the brook bubbling through the garden. Bathrooms are warm and spotless and come with fluffy towels. Breakfast lazily on proper porridge and island produce in the vine-covered conservatory. You can wander Tiroran's 17 pretty acres, but hearty guests may want to make a start on the hundreds of pathways, or climb Ben More, 'the last munro'. If you're really lucky, you'll spot a white-tailed sea eagle.

rooms	6: 3 doubles, 3 twins.
price	£120–£140.
meals	Dinner from £35.
closed	Rarely.
directions	From Craignure or Fishnish car ferries, A849 direction Bunessan & Iona car ferry; right on B8035 for Gruline for 4 miles. Left at converted church. House 1 mile further.

	Laurence Mackay & Katie Munro
tel	01681 705232
fax	01681 705240
email	info@tiroran.com
web	www.tiroran.com

Hotel

The Airds Hotel & Restaurant
Port Appin, Appin, Argyll & Bute PA38 4DF

Faultless service, ambrosial food and warmly cosy interiors make this one of
Scotland's most indulging country-house hotels. Views from the front slide down
to Loch Linnhe, sweep over Lismore Island and cross to the towering mountains
of Ardnamurchan beyond. A small conservatory, candlelit at night, frames the
view perfectly, but in good weather you can skip across the lane to discover a
lawned garden of rainbow colours decked out with tables and parasols. Pre-dinner
drinks are taken in the sitting rooms – open fires, elegant sofas, fresh flowers,
lots of books – after which you're whisked off to the dining room where delicious
food is served on Limoges china. Whatever can be is homemade, so expect the
best, maybe baked goat's cheese with onion confit, cream of cauliflower and
mustard soup, seared fillet of brill in a citrus butter sauce, hot chocolate fondant
with pistachio ice cream. Retire to smart country-house bedrooms (crisp florals,
soft colours, Frette linen, Italian bathrobes) and find your bed turned down, the
curtains drawn. There's pink grapefruit and campari sorbet for breakfast, too.

rooms	12: 6 doubles, 5 twins, 1 suite.
price	Half board £125-£185 p.p.
meals	Half-board only. Lunch £5-£25. Dinner, 4 courses, included; non-residents £49.50.
closed	8-26 January.
directions	A82 north for Fort William, then A828 south for Oban. Right for Port Appin after 12 miles. On left after 2 miles.

	Shaun McKivragan
tel	01631 730236
fax	01631 730535
email	airds@airds-hotel.com
web	www.airds-hotel.com

Hotel

Map 8 Entry 242

The Manor House

Gallanach Road, Oban, Argyll & Bute PA34 4LS

A 1780 dower house for the Dukes of Argyll – their cottage by the sea – built of local stone, high on the hill, with long views over Oban harbour to the Isle of Mull. A smart and proper place, not one to bow to the fads of fashion: sea views from the lawn, cherry trees in the courtyard garden, a fire roaring in the drawing room, a beautiful tiled floor in the entrance hall and an elegant bay window in the dining room that catches the eye. Compact bedrooms are pretty in blues, reds and greens, with fresh flowers, crisp linen sheets, radios, padded headboards and piles of towels in good bathrooms; those that look seaward have pairs of binoculars to scour the horizon. Sample Loch Fyne kippers for breakfast, sea bass for lunch and, if you've room, duck in redcurrant sauce for supper; try their home-baking, too. Ferries leave for the islands from the bottom of the hill – see them depart from the hotel garden – while at the top, overlooking Oban, watch the day's close from McCaig's Folly; sunsets here are really special. *Children over 12 welcome.*

rooms	11: 8 doubles, 3 twins.
price	Half-board £60-£90 p.p.
meals	Half-board only. Lunch £7-£13. Dinner, 5 courses, £32.50.
closed	Christmas.
directions	In Oban, follow signs to ferry. Hotel on right 0.5 miles after ferry turn-off, signed.

	Ann MacEachen
tel	01631 562087
fax	01631 563053
email	info@manorhouseoban.com
web	www.manorhouseoban.com

Hotel

Map 8 Entry 243

Lerags House
Lerags, By Oban, Argyll & Bute PA34 4SE

A spectacular drive down a single track road through lochs and gentle mountains to the lovely house. Built in 1815, the rooms are large and light with high ceilings and sash windows. Cool interiors mix natural colours and light pine surfaces with pale sofas, fresh lilies, straight lines and bold pictures. Charlie and Bella represent an emerging generation of hoteliers: more style, less formality, good prices, great service and Bella's exceptional food. Pan-fried sea bass with rosemary, garlic and lemon-scented puy lentils, chocolate amaretti fudge with vanilla cream…. The menu changes daily. Bedrooms are gorgeous: pale earthy colours, big beds with Italian linen. The suite has a view to the loch and its own sitting area, stylish bathrooms are warm and the towels are big. The delightful garden runs down to tidal mud flats; watch the ebb and flow from the dining room while you breakfast on proper porridge. At the end of the road – a brisk stroll of a mile or so – is a beach for uninterrupted walks, or a constitutional dip. Day trips to Mull, Crinan and Glencoe are all easy, all wonderful.

rooms	6: 4 doubles, 1 twins/doubles, 1 suite.
price	Half board £75 p.p.
meals	Half-board only. Packed lunch £6.
closed	Christmas.
directions	From Oban, south on A816 for 2 miles, then right, signed Lerags for 2.5 miles. House on left, signed.

	Charlie & Bella Miller
tel	01631 563381
email	stay@leragshouse.com
web	www.leragshouse.com

Hotel

Map 8 Entry 244

Ardanaiseig
Kilchrenan, By Taynuilt, Argyll & Bute PA35 1HE

The seduction begins the moment you leave the main road and set off on the twisting, ten-mile track. Such silence, and when you set eyes on the Ardanaiseig you think all is complete: a magical landscape of valley and snow-capped peaks embracing the 1834 baronial mansion that sits on the shores of Loch Awe. But there is more to come. From the big bay windows of the drawing room, watch the peat-burning steamboat pick up fellow guests from the end of the garden to transport them to fairytale castles. There's fun, too, from the art-collecting owner, to add a light touch, and comfortable bedrooms, each one different; 200 acres of woodland gardens with an amphitheatre for concerts; great food. Gary the chef who has been here for six years is "good at everything", creating wonders from scallops from Oban, venison from the woods, beef from Aberdeen. Peter, charming and gentle, is ever-present: all runs smoothly with him at the helm. Venture forth to the village, a three-mile ramble... feel the peace. People come for special occasions – to propose and to marry – but you should find any excuse.

rooms	16: 8 doubles, 8 twins/doubles.
price	£78-£250. Singles £69-£155. Half-board £59-£148 p.p. (min. 3 nights).
meals	Light lunch from £3.75. Afternoon tea £2-£10. Gourmet dinner, 7 courses, £42.
closed	January-mid-February.
directions	A85 to Taynuilt. Left, B845 for Kilchrenan. Then left at Kilchrenan pub; down track for 4 miles.

	Peter Webster
tel	01866 833333
fax	01866 833222
email	ardanaiseig@clara.net
web	www.ardanaiseig.com

Hotel

Map 8 Entry 245

Culzean Castle

The National Trust for Scotland, Maybole, Ayrshire KA19 8LE

Americans in search of ancestors would adore it here. Across the viaduct, under the arch, into the Armoury with its 713 flintlock pistols and 400 swords, and the lift to the top floor. Culzean (pronounced 'Cullane') is Scotland's sixth most popular tourist destination and was built into solid rock a couple of hundred feet above crashing waves. When the Marquess of Ailsa presented the castle to the Scottish people in 1945, Eisenhower was given the top floor suite – Scotland's thank you for his contribution to the war effort. You stay on the same floor where every room is comfortable and spacious; there are glowing fires, cashmere throws, twinkling chandeliers and thrilling sea views – though the most splendid rooms are on the land side. Bathrooms are grandly traditional, service is courteous and thoughtful and the rest is awe-inspiring: hundreds of portraits, a round drawing room that juts out over the sea, a central oval staircase with 12 Corinthian columns. Tour the castle before the tourists invade at 11am, take a stirring cliff walk in 560 idyllic acres, dine together dinner-party style.

rooms	6: 3 doubles, 1 twin/double, 1 four-poster; 1 twin with separate bath.
price	£225-£375. Singles from £140. Whole floor £1,500 per night (includes afternoon tea & evening drinks).
meals	Dinner, 3 courses with wine, £60. By arrangement.
closed	Rarely.
directions	From A77 in Maybole, A719 for 4 miles, signed.

	Mike Schafer
tel	0870 118 1945
fax	01655 884503
email	culzean@nts.org.uk
web	www.culzeanexperience.org

Other Place

Map 8 Entry 246

Knockinaam Lodge
Portpatrick, Dumfries & Galloway DG9 9AD

Lawns run down to the Irish sea, sunsets streak the sky red, roe deer amble down to eat the roses. An exceptional 1869 shooting lodge with unremitting luxuries: a Michelin star in the dining room, 150 malts in the bar and a level of service you might not expect in such far-flung corners of the realm. And history. Churchill once stayed and you can sleep in his big elegant room, where copies of his books wait to be read and where you need steps to climb into an ancient bath. It remains very much a country house: plump cushions on a Queen Anne sofa in an immaculate morning room where the scent of flowers mixes with the smell of burnt wood, invigorating cliff walks, curlews to lull you to sleep, nesting Peregrine falcons, and a rock pool where David keeps lobsters for the pot. In storms, waves crash all around. Trees stand guard high on the hill, their branches buffeted by the wind, bluebells come out by the thousand in spring. Remote, beguiling, utterly spoiling – Knockinaam is worth the detour. John Buchan knew the house and described it in *The Thirty-Nine Steps* as the house to which Hannay fled.

rooms	9: 3 doubles, 5 twins/doubles, 1 suite.
price	Half-board £130-£190 p.p. Singles from £150.
meals	Half-board only. Lunch, by arrangement, £25-£37.50. Dinner, 5 courses, included; non-residents £47.50.
closed	Rarely.
directions	From A77 or A75, for Portpatrick. 2 miles west of Lochans, left at smokehouse. Signed for 3 miles.

David & Sian Ibbotson

tel	01776 810471
fax	01776 810435
email	reservations@knockinaamlodge.com
web	www.knockinaamlodge.com

Hotel

Map 5 Entry 247

Cavens Country House Hotel
Kirkbean, Dumfries & Galloway DG2 8AA

The Fordyces are friendly professionals who put in a huge amount of effort to ensure guests will come back, and they do. It is not just a small, luxury hotel set in a 1750s mansion house, it is also their home. Easy then to sit on a comfortable sofa, dram in hand, and imagine it is yours. Angus is chef and does superb home cooking with a Scottish-French twist, three courses that change every day. A highlight are the cheeses from Loch Arthur Farm, worth leaving home for. Jane does the décor and no two bedrooms are alike; all have comfort, elegance, rich colours, wide beds, padded bedsteads, chintz with swags and tails, books in glass-fronted cases. Views from the vast drawing room sweep down the lovely gardens to a temple at the far end. And you are so near the sea you can smell it. This neck of the woods is a wildlife heaven; birdwatching, shooting, riding, walking, golf. And do visit the gardens that thrive in this climate: the walled garden and glasshouses of Threave nearby, or Logan Botanic Garden, worth the detour.

rooms	6: 4 doubles, 2 twins.
price	£80–£140. Singles from £95.
meals	Dinner, 3 courses, £25. Packed lunch available.
closed	January & February.
directions	From Dumfries, A710 to Kirkbean (12 miles). Hotel signed in village.

	Jane & Angus Fordyce
tel	01387 880234
fax	01387 880467
email	enquiries@cavens.com
web	www.cavens.com

Hotel

Map 5 Entry 248

Greywalls
Muirfield, Gullane, East Lothian EH31 2EG

Gracious, stately and hugely impressive, yet you could curl up on a sofa and feel perfectly at home. Sir Edwin Lutyens built the house in 1901 for a golfer determined to be within a 'mashie niblick' shot of the 18th green; two gate lodges were added for staff, then a nursery wing. Now it's half hotel, half private home – held in equal affection by family and guests. Greywalls is discreet, peaceful, welcoming and unpompous – one guest said staying here was like "breathing silk". Enter a charmed world of log fires, French windows, family portraits, parquet floors. Benches on the lawn look directly onto Muirfiled golf course; Nicklaus stayed in 1966, Watson in 1980, Els in 2002 – all went on to win the Open. There's a panelled library, a cosy bar, chintz in the bedrooms and a dedicated team in the kitchen – the food is sublime. Bedrooms – six in the lodges, more in the house – have everything you could wish for, and there's the Colonel's House for private groups. The walled garden was designed by Gertrude Jekyll: a delightful tapestry of arbours, arches, peonies, lavender and immaculate lawns.

rooms	23: 20 twins/doubles, 3 singles.
price	£285. Singles £135.
meals	Lunch £20-£25 (Friday-Sunday). Dinner £45.
closed	January & February.
directions	A198 from A1 & take last road at east end of Gullane village.

Giles Weaver

tel	01620 842144
fax	01620 842241
email	hotel@greywalls.co.uk
web	www.greywalls.co.uk

Hotel

Map 9 Entry 249

The Inn at Lathones

Lathones, St Andrews, Fife KY9 1JE

Once upon a time in the Kingdom of Fife, two people fell in love, married and lived happily ever after in this old inn; beer flowed, food was plentiful, customers burst into song, even a dwarf highwayman dropped in after work. Legend says when the landlady died in 1736, the wedding stone above the fireplace in the lounge cracked, so strong was their love. Today, she and her horse haunt the wonderful Stables, the oldest part of the inn, with its garlands of hops and bottle-green ceiling – but in the friendliest way. Lathones could charm even the most cantankerous ghost: superb food, the draw of an open fire, leather sofas to sink into, and a warm Scottish welcome. Walk into the bar to find bottles of grappa and eau-de-vie asking to be sampled, while Martin Avey's menu is mouthwatering: try red-wine marinated halibut followed by chocolate trio with kumquat marmalade. Comfortable, traditional-style bedrooms are split between a coach house and an old blacksmith's house either side of the inn. Historic St Andrews and the East Neuk of Fife fishing villages are close.

rooms	13 twins/doubles.
price	£150-£220.
meals	Lunch £14.50. Dinner, à la carte, from £22. Packed lunch from £12.
closed	Christmas; 2 weeks in January.
directions	From Kirkcaldy, or St Andrews, A915 to Largoward. Inn 1 mile north on roadside.

Nick White

tel	01334 840494
fax	01334 840694
email	lathones@theinn.co.uk
web	www.theinn.co.uk

Inn

Map 9 Entry 250

Rab Ha's

83 Hutcheson Street, Glasgow G1 1SH

Lively, full of soul, and the price isn't bad either. Down in the trendy Merchant City, Rab Ha's puts on a good show, the cast comprising a collection of bon vivants who gather at night for the odd malt, a drop of beer, a glass of Spanish wine or even a cocktail. Flames fly in a stone fireplace in the candlelit panelled bar, waiters whisk plates to your table in the stylish cellar restaurant. Fabulous food gives lots of choice, anything from traditional favourites like haggis, neaps and tatties to saddle of Rannoch Moor venison; the pre-theatre menu is exceptionally well-priced and they also do a mean Sunday lunch. Bedrooms are modern and spruce with crisp white linen, yellow walls and curvaceous twiggery; excellent bathrooms may come with a claw-foot bath. Don't expect peace and quiet until late; hushed it is not! Continental breakfast can be delivered to your room or there's the full Scottish works in the bar. Extravagant, energetic Glasgow can be explored by foot: chic shops, groovy galleries and cool clubs are all close. But you may just want to stay put and join in the fun.

rooms	4: 3 doubles, 1 twin/double.
price	£75–£95.
meals	Bar menu, 2 courses, from £11. Lunch & dinner: main courses £12.50–£15.95.
closed	Christmas Day.
directions	5-minute walk from Queen Street station.

	Andy Young
tel	0141 572 0400
fax	0141 572 0402
email	e.management@rabhas.com
web	www.rabhas.com

Restaurant with Rooms

Map 8 Entry 251

The Pines

Woodside Avenue, Grantown-on-Spey, Moray PH26 3JR

A stone's throw from the town, The Pines – with its woodland grounds that lead to the beautiful river Spey – is an interesting find. Gwen is a gifted cook and Michael chatty and debonair; you'll soon feel at home. Downstairs rooms – a deep red dining room and conservatory with garden views, an attractive sitting room – are bright with patterned carpets, and paintings crowd every wall. Mainly Scottish artists are represented, but this is a good international collection from traditional to modern. The upstairs drawing room has deep sofas; borrow a book from the library and settle here. Expect delicious food: venison from a local estate, gravadlax from Strathaird, eggs free-range, bread homemade. Bedrooms vary in size but all have excellent beds with good linen, and there are spoiling touches with fresh flowers and fruit, an evening turn-down and spotless bathrooms. Stroll through the attractive garden which is bordered on the far side by coniferous woodland; a bat box, squirrel feeders, bird boxes and a bee house will provide the entertainment. Come for peace and quiet and a bit of cossetting.

rooms	8: 3 doubles, 4 twins/doubles, 1 single.
price	£98–£116. Singles from £55. Half-board £75–£88 p.p.
meals	Dinner, 4 courses, £30. Packed lunch available.
closed	November–February.
directions	A95 north to Grantown. Right at 1st traffic lights; A939 for Tomintoul, 1st right into Woodside Ave. 500 yds on left.

Michael & Gwen Stewart

tel	01479 872092
fax	01479 872092
email	info@thepinesgrantown.co.uk
web	www.thepinesgrantown.co.uk

Hotel

Map 9 Entry 252

Minmore House
Glenlivet, Banffshire AB37 9DB

Driving up from Balmoral in the late afternoon sun, you could be forgiven for thinking the colour green was created here. The east of Scotland often plays second fiddle to its 'other half' in the west, but this lush cattle-grazing land is every inch as beautiful. Amid it all is Minmore, a great wee pad run with breezy good cheer by Victor and Lynne. They used to run a restaurant in South Africa and once cooked for Prince Philip; their food continues to win rave reviews. Their kingdom stretches to seven spotless bedrooms and a couple of suites that Lynne describes as "very zoosh". Guests swap highland tales in a pretty sitting room or, best of all, in a carved wooden bar, half-panelled, with scarlet chairs, the odd trophy and 104 malts. The garden is a birdwatcher's paradise, with lapwing, curlew and a rare colony of oyster-catchers; free-range chickens, source of your breakfast eggs, roam. Visit the famous Glenlivet distillery nearby, or cycle deep into the Ladder Hills where buzzard, falcon and even eagles soar; then back to Lynne's irresistible chocolate, whisky and yogurt cake and a blazing fire.

rooms	9: 3 doubles, 4 twins, 2 suites.
price	£96–£196. Suites £144–£260. Half-board from £86 p.p.
meals	Light lunch £15. Dinner, 4 courses, £38. Full picnic £10.
closed	26 November–28 December.
directions	From Aviemore, A95 north to Bridge of Avon; south on B9008 to Glenlivet. At top of hill, 400 yds before distillery.

	Victor & Lynne Janssen
tel	01807 590378
fax	01807 590472
email	enquiries@minmorehousehotel.com
web	www.minmorehousehotel.com

Hotel

Map 9 Entry 253

Woodwick House

Evie, Orkney KW17 2PQ

Trees are in short supply on Orkney but Woodwick sits in a sycamore wood fed by a burn that tumbles down to a seaweedy bay overlooking the Island of Gairsay; walk through wild flowers, past lichen-covered trees to the sound of rushing water and babbling crows – magical. Woodwick promotes "care, creativity and conservation", so come here to think, free of distraction. Manager James and his young staff are quietly charming, and the house is nothing fancy, just nicely fashioned and homely. Built in 1912, it stands on the site of a larger building destroyed during the Jacobite rebellion – a remarkable 'doocot' remains. There's a wisteria-filled conservatory, a hushed dining room (food is delicious, much of it organic), two sitting rooms, an open fire, a piano, books and lots of good old films. Outside, a half-wild garden, clucking hens, distant sheep and a pathway down to the small bay where seals nose about. A nearby ferry takes you to some of the smaller islands, while the Italian Chapel and numerous ancient sites are an absolute must. *Pets £7 for duration of stay.*

rooms	8: 3 doubles, 1 twin; 2 doubles, 1 twin, 1 single, with basins, all sharing bathroom.
price	£64-£92. Singles £32-£60.
meals	Lunch & packed lunch by arrangement. Dinner £28.
closed	Rarely.
directions	From Kirkwall, A965 to Finstown; A966 for Evie. Right after 7 miles; next right past Tingwall ferry turning, left down track to house.

	James Bryan
tel	01856 751330
fax	01856 751383
email	mail@woodwickhouse.co.uk
web	www.woodwickhouse.co.uk

Other Place

Map 12 Entry 254

Killiecrankie House Hotel

Pass of Killiecrankie, By Pitlochry, Perth & Kinross PH16 5LG

In the one-time dower house to Blair Castle, you are ideally positioned for all things Highland: the games at Braemar, the festival at Pitlochry, fishing, walking, castles, golf... and whisky, about which Tim, once a big mover and shaker in the wine trade, knows a thing or two. He and Maillie have come north of the border to cook great food, to serve good wines and to provide the sort of comfortable indulgence that caps a hard day's pleasure with rod, club or map. Food is top of the list, with an ever-changing menu of fresh fish and local meat and game, home-grown soft fruits, potatoes, asparagus, leeks and mangetout. Wine buffs will be in heaven: reasonably priced wine by the glass complements each course and the special vegetarian menu could convert an ardent carnivore... for an evening at least. Newly refurbished bedrooms are a good size, cosy, carpeted, warm and light, with views down the Garry Valley. There's a small bar, a snug sitting room with books and games, beautifully maintained grounds and an RSPB sanctuary near the house that's home to buzzards. Bring the binoculars.

rooms	10: 4 doubles, 4 twins/doubles, 2 singles.
price	Half-board £84-£99 p.p.
meals	Half-board only. Lunch from £3.25. Dinner, 4 courses, £34.
closed	January-March.
directions	A9 north of Pitlochry, then B8079, signed Killiecrankie. Straight ahead for 2 miles. Hotel on right, signed.

Tim & Maillie Waters

tel	01796 473220
fax	01796 472451
email	enquiries@killiecrankiehotel.co.uk
web	www.killiecrankiehotel.co.uk

Hotel

Map 9 Entry 255

Loch Tummel Inn

Strathtummel, By Pitlochry, Perth & Kinross PH16 5RP

A super little inn with huge views from the front that shoot across a shimmering Loch Tummel to a mountain of forest beyond. This is Rob Roy country; legend has it that his hideout, McGreggor's Cave, lies in the forest; pull on your boots and search the far shore while eagle, buzzard and falcon spiral above. For something more adventurous, Robert runs an outdoor sports centre and white-water rafting, mountain biking, kayaking, trekking and riding can all be arranged. Back at the inn a huge window in the first-floor sitting room frames the view, the terrace is shaded by honeysuckle, perfect for lazy lunches; and there's a beer garden across the road for pre-dinner drinks. Inside, tartan carpets run throughout giving a smart country-inn feel. There are 80 malts and a wood-burner in the bar, a pitched pine roof and exposed stone walls in the restaurant; grab the window seats and sit down to a bowl of mussels or an Aberdeen Angus steak. Airy bedrooms have warm colours, pretty fabrics, crisp linen, big beds, spotless bathrooms and DVD players; all but one has loch views.

rooms	6: 2 doubles, 4 twins/doubles.
price	£65-£120. Singles from £40.
meals	Bar meals from £8.
	Dinner, 3 courses, £26.
closed	Never.
directions	From Perth, A9 north, turn off after Pitlochry, for Killicrankie. Left onto B8019 for Tummel Bridge & Kinloch Rannoch; inn 8 miles on right.

Robert Gilmour

tel	01882 634272
fax	01882 634272
email	info@lochtummelinn.co.uk
web	www.lochtummelinn.co.uk

Inn

Map 8 Entry 256

The Ardeonaig Hotel

South Loch Tay Side, By Killin, Perth & Kinross FK21 8SU

A little bit of heaven on the quiet side of Loch Tay. This is a seriously spoiling hotel, the epitome of 21st-century deep country chic. Whitewashed walls and hanging baskets give way to an idyllic courtyard where stone flowerbeds tumble with colour. Best of all is the first-floor library in varnished pine with its enormous window framing imperious views of field, loch and mountain. There are plump sofas, leather armchairs, books and maps, binoculars, too. Elsewhere, a snug bar in tartan, a peat fire in a sparkling sitting room, and views of a tumbling burn through dining room windows. Pete, a South African, had Fish Hoek in London and made quite a splash cooking up fabulous things, so expect seriously good food, perhaps smoked salmon salad, roast saddle of local hare, then purple figs with honey and ginger. Stylish, uncluttered bedrooms are blissfully free of TVs and come in creams and browns, with good art, halogen lighting and cedarwood blinds. Those at the back have exquisite views. Stroll down to the water and find a flotilla of fishing boats; the hotel has rights, so bring your rod.

rooms	20: 11 doubles, 6 twins, 3 suites.
price	£120–£170. Singles from £75. Suites £220–£250. Half-board £90–£150 p.p.
meals	Bistro meals from £6.50. Dinner £26.50–£40. Tasting menu £49.50.
closed	Never.
directions	A9, then A827 to Kenmore via Aberfeldy. In Kenmore take south side road along Loch Tay for 10 miles. On right.

	Peter & Sara Gottgens
tel	01567 820400
fax	01567 820282
email	info@ardeonaighotel.co.uk
web	www.ardeonaighotel.co.uk

Hotel

Map 8 Entry 257

Monachyle Mhor

Balquhidder, Lochearnhead, Perth & Kinross FK19 8PQ

Loch Voil washes the shores at the bottom of the hill, mountains surround, skylarks sing on the breezes and cars pass at the rate of one an hour; the twisty road ends two miles up the track. The 1600s farmhouse, warm and unpretentious, is stylish, modern and vibrant within. Rambling Monachyle has glorious colours, lashings of comfort and a lovely, laid-back feel. Best of all: it has food cooked by Tom. The freshest that Scotland has to offer is what sparks his imagination: game, fish, wild berries, artichokes from the organic garden, mushrooms foraged the day before… sensational. This is a family affair and they started here as farmers – still are – then began doing B&B and now that has evolved too_. The restaurant is London-swish with Scottish views; the panelled bar with its wood fire deliciously snug. Bedrooms, split between house, barns and coach house, are to die for: huge beds, clean lines, rugs on creaking wooden floors, bathrooms with slate floors, huge showers. Walkers and dogs are welcome, locals fill the place at weekends and there's jazz on the 'lawns' in summer.

rooms	11: 3 doubles, 1 twin, 7 suites.
price	£95–£220. Singles from £85. Suites £150–£220.
meals	Sunday lunch £29. Dinner £44.
closed	January.
directions	M9, junc. 10, onto A84 17 miles north of Callander; left at Kings House Hotel, following signs to Balquhidder. 6 miles along road. Along Loch Voil. Hotel on right up drive, signed.

Tom Lewis

tel	01877 384622
fax	01877 384305
email	info@monachylemhor.com
web	www.monachylemhor.com

Hotel

Map 8 Entry 258

Creagan House
Strathyre, Callander, Perth & Kinross FK18 8ND

Run with huge skill and passion by Gordon and Cherry, it is decorated not by numbers, nor by fashion, but by enthusiasm, evolving slowly and naturally. The welcome is second to none and the food magnificent – carefully sourced and cooked with great flair by Gordon. Meat and game from Perthshire, seafood straight from the boats (local as much as possible) and served on Skye pottery at long polished oak tables in a baronial dining room. There's a smallish sitting room with a log-effect fire, new blue carpeting in the bar and 45 malt whiskies with a guide to help choose. No airs and graces, just the sort of attention you get in small, owner-run places. Bedrooms at the front, facing the quiet road, look to meadow, river and mountain – fabulous. All are a decent size for a cottagey house, all are spic and span and the twin is on the ground floor. Canopies on beds, Sanderson wallpaper, solid furniture, no TVs; "you don't come to Creagan to watch a box," says Cherry. Bag a munro instead – walking sticks at the door will help you up Beinn An T-Sidhein.

rooms	5: 4 doubles, 1 twin.
price	£110. Singles £65.
meals	Dinner £28.50.
closed	February.
directions	From Stirling, A84 north through Callander to Strathyre. Hotel 0.25 miles north of village on right.

	Gordon & Cherry Gunn
tel	01877 384638
fax	01877 384319
email	eatandstay@creaganhouse.co.uk
web	www.creaganhouse.co.uk

Restaurant with Rooms

Map 8 Entry 259

Ballochneck

Buchlyvie, Stirling FK8 3PA

Up the long rutted drive, past the curling pond (you can in winter) to Donnie and Fiona's 'big hoose' and a rocking good time. The house looks imposing, big and Scottish, but Donnie (also big and Scottish) is down the high steps with a smile and some banter in record time. He wants to show you his fires (blazing away in every room) and the enormous, beautiful bedrooms in sumptuous colours with bâteau beds and acres of crisp linen. There's the copper bathroom to marvel at (with another working fire) and several stunning views. He'll also want to tell you little stories about a picture, perhaps, or some evening or other he had with so-and-so — and take you to the games room at the top of the house with the full-sized billiard table and the purple walls. His charming wife Fiona (who has a gift for interior design using quirky colour combinations) is the perfect foil, calmly efficient and an accomplished cook. Only food and wine are taken seriously; the rest is laid back. Shooting, fishing, walking and the divine Donnie: what an antidote to work and the city! *Children over 12 welcome.*

rooms	3: 1 double; 1 double, 1 twin sharing bathroom (let to same party only).
price	£145-£160.
meals	Lunch, 4 courses, £20, by arrangement. Dinner, 4 courses, £32.50. Packed lunch £10.
closed	Christmas & New Year
directions	At Buchlyvie, right onto B835 towards Aberfoyle. Entrance 200 yds on left after bridge. 1 mile along drive to house.

	Donnie & Fiona Allan
tel	01360 850216
fax	01360 850376
email	info@ballochneck.com
web	www.ballochneck.com

B&B

Map 8 Entry 260

Mackay's Rooms & Restaurant
Durness, Sutherland, The Highlands IV27 4PN

White beaches, turquoise sea, waves, cliffs, waterfalls, huge tumbling skies and mountains. Robbie and Fiona (local, young and brimming with energy) have brought it all inside with natural wood, stone, slate, seagrass and colours that relect the landscape – heathers, blues and neutrals. Downstairs is comfortable and intimate – vanilla candles flickering in glass, a merry fire burning away, an interesting mix of modern and old furniture. Bedrooms are individual in style and vary much in size but all have excellent new beds, contemporary lighting, flat-screen TVs, DVD players, iPods and the same gorgeous natural colour schemes; purple saxifrage, moss campion and primrose yellow. Bathrooms are new, some with power showers, all with thick white towels and slate soap dispensers. Eat sublime food: cullen skink (fish soup), local venison, Highland beef, homemade puddings at chunky tables with high-backed leather chairs. The smell of peat fires drifts in the wind, gulls cry and the sea soothes – a place to free the heart and restore one's soul.

rooms	7: 4 doubles, 2 twins, 1 single.
price	£70-£100.
meals	Dinner, 3 courses, from £24.
closed	November-Easter.
directions	A838 north from Rhiconich. After 19 miles enter Durness village. Mackay's is on the right hand side opposite memorial.

	Fiona Mackay
tel	01971 511202
fax	01971 511321
email	fiona@visitmackays.com
web	www.visitmackays.com

Restaurant with Rooms

Map 11 Entry 261

2 Quail Restaurant & Rooms

Castle Street, Dornoch, Sutherland IV25 3SN

The Royal Burgh of Dornoch feels prosperous and assured. It has a world-class golf course, sandy beach and a pretty, shop-lined high street; Madonna christening her child in the cathedral did nothing to harm visitor numbers. Such a town deserves a smart restaurant and 2 Quail is it. It's central, sparkling and atmospheric and upholds with ease its reputation as one of Scotland's best eating places. You step into an instantly welcoming atmosphere and the hard-working Michael and Kerensa look after you impeccably; their standards are high and they employ no staff, preferring to run the show themselves. Michael, a gifted chef, employs a light touch with the freshest ingredients – potted langoustine with tomato confit and a truffle salad, halibut with an orange crust, loin of roe deer, caramelised raspberry tart – while Kerensa really knows her wines. The rooms upstairs are the icing on the cake: spotlessly clean and stylish, with excellent bathrooms and a generous supply of first-class bubbles and shampoos. Perfect.

rooms	3: 1 double, 1 twin, 1 twin/double.
price	£75–£95.
meals	Dinner, 4 courses, £35.50.
closed	Christmas; February & March.
directions	From Inverness, A9 north for 44 miles, then right on A949, for Dornoch. Restaurant on left before cathedral.

	Michael & Kerensa Carr
tel	01862 811811
email	stay@2quail.com
web	www.2quail.com

Map 11 Entry 262

Glenmorangie, The Highland Home at Cadboll

Fearn, By Tain, The Highlands IV20 1XP

Glenmorangie — glen of tranquillity. And so it is; this is heaven. Owned by the eponymous distillery, this 1700s farmhouse of thick walls and immaculate interiors stands in glorious country, with a tree-lined path down to the beach; see your supper landed by fishermen, or search for driftwood instead. A perfect place and a real find, with levels of service to surpass most others, where staff are attentive yet unobtrusive, and where the comforts seem unending. Bedrooms are exceptional: decanters of whisky, *fleur de lys* wallpaper, tartan blankets and country views. Rooms flood with light, there are bathrobes and piles of towels, the best linen and blankets, and the cottage suites are perfect for families. Downstairs, the portrait of the Sheriff of Cromarty hangs on the wall, a fire crackles between plump sofas in the drawing room, and views of the garden draw you out. The walled half-acre garden is both beautiful and productive, with much for your plate: superb dinners are served in intimate dinner party style. All this, and golf at Royal Dornoch, Tain and Brora.

rooms	9: 6 twins/doubles, 3 cottage suites.
price	Half-board £160-£190 p.p.
meals	Half-board only.
	Light lunch from £7.
	Dinner, 5 courses, included;
	non-residents £45.
closed	3-23 January.
directions	A9 north from Inverness for
	33 miles to Nigg r'bout. Right on
	B9175, for Nigg, over r'way crossing
	for 1.5 miles, then left, following
	signs to house.

	Martin Baxter
tel	01862 871671
fax	01862 871625
email	relax@glenmorangieplc.co.uk
web	www.theglenmorangiehouse.com

Hotel

Map 11 Entry 263

Stein Inn

Stein, Waternish, Isle of Skye IV55 8GA

The drive here is a treat and you sense that you'll find something special at the end of the gently undulating road. Waternish is a gem – Skye at its softest – and the Stein Inn sits snugly on the quay alongside bobbing boats; dating from 1790, it's the oldest on the island. Angus stocks over 100 single malts, thirst-quenching ales and seasoned opinion in the little wooden-clad bar. In good weather, sit by the shore of the sea loch: across the water, the headland rises; to the north, low-slung islands lie scattered. Lose yourself with a pint watching locals potter about in their boats against a setting sun, then step inside to the simple little dining room with a fire and pine tables. The daily specials menu includes fish from Loch Dunvegan, local meat and cheeses and scrummy puddings; try chocolate bread pudding or apple and cherry tart. Rooms are neat and tidy with bright blue carpets, pine furniture and jolly quilts. There's a pool room, a play area, a place for afternoon tea, and the affable Angus and Teresa are refreshingly child-friendly.

rooms	5: 2 doubles, 2 family, 1 single.
price	£52–£72. Singles £26–£36.
meals	Bar lunch from £5. Dinner, 3-courses, around £13.
closed	Christmas Day & New Year's Day.
directions	From Isle of Skye bridge, A850 to Portree. Follow sign to Uig for 4 miles, left on A850 for Dunvegan for 14 miles. Hard right turn to Waternish on B886. Stein 4.5 miles along loch side.

	Angus & Teresa McGhie
tel	01470 592362
fax	01470 592362
email	angus.teresa@steininn.co.uk
web	www.steininn.co.uk

Inn

Map 10 Entry 264

Greshornish House Hotel

By Portree, Isle of Skye IV51 9PN

A wise man once said, "Skye is not a place, but an intoxication." This low-slung, white-painted manor house sits right beside the loch and the views stretch as far as the Trotternish peninsula. Neil and Rosemary have only been here a couple of years but already they've stamped their personality on the place; the rooms they have done so far are warm, peaceful, calming and relaxing. Bedrooms are mostly large, some still waiting for the magic wand, but all have excellent views over the water or the gardens, expensive bed linen and deep peace. In the restaurant, fish is as fresh as it can be, with scallops straight from the loch, and langoustine and lobster plucked from Dunvegan Bay. Dig into Talisker crab cakes, pan-fried halibut, basil pannacotta and a strawberry consommé. The hearty appetite of the walker is well understood here and conservatory breakfasts will set you up for anything; a game of tennis or croquet, a stroll around the garden or an energetic walk. Take your binoculars for otter, eider, heron and maybe a sea eagle – and watch out for sheep on the road to get here.

rooms	9: 4 doubles, 2 twins/doubles, 1 twin, 2 family.
price	£100–£160.
meals	Lunch, 2 courses, from £14.95, by arrangement. Dinner from £32.50. Packed lunch about £5.
closed	Christmas. Occasionally in winter.
directions	A87 through Portree towards Dunvegan. 4 miles after Portree left on A850 for Dunvegan; signed to the right, 2 miles down single track road.

Neil & Rosemary Colquhoun

tel	01470 582266
fax	01470 582345
email	info@greshornishhouse.com
web	www.greshornishhouse.com

Hotel

Viewfield House

Portree, Isle of Skye IV51 9EU

A fabulous legacy of a mix; Scottish aristocracy with high colonialism. From its hall to its tiny, turret bedroom, the Victorian factor's house is stuffed with hunting trophies, eastern ornaments and heavy antiques, blending grandeur with odd touches of humour brilliantly. It's a fine ancestral seat, built in 1790, with huge windows in the sitting room, roaring fires, dark panelling, oriental rugs and some unique 100-year-old wallpapers upstairs. At 7.30 each evening a gong summons guests to dinner – Hugh and Linda take it in turns to cook. Food is seasonal and delicious, be it crab and tomato tart, fillet of pork with apricot and coriander or hazelnut cake with mascarpone cream. Each night Hugh dons a kilt in the family tartan while Linda, a Californian, remains delightfully unfazed by the splendour of the surroundings: beautiful period furniture and ancestors peering down from the walls. Upstairs is a warren of bedrooms ranging from big to vast and all are comfy and good: traditional fabrics, well-laundered sheets. Outside, climb through woods to Fingal's Seat for 360° views, or swim in a loch.

rooms	12: 4 doubles, 3 twins/doubles, 2 twins, 1 single; 1 double, 1 single sharing bath & shower.
price	£80-£110. Singles £40-£60. Half-board £65-£85 p.p.
meals	Dinner, 4 courses, £28. Packed lunch £5.20.
closed	Mid-October-mid-April.
directions	On A87, coming from south, driveway entrance on left just before the Portree National filling station.

	Hugh & Linda Macdonald
tel	01478 612217
fax	01478 613517
email	info@viewfieldhouse.com
web	www.viewfieldhouse.com

Hotel

Map 10,11 Entry 266

Hotel Eilean Iarmain

Eilean Iarmain, Sleat, Isle of Skye IV43 8QR

One of the prettiest spots on Skye – a whitewashed hamlet at the end of the road. The Sound of Sleat wraps itself around the place and fishermen still land their catch 30 paces from the front door. Across the water Robert Louis Stevenson's lighthouse paddles in the shallow and the mountains of the mainland rise. Inside, the Hebrides of old survives, part shooting lodge, part gentlemen's club: tartan carpets, hessian on the walls, the papers by the fire in the morning room and a new Smuggler's Den where Gaelic whiskies can be savoured. Bedrooms in smart country style are split between the main house, the garden house and the stables, the latter for sparkling two-storey suites that sport crisp fabrics and new pine. Next door in the bar, the occasional ceilidh breaks loose and fiddles fly, but there's also a touch of refined culture in the art gallery round the corner. Sir Iain – born in Berlin, christened in Rome, schooled in Shanghai – is Skye through and through, and deeply involved in regenerating the woodland terrain to the south of the island. He'll teach you the odd word of Gaelic, too. Bring your kilt.

rooms	15: 7 doubles, 4 twins, 4 suites.
price	£100–£190. Singles from £75. Suites £200–£220.
meals	Bar meals from £7.50. Lunch £12.50. Dinner, 4 courses, £31.
closed	Rarely.
directions	A87 over Skye Bridge (toll £5.50), then left after 7 miles onto A851, signed Armdale. Hotel on left after 8 miles, signed.

Sir Iain & Lady Noble

tel	01471 833332
fax	01471 833275
email	hotel@eileaniarmain.co.uk
web	www.eileaniarmain.co.uk

Hotel

Kinloch Lodge
Sleat, Isle of Skye IV43 8QY

Skye is Scotland at its softest and the Sleat peninsula is positively velvety.
Shimmering waters, lochs giving onto the Sounds of Sleat and Cullin, boats
bobbing and drifting... Kinloch Lodge sits in Clan Donald territory; Godfrey is
the High Chief and ancestors look down from the regal green walls. The family-
run hotel feels just the right size – big enough to find a quiet corner and be
private and small enough to feel personal – and Lady Macdonald's daughter,
Isabella, and son-in-law Tom take day-to-day care of the hotel with a charming
exuberance. Rooms are very comfy: chintzes and tartans, bathrobes and smellies;
they vary in size and outlook – this was built as a shooting lodge, not a hotel – but
dig deeper and grab yourself a dreamy view of Loch Na Dal, the lighthouse and
Knoydart or the Cullins. At dinner, Tom glides between tables helping with wine
choices and the chef trips out Skye crab tart with crisp mustard pastry, maybe
salmon with sautéed fennel. Portions are generous; afterwards take a slow walk to
a fireside seat in one of the three drawing rooms for coffee and homemade fudge.

rooms	14: 7 twins/doubles. Annexe: 5 twins/doubles; 2 doubles with separate shower or bath.
price	Half-board £95-£150 p.p. Singles by arrangement.
meals	Half-board only. Lunch from £4.50.
closed	22-28 December.
directions	From Skye Bridge follow signs south on A851 to Armadale-Mallaig ferry. Lodge signed on left down forestry road, approx. 20 minutes from bridge.

	Lady Macdonald
tel	01471 833214
fax	01471 833277
email	bookings@kinloch-lodge.co.uk
web	www.kinloch-lodge.co.uk

Hotel

Tigh an Eilean

Shieldaig, Loch Torridon, The Highlands IV54 8XN

Tigh an Eilean is the Holy Grail of the west coast – when you arrive you realise it's what you've been looking for all these years. A perfect place in every respect, from its position by the sea in this very pretty village, to the magnificence of the Torridon mountains that rise all around... this area is one of the wonderlands of the world. And Shieldaig itself has a strong sense of community, the hub of which is the pub – like the shop, owned by the hotel – where locals come to sing their songs, play their fiddles, drink their whisky, and talk. Most surprising of all is the hotel. Christopher and Cathryn, ex-London lawyers loving their new career, run an airy and stylish inn – all tartan cushions on window seats, sensational views, homemade shortbread, bedrooms that are comfy and bathrooms that sparkle. No TVs, no telephones, but kind, gentle staff who chat and advise. Friendly sitting rooms have plump sofas, Farrow & Ball colours and the odd tweed chair, an honesty bar and an open fire. Dine on Hebridean scallops in the restaurant, or try the pub: fewer frills but lots of fun.

rooms	11: 5 doubles, 3 twins, 3 singles.
price	£144. Single £68. Half-board from £110 p.p.
meals	Bar meals from £5. Restaurant dinner £41.
closed	November–March.
directions	On loch front in centre of Shieldaig.

Christopher & Cathryn Field
tel   01520 755251
fax   01520 755321
email   tighaneileanhotel@shieldaig.fsnet.co.uk

Hotel

Map 11 Entry 269

Doune

Knoydart, Mallaig, The Highlands PH41 4PL

Drive for miles and arrive at the water's edge where the mighty mountains of Knoydart rise to the east and Loch Nevis fuses with the sea. Be met by boat at Mallaig and taken to one of the most inaccessible parts of the Scottish mainland. Ever imagined landing in paradise? Here is a village of three families with no roads and a glorious view – Skye across the Sound of Sleat. Hear the water lapping, the call of a bird… and the whoops of joy of other guests as the combination of solitude, beauty, comfort and hospitality triggers an overpowering happiness. Hike (with a guide if you wish) and see no one all day, dive and find your own supper. Food is exceptional – maybe something from the sea, then a perfect venison pie. Along the veranda are three little pine-lined bed and shower rooms, with bunk galleries for children, hooks for clothes, easy chairs for watching the weather. And a further log cabin, with simple bedrooms, kitchen and an open-plan lay-out. The sunsets are breathtaking, the wind whistles, and townies will never know darkness like this. *Boat pick-up Tues & Sat only. Minimum stay three nights.*

rooms	3 + 1: 2 doubles, 1 twin. Self-catering lodge for 12.
price	Full-board £65 p.p. per night; £390 p.p. per week. Lodge from £3,400 per week.
meals	Full-board (includes packed lunch) except in Lodge.
closed	October-Easter.
directions	Park in Mallaig; the boat will collect you at an agreed time.

Martin & Jane Davies

tel	01687 462667
fax	08700 940428
email	martin@doune-knoydart.co.uk
web	www.doune-knoydart.co.uk

Other Place

Map 8 Entry 270

Tomdoun Sporting Lodge
Glengarry, Invergarry, The Highlands PH35 4HS

A quirky little place wrapped up in the middle of nowhere: in good weather Reception moves onto the veranda and the dogs sunbathe on lilos. Below, the blissful river Garry jumps from one loch to another; beyond, Glas Bheinn rises from the forest. Interiors are stylishly unpretentious (posh, but old!) with piles of logs and vintage luggage in the hall, a country-house dining room for communal breakfasts, and a smouldering coal fire in the lively bar. Come to fish – the hotel has rights on the loch and river – and if you're lucky, they'll cook your catch for supper. If not, settle for langoustine and cockles from Skye, or halibut fresh from Lochinver. A French filmmaker liked the place so much he returned to shoot a movie; Sheila is now a star. Exquisite walking in the wild and peaceful glen, with Loch Horn 20 miles upstream (where the road runs out). Bedrooms are simple, homely, nicely priced, full of colour; those at the front have huge Glengarry views. There's loads to do: clay-pigeon shooting, white-water rafting, water-skiing, abseiling, mountain biking.

rooms	10: 3 doubles, 2 family; 3 doubles, 1 twin, 1 single all sharing 2 baths.
price	£70–£100. Singles from £35.
meals	Packed lunch £7.95. Bar meals from £7. Dinner, 3 courses, from £18.95.
closed	24-25 December.
directions	A82 north from Fort William, then A87 west from Invergarry. After 5 miles, left for Glengarry. Hotel 6 miles up on right.

	Michael & Sheila Pearson
tel	01809 511218
email	enquiries@tomdoun-sporting-lodge.com
web	www.tomdoun-sporting-lodge.com

Hotel

Map 8 Entry 271

Kilcamb Lodge
Strontian, Argyll PH36 4HY

A stupendous setting, with Loch Sunart at the end of the garden and Glas Bheinn rising beyond. As for Kilcamb, it has all the ingredients of the perfect country house: a smart yellow drawing room with a roaring fire, a dining room that's won just about every award going and super-comfy bedrooms that don't stint on colour. The feel here is shipwreck-chic. There's a 12-acre garden with half a mile of shore, so follow paths to the water's edge and look for dolphins, otters and seals or watch duck and geese; if you're lucky, you may see eagles. Back inside you'll find stained-glass windows on the landing, a ship's bell in the bar, fresh flowers in the bedrooms. Come down at eight for a four-course dinner and feast on goat's cheese and chive mousse, cream of celery and stilton soup, roast venison with a juniper jus, then lemon curd crème brûlée. Warmly decorated bedrooms have all the trimmings: super king-size beds, padded headboards, big white towels, shiny bathrooms. Ardnamurchan Point is up the road and worth a visit: it's the most westerly point in mainland Britain.

rooms	9: 5 doubles, 1 twin, 3 suites.
price	£142–£165. Suites £196. Singles from £90.
meals	Lunch from £6. Dinner, 4 courses, £42.
closed	Rarely.
directions	From Fort William, A82 south for 10 miles to Corran ferry, then A861 to Strontian. Hotel west of village on left, signed. A830 & A861 from Fort William takes an hour longer.

David & Sally Ruthven-Fox

tel	01967 402257
fax	01967 402041
email	enquiries@kilcamblodge.co.uk
web	www.kilcamblodge.co.uk

Hotel

Map 8 Entry 272

Scarista House
Isle of Harris, Western Isles HS3 3HX

All you need to know is this: Harris is one of the most beautiful places anywhere in the world. Beaches of white sand that stretch for a mile or two are not uncommon. If you bump into another soul, it will be a delightful coincidence, but you should not count on it. The water is turquoise, and coconuts sometimes wash up on the beach. The view from Scarista is simple and magnificent: field, ridge, beach, water, sky. Patricia and Tim are the kindest people, quietly inspiring. Their home is island heaven: coal fires, rugs on painted wooden floors, books everywhere, old oak furniture, a first-floor drawing room, fresh flowers and fabulous Harris light. The golf club has left a set of clubs by the front door in case you wish to play (the view from the first tee is one of the best in the game). A corncrake occasionally visits the garden. There are walking sticks and Wellington boots to help you up the odd hill. Kind local staff may speak Gaelic. And the food is exceptional, maybe twice-baked crab soufflé, seared loin of Harris lamb, marmalade tart with plum compote. A perfect place.

rooms	5: 3 doubles, 2 twins.
price	£175–£199. Singles from £120.
meals	Dinner, 3 courses, £43.50. Packed lunch £5.50.
closed	Christmas.
directions	From Tarbert, A859, signed Rodel. Scarista 15 miles on left, after golf course.

	Patricia & Tim Martin
tel	01859 550238
fax	01859 550277
email	timandpatricia@scaristahouse.com
web	www.scaristahouse.com

Hotel

Map 10 Entry 273

Tigh Dearg

Lochmaddy, Isle of North Uist, Western Isles HS6 5AE

This far-flung island chain is worth every second it takes to get here. Come for huge skies, sweeping beaches, carpets of wild flowers in the machair in summer, stone circles, ancient burial chambers, white-tailed eagles and fabulous Hebridean light. It's hard to overstate the sheer wonder of these bleakly beautiful islands, five of which are connected by a causeway, so drop south to Benbecula (*Whisky Galore* was filmed here) or Eriskay (for the Prince's Strand, where Bonnie Prince Charlie landed). Up on North Uist, you'll find 1,000 lochs, so climb North Lees for wonderful watery views, then tumble back down to the island sanctuary of Tigh Dearg. The house is a delight, immensely welcoming, full of colour, warmly contemporary, with windows that flood the place with light. Swanky bedrooms come with suede bedheads, power showers, bathrobes and beach towels, bowls of fruit and crisp white linen. In the restaurant, lobster, crab, squid, sole all come straight from the water. Walk, ride, fish, canoe, then return and try the sauna. Come in November for the northern lights. Fabulous.

rooms	8 twins/doubles.
price	£80–£139.
meals	Bar meals from £7.50. Dinner, 3 courses, £25.
closed	Never.
directions	North into Lochmaddy. Left, signed Police Station. Hotel on left after 200 yds.

	Iain MacLeod
tel	01876 500700
email	info@tighdearghotel.co.uk
web	www.tighdearghotel.co.uk

Hotel

Map 10 Entry 274

Wales

Neuadd Lwyd
Penmynydd, Anglesey LL61 5BX

Tudor kings came from this village, their forefathers buried in the tiny church that stands beyond the garden gate. Six sublime acres wrap around you, sheep graze in the fields, views shoot off to a distant Snowdon. The house, an 1854 rectory cloaked in wisteria, has been refurbished in lavish style and smart Victorian interiors shine. The drawing room floods with morning light, has deep sofas, polished wood floors, loads of books and a crackling fire; French windows open onto the south-facing terrace for sunny afternoons. High-ceilinged bedrooms are immaculate and full of beautiful things: cut-glass Venetian mirrors, ornate marble fireplaces, beautifully upholstered armchairs, Provençal eiderdowns; the two bigger rooms have slipper baths. Best of all is the cooking. Susannah and co-chef Delyth trained at Ballymaloe and whatever can be is homemade; delicious breads, fabulous oat cakes, jams, compotes, sorbets, ice creams. You may get Gorau Glas cheese soufflé, rack of Anglesey lamb with minted pea purée, warm pear and frangipani tarte, a plate of Welsh cheeses. Coastal paths will help you atone.

rooms	4: 3 doubles, 1 twin.
price	£125–£145. Singles £80–£110. Half-board from £82.50 p.p.
meals	Dinner, 4 courses, £35.
closed	Sundays & Mondays.
directions	A55 north over Britannia Bridge. 2nd exit (A5025) for Amlwch, then left for Llangefni (B5420). After 2 miles, right signed St Gredifael's Church. 1 mile up lane; on right.

Susannah & Peter Woods
tel	01248 715005
fax	01248 715005
email	post@neuaddlwyd.co.uk
web	www.neuaddlwyd.co.uk

Restaurant with Rooms

Map 5 Entry 275

Jolyon's Boutique Hotel
5 Bute Crescent, CF10 5AN

Down in Butetown, the captain's house stands on Cardiff Bay's oldest residential street. Bang opposite, the regenerated docks are home to the Welsh Assembly, the Norwegian Church and the Millennium Centre. At Jolyon's boutique B&B hotel run in the Mediterranean style, you get quietly groovy interiors. Bedrooms start on the ground floor and work their way skywards to the one at the top with a private roof terrace. The higher you go, the better the view. In the basement is a bar made from reclaimed 1840 timbers encased in stainless steel; stop for an espresso, a trappist beer or a glass of pear and strawberry cider. An old harmonium rests against an exposed stone wall; sink into red leather sofas and gaze at contemporary art. Spotless bedrooms aren't huge, but nor are they small, and light floods in so none feel cramped. You find Moroccan lanterns, French armoires, Dutch marble, Canadian oak, Indian teak, Philippe Starck loos in airy bathrooms (you can watch TV while you soak in a couple). Jolyon will tell you where to eat: Capsule, for cocktails and *calzone*, is a must.

rooms	6 doubles.
price	£85-£140.
meals	Cheese plates from £10.
closed	Never.
directions	M4 junc. 29, then A48(M) for Cardiff. Take exit marked 'Docks and Bay'. Straight ahead, past Millenium Centre & 1st left.

	Jolyon Joseph
tel	02920 488775
fax	02920 488775
email	info@jolyons.co.uk
web	www.jolyons.co.uk

Hotel

Map 2 Entry 276

The Big Sleep Hotel
Bute Terrace, Cardiff CF10 2FE

Cheap but sure damn groovy, this novel and gutsy designer hotel is a good launch-pad from which to discover a regenerated Welsh capital. Retro 1970s style and 1990s minimalism co-join inside a ten-storey former office block opposite Cardiff International Arena. The building was resurrected as The Big Sleep by two innovators with flair and a friend in the actor John Malkovich, who helped back the project. To keep costs down, Cosmo supplied the formica from his Bath-based factory – the first in Britain to bend the material – and Lulu sourced the teddy-bear fur to make full-length curtains and to carpet the fun penthouse suite. Cool blues and stark white walls were inspired by 1950s architect Gio Ponti. Most rooms have glittering city views at night; we suggest you pay extra for one of the two suites on the tenth floor. Elsewhere, modular seating re-upholstered in white PVC, a handy 'ironing station', a colourful lobby, and deep red 1960s wallpaper in the busy bar. Good value for this city hotel, described as a "travel lodge with sex appeal."

rooms	81: 42 doubles, 30 twins, 7 family, 2 suites.
price	£45–£135.
meals	Continental breakfast included.
closed	Christmas Day & Boxing Day.
directions	M4, junc. 29, A48(M), for Cardiff East. 3rd junc., A4232 to city centre. At 1st r'bout, 2nd exit, 1 mile past Lloyds TSB, left at lights on A4160. Right at 3rd set of lights, under bridge. On left.

Cosmo Fry & Lulu Anderson

tel	02920 636363
fax	02920 636364
email	bookings.cardiff@thebigsleephotel.com
web	www.thebigsleephotel.com

Hotel

Map 2 Entry 277

SACO Serviced Apartments

76 Cathedral Road, Cardiff CF11 9LN

Folk intent on corporate lets, house-hunting, student-offspring-visiting or away for a family celebration are discovering the advantages of serviced-apartment independence. Kick off your shoes, pour yourself a glass of wine and settle down on a spotless burgundy sofa to satellite TV – it's like home, only neater. The immaculate apartments, whose Victorian sash windows overlook pleasant, wide, tree-lined Cathedral Road, have their bedrooms quietly at the back. You get oatmeal carpeting, padded dining chairs, a spotlit kitchen, a smart little bathroom (and extra shower room in the apartments for four) all mod cons and a friendly local rep. Beds are king-size, with white duvets and fat pillows, bedroom furniture is attractively colour-washed, cots and broadband are on request. It's a neutral, contemporary and functional open-plan space that is, frankly, hard to fault. Best of all, you are a short walk from Cardiff Castle, the Millennium Stadium and the pedestrianised shopping centre. *Long-stay rates available.*

rooms	15 apartments for 2 or 4.
price	£69-£110 + VAT.
meals	Restaurants within walking distance.
closed	Rarely.
directions	5-minute taxi ride from railway station.

	Jo Redman
tel	0845 122 0405
fax	0117 974 5939
email	cardiff@sacoapartments.co.uk
web	www.sacoapartments.co.uk

Other Place

Map 2 Entry 278

Ty Mawr Country Hotel
Brechfa, Carmarthenshire SA32 7RA

Ty Mawr translates as 'big house' and this is a classic Welsh building, all 15th-century stones, low beams, log fires and low-slung sash windows. Steve and Annabel have worked in the business for years, took time off to trot the globe, then settled into this peaceful part of the Brechfa forest to show off their skills. Steve is in charge of the kitchen and his philosophy is simple: use the best local and seasonal ingredients and you don't need to tamper with it much. There's organic Welsh Black beef from the neighbouring farm, fruit, veg and honey from another nearby, fish and shellfish from a fisherman in Cardigan with a license to coracle fish on the Teifi. Annabel does 'front of house' and the whole place has an inviting, fresh and friendly feel. In winter, the scent of woodsmoke infuses the sitting room; in summer, dining room doors open to a birdsung terrace and a pretty garden with a gurgling brook. Local art enlivens the walls and bedrooms are freshly cosy: embroidered bedcovers, window seats with bolsters, claw-foot baths and comfy pine beds. A sweet sanctuary, and they brew their own beer, too.

rooms	5: 3 doubles, 1 twin; 1 double with separate bath.
price	£95–£105. Singles £65. Half-board £70 p.p. (min. 2 nights).
meals	Sunday lunch £13.50–£16.50. Dinner £26–£29. Packed lunch from £5.
closed	Rarely.
directions	M4 west onto A48, then B4310 exit, for National Botanic Gardens, north to Brechfa. In village centre.

	Steve & Annabel Viney
tel	01267 202332
email	info@wales-country-hotel.co.uk
web	www.wales-country-hotel.co.uk

Hotel

Map 2 Entry 279

Escape Boutique B&B

48 Church Walks, Llandudno, Conwy LL30 2HL

Bill Bryson raved about Llandudno – the unspoilt front with its bright white hotels and pier, the bustling shops and restaurants behind. Just a short walk from the sea, the house on the hill with its Victorian features intact – stained-glass windows, ornate carved fireplaces – has been stunningly transformed into a world of wood floors, cool neutral colours, Italian cream leather and glass chandeliers. Sam and Gaenor have cut not one corner so everything is the best: huge pocket-sprung mattresses, Farrow & Ball colours, acres of crisp linen, gorgeous goose down, beautifully designed bathrooms with a roll top bath or a drench-me shower. Bedrooms are spotless, some have sea views and breakfast is a feast of Conwy Gold Award sausages and serious coffee. Best of all are the easy-going owners who organise pretty much anything you want – or leave you to your own devices. The comfortable sitting room with honesty bar would make this a great place for a weekend house party; there's even a pretty garden in which to sip something cool before a stroll into town.

rooms	9 doubles.
price	£75-£105.
meals	Restaurants & pubs within walking distance.
closed	Rarely.
directions	A55 from Chester into North Wales; junc. 18 Llandudno (A470). Follow signs to promenade; left into Church Walks & past Great Orme Tramway. House on right.

Sam Nayar

tel	01492 877776
fax	01492 878777
email	info@escapebandb.co.uk
web	www.escapebandb.co.uk

B&B

Map 5 Entry 280

The Kinmel Arms

The Village, St George, Abergele, Conwy LL22 9BP

St George — just a handful of cottages — so the locals must be pleased that one of their own (the lovely Lynn, who grew up near here) has returned, with husband Tim, to turn the old place into a sparkling restaurant with rooms. Walk in to a light, open-plan space of cool, neutral colours, hard wood floors and a central bar with new stained-glass detail above; then through to a conservatory-style restaurant painted a cheery yellow, with marble-topped tables and Tim's photographs and paintings on all the walls, inspired by the North Wales landscape and his climbing travels. Behind are four gorgeous suites, each with wide French windows to a decked seating area facing east for glorious sunrises — you breakfast here on goodies from your own fridge. Expect huge beds with crisp linen, high ceilings and fresh yellow walls, flat-screen TVs, luxurious porcelain bathrooms with vast towels and designer radiators. Everything is geared towards relaxation — the rooms, the food, the wine, the independence. You're a hop from that stunning coast — and Snowdonia — while great walks start from the door. Fabulous.

rooms	4 suites.
price	£135–£175.
meals	Continental breakfast. Light lunches £3.25–£8.95. Dinner, 2 courses, from £15.
closed	Sunday evenings & Mondays.
directions	A55, junc. 24 from Chester; left; 0.25 miles to top of Primrose Hill.

Tim Watson & Lynn Cunnah-Watson

tel	01745 832207
fax	01745 822044
email	info@thekinmelarms.co.uk
web	www.thekinmelarms.co.uk

Restaurant with Rooms

Map 5 Entry 281

Tyddyn Llan

Llandrillo, Corwen, Denbighshire LL21 0ST

Everything is orchestrated superbly here. Your entry is into a smart country home – there's no reception desk – where owners Bryan and Susan Webb greet you with the promise of deep comfort and some exquisite modern cooking. There are three sitting rooms, a log fire, carefully chosen antiques and a dining room with a gentle, French country feel: blue-grey panelling and soft floral drapes. Eat at white-clothed tables on fresh, locally sourced produce lovingly cooked: grilled scallops, Welsh black fillet of beef au poivre, calves' sweetbreads with pancetta, whimberry crème brûlée. Bedrooms vary in size but all are cosy and well-designed in a traditional style with warm colours, lush towels and every indulging extra. Treat yourself to tea on the veranda after a game of croquet on the lawn... or walk the Berwin Ridge which rises to 2,000 feet. Or come with rod and wellies to fish trout and grayling on the river Dee. Great comfort and fine food in an astonishingly beautiful Welsh valley.

rooms	13: 8 doubles, 4 twins, 1 garden suite.
price	£110-£240. Singles from £95. Half-board £95-£150 p.p.
meals	Lunch £19.50-£25. Dinner £35-£40; tasting menu £55.
closed	Two weeks in January.
directions	From A5 west of Corwen, left on B4401 to Llandrillo. Go through village, entrance on right after tight bend.

Bryan & Susan Webb

tel	01490 440264
fax	01490 440414
email	tyddynllan@compuserve.com
web	www.tyddynllan.co.uk

Hotel

Map 5 Entry 282

Denbighshire

The Hand at Llanarmon
Llanarmon Dyffryn Ceiriog, Llangollen, Denbighshire LL20 7LD

Single-track lanes plunge you into the middle of nowhere. Lush valleys rise and fall, so pull on your boots and scale a mountain or find a river and jump into a canoe. Back at the Hand, a 16th-century drovers' inn, the pleasures of a country local are hard to miss. A coal fire burns on the range in reception, a wood fire crackles under brass in the front bar and a wood-burner warms the lofty dining room. Expect exposed stone walls, low beamed ceilings, old pine settles and candles on the mantelpiece. There's a games room for darts and pool, a quiet sitting room for maps and books. Delicious food is popular with locals, so grab a table and enjoy seasonal menus — perhaps game broth, lamb casserole, and orange and coriander sponge served warm with a cointreau syrup. Bedrooms are just as they should be: not too fancy, cosy and warm, spotlessly clean and with crisp white linen. A very friendly place. Martin and Gaynor are full of quiet enthusiasm and have made their home warmly welcoming. John Ceiriog Hughes, the Welsh Shakespeare, came from these hills. Special indeed.

rooms	13: 8 doubles, 4 twins, 1 suite.
price	£85–£110.
meals	Lunch from £4.50.
	Sunday lunch £17.
	Dinner £8–£25.
closed	24-26 December.
directions	Leave A5 south of Chirk for B4500. Village 11 miles ahead and signed.

Gaynor & Martin De Luchi

tel	01691 600666
fax	01691 600262
email	reception@thehandhotel.co.uk
web	www.thehandhotel.co.uk

Inn

Map 5 Entry 283

West Arms Hotel

Llanarmon Dyffryn Ceiriog, Denbighshire LL20 7LD

Come here if you dream of a traditional place in a gorgeous village where the road ends and the real country begins. The smell of fresh bread may greet you, perhaps the scent of flowers, or woodsmoke from the fire. Hear the sound of the river Ceiriog through the open front door; sit in the half-glow of the dimly-lit bar, warm and cosy. It's as a 16th-century inn should be, of flagstone, beam and leaded window. Décor is simple, the layout rambling, with old Welsh colours, floral sofas, a few antiques, a glowing inglenook. Bedrooms are clean and modest, on different levels, some with oak beams and low ceilings, those at the back with pastoral views; bathrooms are freshly new. You could sit in the garden for hours, what with the stream and the view. Lee, Sian and Grant are laid-back but dedicated, thoroughly at one with what they're doing. The chef is Welsh and superb – a local TV celebrity no less! – and backed by two others. Walk the rolling Berwyn Hills and return in muddy boots – no-one will turn a hair. All manner of country pursuits can be arranged, and sheepdog trials are held in the village.

rooms	15: 2 doubles, 2 twins, 9 twins/doubles, 2 suites.
price	£95-£174. Singles £53.50-£94.
meals	Bar meals from £4.45. Dinner from £28. Packed lunch from £8.
closed	Never.
directions	From Shrewsbury, A5 north to Chirk. Left at r'bout on B4500, signed Ceiriog Valley, for 11 miles to Llanarmon Dyffryn Ceiriog. Hotel in centre.

Sian & Lee Finch & Grant Williams

tel	01691 600665
fax	01691 600622
email	gowestarms@aol.com
web	www.thewestarms.co.uk

Hotel

Map 5 Entry 284

Plas Bodegroes
Pwllheli, Gwynedd LL53 5TH

Close to the end of the world and worth every second it takes to get here. Chris and Gunna are inspirational, their home a temple of cool elegance, the food possibly the best in Wales. Fronted by an avenue of 200-year-old beech trees, this Georgian manor house is wrapped in climbing roses, wildly roaming wisteria and ferns. The veranda circles the house, as do long French windows that lighten every room; open one up, grab a book and pull up a chair. Not a formal place – come to relax and be yourself. Bedrooms are wonderful, the courtyard rooms especially good; exposed wooden ceilings and a crisp clean style give the feel of a smart Scandinavian forest hideaway. Best of all is the dining room, almost a work of art in itself, cool and crisp with exceptional art and Venetian carnival masks on the walls – a great place to eat Chris's Michelin-starred food. How about French onion soup, roast mountain lamb with rosemary jus, and apricot and ginger parfait with pistachio praline? Tear yourself away and explore the Lleyn peninsula: sandy beaches, towering cliffs and country walks all wait. Snowdon is close, too.

rooms	11: 7 doubles, 2 twins, 1 four-poster, 1 single.
price	£110–£170. Singles £50–£80. Half-board from £80 p.p.
meals	Sunday lunch £17.50. Dinner £40. Not Sunday evenings.
closed	December–February; Sunday & Monday.
directions	From Pwllheli, A497 towards Nefyn. House on left after 1 mile, signed.

	Chris & Gunna Chown
tel	01758 612363
fax	01758 701247
email	gunna@bodegroes.co.uk
web	www.bodegroes.co.uk

Hotel

Map 5 Entry 285

Penmaenuchaf Hall

Penmaenpool, Dolgellau, Gwynedd LL40 1YB

A long, windy road leads to the Hall and it's worth taking just for the views. Stand at the front of the house, on the Victorian stone balustrade, and gaze down on the tidal ebb and flow, or amble round the back to banks of rhododendrons, azaleas and camellias and a rising forest behind. Inside, all is immaculate bordering on sumptuous: rugs, wooden floors and oak panelling, flowers erupting from jugs and bowls, leather sofas and armchairs, open fires and lavish drapes. And, everywhere, those views. Impressive detail in the bedrooms too, with their vanity mirrors, underfloor heated bathrooms and every spoiling extra. They come in all shapes and sizes, the big being *huge*, the small being warm and cosy; one room up in the eaves has a fine bergère bed. In the dining room, stiff white napery, a dress code and the best of modern British, with fresh local produce and herbs from the garden. Fish in their 13 miles of salmon river, return to snooker, backgammon and a grand piano. You'll warm to Mark's sense of humour, too. *Children over six welcome. Pets by arrangement.*

rooms	14: 7 doubles, 5 twins/doubles, 1 four-poster, 1 family room.
price	£130–£200. Singles £75–£135.
meals	Lunch £4–£18. Afternoon tea from £6. Dinner, 4 courses, £35. Also à la carte.
closed	Rarely.
directions	From Dolgellau, A493 west for about 1.5 miles. Entrance on left.

	Mark Watson & Lorraine Fielding
tel	01341 422129
fax	01341 422787
email	relax@penhall.co.uk
web	www.penhall.co.uk

Hotel

Map 5 Entry 286

The Bell at Skenfrith
Skenfrith, Monmouthshire NP7 8UH

Indulge the senses at this classy 17th-century coaching inn on the banks of the Monnow – a blissful village setting, with a ruined Norman castle and an ancient humpback bridge. Inside is immaculately done but informal, and is run with warmth – Janet treats young staff like members of the family. Expect the best of everything: coffee from a proper cappuccino machine, food mostly organic, wine and cognacs superb – there's even an organic menu for children (Mash Bang Wallop etc). Bedrooms, all different, are understatedly elegant with Farrow & Ball colours and beds dressed in cotton piqué and Welsh wool; you get homemade biscuits, Cath Collins toiletries and a hi-tech console by the bed so you can listen to music in your bath. After an energetic day out on the hills or the river, settle down to Usk Valley lamb and tarte tatin in the restaurant overlooking the terrace. Toast the occasion with local cider or champagne from a great list, then flop into one of the big sofas next to a roaring fire. Fine indeed.

rooms	8: 3 doubles, 1 twin/double, 2 four-posters, 2 attic suites.
price	£100-£180. Singles from £75 (Mon-Fri).
meals	Bar lunch from £15. Sunday lunch £21.50. Dinner, à la carte, £27-£32.50.
closed	Mondays November to Easter; 2 weeks January-February.
directions	From Monmouth, B4233 to Rockfield; B4347 for 5 miles; right on B4521, Skenfrith 1 mile.

William & Janet Hutchings

tel	01600 750235
fax	01600 750525
email	enquiries@skenfrith.co.uk
web	www.skenfrith.co.uk

Inn

Map 2 Entry 287

Beaufort Arms

High Street, Raglan, Usk, Monmouthshire NP15 2DY

A 16th-century village inn with a terrace at the front for a pint in summer, a snug beamed bar for the rugby, and a music festival in the second week of June (hop from pub to church for rock, jazz, folk and classical). At the inn flagged floors, exposed stone walls and low beamed ceilings have been spruced up to give a fresh traditional feel; not contemporary, just warmly inviting. A pretty entrance hall of half-panelled walls and rippling glass takes you back to the 1920s. A very friendly place with lots to drink: local ales, Belgian beers, French coffee, New World wines. Chose from boarded menus in the big bar (Slovakian meatballs, beer-battered hake) or skip over to the dining room for something more fancy (pan-fried monkfish with a peach and rocket salad). Bedrooms in the main house are stylish. Some have pleasant views, a couple have sleigh beds, all come with crisp white linen and pretty throws; those in the old stables are simpler, smaller, less expensive. The A40 passes quietly nearby, making access easy. Raglan's exquisite medieval castle is close, as are the mighty Brecon Beacons.

rooms	15: 7 doubles, 7 twins, 1 single.
price	£65–£95. Singles from £55.
meals	Lunch & dinner £5–£25. Sunday lunch £11.25–£14.25.
closed	Christmas.
directions	M4 junc. 24, A449 north, then A40 west and immediately left into village. On right opposite church.

Eliot & Jana Lewis

tel	01291 690412
fax	01291 690935
email	thebeauforthotel@hotmail.com
web	www.beaufortraglan.co.uk

Inn

Map 2 Entry 288

The Crown at Whitebrook

Whitebrook, Monmouth, Monmouthshire NP25 4TX

An unbeatable combination of attentive service, sublime food and impeccable style make this a real find for those in search of affordable luxury. The Crown is a small restaurant with rooms in a tiny village that's wrapped up in the Wye Valley. Forest rises all around, goats graze in fields, deer amble by in summer. Walks start from the front door, so climb to the ridge for imperious views or head south to Tintern Abbey. Don't stray too far. Bedrooms are a real treat, seriously comfortable, with crisp linen, pretty colours, decanters of sherry and fluffy white bathrobes. The smaller rooms are exceptional value, but splash out on bigger ones for sofas, armchairs and a little more space, huge walk-in showers, sparkling deep baths, perhaps a four-poster bed; all come with an astonishing array of hi-tech gadgetry including a movie library and internet access through the TV. As for the food, expect something very special, perhaps seared langoustine and crab risotto, chargrilled loin of wild venison, then confit of rhubarb with apple sorbet. Whatever can be is homemade and flavour floods from every bite. Brilliant.

rooms	8: 6 doubles, 2 twins/doubles.
price	£100–£120. Singles from £75.
meals	Lunch (Tues–Sun), from £19.50. Dinner, 3 courses, £37.50. Not Sunday eves or Mondays.
closed	Late December to early January.
directions	M48 junc. 2, then A466 north. Through Llandogo, left immediately before bridge over river. 2 miles to village, house signed left.

	Michael Obray
tel	01600 860254
fax	01600 860607
email	info@crownatwhitebrook.co.uk
web	www.crownatwhitebrook.co.uk

Restaurant with Rooms

Map 2 Entry 289

Lake Vyrnwy Hotel

Llanwddyn, Montgomeryshire SY10 0LY

A blissful pocket of rural Wales. High hills of forest and ancient grazing land cradle majestic Lake Vyrnwy; it was excavated by hand, completed in 1891 and now provides Liverpool's water (it took two years to fill). The hotel was built shortly afterwards so civic dignitaries could come to ogle the dam. They also came to fish the 400,000 trout that were released into the water. The view is *stupendous*, the lake stretching five miles into the distance, home to rolling mists and sunburst. Walk or cycle round it, canoe, sail or fish on it, all can be arranged. Birdwatchers will be in heaven, the walking is fabulous, but if you want to hole up in country-house comfort, you can; a plush drawing room, an arm-chaired library, a new conservatory, a terraced bar and an award-winning restaurant for fresh local produce all look the right way. Some rooms in the house are seriously grand (in one you can soak in a claw-foot bath while gazing down the lake), others are snug in the eaves and come in warm country colours. A spa is opening in 2007, as are 14 new bedrooms, all with balconies. A place to return to again and again.

rooms	38: 35 twins/doubles, 2 four-posters, 1 suite.
price	£100–£210. Singles from £90. Half-board £67.50–£120 p.p.
meals	Lunch from £8.50. Bar meals from £8. Dinner, 3 courses, £34.
closed	Rarely.
directions	A490 from Welshpool; B4393 to Lake Vyrnwy. Brown signs from A5 at Shrewsbury as well.

	The Bisiker Family
tel	01691 870692
fax	01691 870259
email	res@lakevyrnwy.com
web	www.lakevyrnwy.com

Hotel

Map 5 Entry 290

Cnapan

East Street, Newport, Fishguard, Pembrokeshire SA42 0SY

Cnapan is a way of life – a family affair with three generations at work in harmony. Eluned makes the preserves, John bakes the bread, Judith excels in the kitchen, Michael looks after the bar and Oliver, the newest recruit, serves a mean breakfast. It is a very friendly place with locals popping in to book tables and guests chatting in the bar before dinner. As for the house, it's warm and cosy, charmingly home-spun, with whitewashed stone walls and old pine settles in the dining room, comfy sofas and a wood-burner in the sitting room, and a tiny telly in the bar for the odd game of rugby (the game of cnapan, rugby's precursor, originated in the town). There are maps for walkers, bird books, flower books, the daily papers, too. Spill into the garden in summer for pre-dinner drinks under the weeping willow, then slip back in for Judith's delicious food, perhaps parsnip soup, breast of Gressingham duck, honey ice cream. Comfy bedrooms, warmly simple, are super value for money. You're in the Pembrokeshire National Park here; beaches and clifftop coastal walks beckon.

rooms	5: 1 double, 3 twins, 1 family. Extra bath available.
price	£76. Singles £45.
meals	Lunch from £7.50. Dinner from £26. Not Tuesday evenings from Easter to October.
closed	Christmas, January & February.
directions	From Cardigan, A487 to Newport. 1st pink house on right.

	John & Eluned Lloyd, Michael & Judith Cooper
tel	01239 820575
fax	01239 820878
email	cnapan@online-holidays.net
web	www.cnapan.co.uk

Restaurant with Rooms

Map 1 Entry 291

Penally Abbey

Penally, Tenby, Pembrokeshire SA70 7PY

A fabulous position up on the hill with a ridge of sycamore and ash towering above and huge views to the front of Carmarthen Bay. Caldy island lies to the east, the road ends at the village green, a quick stride across the golf course leads to the beach. Up at the house, a fine arched window by the grand piano frames the view perfectly, so sink into a chesterfield in front of the fire and gaze out to sea. The house dates to 1790 and was once an abbey; you'll also find St Deiniol's, a ruined 13th-century church that's lit up at night. Sprawling lawns are yours to roam, bluebells carpet the wood in May. Bedrooms are all different: grand four-posters and wild flock wallpaper in the main house; a simpler cottage feel in the coach house; warm contemporary luxury in St Deiniol's Lodge. Steve's gentle, unflappable manner is infectious and hugely relaxing; don't expect to feel rushed here. Elleen cooks in the French style, much of it picked up in the kitchen of a château many years ago; her Tenby sea bass is exquisite. The Pembrokshire coastal path passes by outside. An extremely comfortable house; don't miss it.

rooms	17: 6 doubles, 1 twin; 1 double with separate bath. Coach house: 4 doubles. Lodge: 5 twins/doubles.
price	£130-£195. Half-board from £100 p.p.
meals	Lunch by arrangement. Dinner, 3 courses, £35.
closed	Never.
directions	From Tenby, A4139 for Pembroke. Right into Penally after 1.5 miles. Hotel signed at village green. Train station 5 mins walk.

	Steve & Elleen Warren
tel	01834 843033
fax	01834 844714
email	info@penally-abbey.com
web	www.penally-abbey.com

Hotel

Map 1 Entry 292

Milebrook House Hotel

Milebrook, Knighton, Powys LD7 1LT

Your arrival at the old family home of writer and explorer Wilfred Thesiger (he lived here from 1922 to 1939) is expectedly comforting. The parquet floor in the hall smells of lavender floor wax, the clock ticks quietly, the flowers are fresh and Beryl is likely to come out of the kitchen in her apron to greet you. Much space and comfort in the bedrooms where fabrics are blended, beds excellent, lighting adjustable, the furniture modern and the service attentive and unobtrusive. In the walled kitchen garden flowers and vegetables are grown for the table — a table to reckon with, by all accounts; the new chef is winning recognition for his skilful British cooking. Outside, wild terrain, too, devoted to a mature arboretum and wildlife pond, and terracing, a gazebo, a pergola with roses growing over obelisks and a croquet lawn. At the end of these gorgeous gardens are pheasants, moorhens, red kites, kingfishers, herons and the Welsh border; you may fish on their stretch of the river Teme. The countryside belongs to a portion of Britain — sadly decreasing — that is still called 'tranquil'. A wonderful place to unwind.

rooms	10: 5 doubles, 4 twins, 1 family.
price	£92–£98. Singles £59.50–£63.50. Half-board (min. 2 nights) £79.75–£83.25 p.p.
meals	Lunch from £11.95. Not Monday lunchtimes. Dinner £29.50.
closed	Rarely.
directions	From Ludlow, A49 north, then left at Bromfield on A4113 towards Knighton for 7 miles. Hotel on right.

	Rodney & Beryl Marsden
tel	01547 528632
fax	01547 520509
email	hotel@milebrook.kc3ltd.co.uk
web	www.milebrookhouse.co.uk

Hotel

Map 2 Entry 293

Carlton House

Dolycoed Road, Llanwrtyd Wells, Powys LD5 4RA

A Welsh spa town – Wales's prettiest – with one of the most talented chefs in Britain. Mary Ann joined the cooking elite in 2002, winning a Michelin star; high time, said her legion of fans. They've been coming to this marvellously eccentric restaurant with rooms for years. Victorians flocked to Llanwrtyd Wells in the 1800s, drawn in the belief that the natural springs could cure everything from a troubled soul to a wart on the toe. This 1900 townhouse is about food, not décor; the modest but, in places, bravely colourful rooms are just somewhere to rest your sated self. The Gilchrists are old pros, and great company. Alan, an ever-engaging and unflappable host, orchestrates all in the ground-floor restaurant, full of madly colourful modern furniture and screened off by book shelves. Mary Ann is entirely self-taught and cooks with instinctive brilliance... scallops with crisped Carmarthen ham, fruit sorbets with Earl Grey syrup; she decides what to cook only hours before she puts on her apron. Ponytrekkers, cyclists and walkers fill the town in summer; Carlton suits all year.

rooms	6: 4 doubles, 2 twins/doubles.
price	£60–£90. Singles £45. Half-board from £64 p.p. (min. 2 nights).
meals	Lunch (Tuesday-Friday) by arrangement. Dinner £25–£42 (not Sundays).
closed	Last 2 weeks December (open for New Year).
directions	From Builth Wells, A483 to Llanwrtyd Wells. 1st right in town. House 50 yds on right.

	Alan & Mary Ann Gilchrist
tel	01591 610248
email	info@carltonrestaurant.co.uk
web	www.carltonrestaurant.co.uk

Map 2 Entry 294

The Lake Country House & Spa
Llangammarch Wells, Powys LD4 4BS

Deep in the silence of Wales, a country house intent on pampering you rotten. Fifty acres of lawns, lake and ancient woodland sweep you clean of city cobwebs, and if that's not enough a spa has been added, with an indoor pool, treatment rooms and a tennis court by the lake. Sit in a hot tub and watch guests fish for their supper, try your luck on the nine-hole golf course, or saddle up near by and take to the hills. Come home to afternoon tea in the drawing room, where beautiful rugs warm a brightly polished wooden floor and chandeliers hang from the ceiling. The hotel opened over 100 years ago and the leather-bound fishing logs go back to 1894. A feel of the 1920s lingers. Fires come to life in front of your eyes, grand pianos and grandfather clocks sing their songs, snooker balls crash about in the distance. Dress for a delicious dinner – the food and wines deserve it – then retire to cosseting bedrooms. Most are suites: those in the house are warmly traditional, those in the lodge are softly contemporary. The London train takes four hours and stops in the village. Resident geese waddle. Marvellous.

rooms	30: 6 twins/doubles, 12 suites. Lodge: 12 suites.
price	£160–£190. Singles from £130. Suites £200–£240. Half-board £105–£150 p.p.
meals	Lunch, 3 courses, £24.50. Dinner, 3 courses, £39.50.
closed	Rarely.
directions	From Builth Wells, A483 west for 7 miles to Garth. Signed from village.

	Jean-Pierre Mifsud
tel	01591 620202
fax	01591 620457
email	info@lakecountryhouse.co.uk
web	www.lakecountryhouse.co.uk

Hotel

Map 2 Entry 295

Pwll-y-Faedda

Erwood, Builth Wells, Powys LD2 3YS

Who would not want to live here, on the salmon river? The big, elegant, 1920s fishing lodge, set beneath plunging hills and moorland, has been given a new lease of life; sit back and let the river tumble past your window. There's a soft-carpeted, country-house glow here, with English antiques and a dash of oriental spice: rooms are full of interest, with rugs and paintings from far-flung travels. The entrance hall and library are quintessential wood-panelled 'hunting lodge' – minus antlers on the walls. First-floor bedrooms have fine proportions and a light, harmonious feel; creamy carpets, rich wall hangings, generous beds and (all bar one) waterside views. Those that look downriver are as big as suites. Yolande has an eye for every little extra, gives you breakfast when you like and is a terrific cook; don't miss her sticky toffee pudding. If you're an angler like your host, there are 800 yards of double-bank salmon and trout fishing to cast your line in – and 27 acres of grounds. Pwll-y-Faedda runs on oiled wheels and is great for weddings and house parties. *Fishing by advance booking.*

rooms	6: 5 doubles, 1 twin.
price	£80–£98. Singles £70.
meals	Dinner, 3 courses, £28.
closed	Rarely.
directions	From Abergavenny towards Crickhowell, then right, through Talgarth, towards Builth Wells. After Erwood look for lay-by & discreet sign on right which is entrance to drive.

Jeremy & Yolande Jaquet

tel	01982 560202
email	info@pwllyfaedda.co.uk
web	www.pwllyfaedda.co.uk

Hotel

Map 2 Entry 296

Llangoed Hall

Llyswen, Brecon, Powys LD3 0YP

One of the most refined hotels in Britain, Llangoed Hall rests in the valley of the Wye with glorious views to the Black Mountains and Brecon Beacons. It was Sir Bernard's dream to restore this Clough Williams-Ellis house, and the magnificent Edwardian manor has risen like a phoenix. Liveried butlers, cut-glass decanters, a million deep sofas, crackling logs and remarkable artefacts from around the world, from old Penguin editions to rare Whistler lithographs, are all brought together with magnificent style. Sweep up the carved staircase to big bedrooms – some with spectacular views. The restaurant is another reason for staying here: decorated in Elanbach blue and white, it's a sumptuous match for the food. Outside, clipped hedges, giant Wellingtonia, a maze big enough to get lost in and a private path to the river Wye for fishing and picnics on a private beach. Hushed afternoon tea served on a silver tray is sheer indulgence – as is Welsh black fillet steak for dinner, followed by dark chocolate fondant. It's all done in house-party style, and you're invited.

rooms	23: 20 twins/doubles, 3 suites.
price	£195-£385. Suite £350-£385. Half-board £265-£430 per room.
meals	Lunch from £4.50. Afternoon tea £8-£14.50. Dinner from £43.
closed	Rarely.
directions	From Brecon, A470 for Builth Wells for about 6 miles; left on A470 to Llyswen. Left in village at T-junc. Entrance 1.5 miles further on right.

	Calum Milne
tel	01874 754525
fax	01874 754545
email	enquiries@llangoedhall.com
web	www.llangoedhall.com

Hotel

Map 2 Entry 297

The Felin Fach Griffin

Felin Fach, Brecon, Powys LD3 0UB

Stylish but cosy, fresh but not fussy. This bold venture mixes the buzz of a smart city bistro with the easy-going pace of Welsh country living – it's hugely popular. Full of bright elegance, downstairs fans out from the bar into several eating and sitting areas, with stripped pine and old oak furniture. Make for three giant leather sofas around a raised hearth and settle in, or opt for the rustic charm of the chatty backroom bar. A Dutch chef stars in the kitchen, conjuring up simple but sensational dishes for smartly laid tables: fruit, vegetables and leaves are mostly from their own kitchen garden. Langoustines with quinoa grain, Welsh rack of lamb, tasty mash, vanilla crème brûlée. Breakfast is served around one table in the morning room. Wallow with the papers and make your own toast on the Aga, as you like it – or have it as it comes. Bedrooms are in a modern style, clean and simple, with a few designer touches; tulips in a vase, muslin round the four-posters. Outside, the Breacon Beacons all around, so don't forget your hiking boots.

rooms	7: 2 doubles, 2 twins/doubles, 3 four-posters.
price	£97.50–£125. Singles from £67.50.
meals	Lunch from £15. Dinner from £25. Not Monday lunchtimes.
closed	Christmas Day, Boxing Day & occasionally.
directions	From Brecon, A470 for Builth Wells to Felin Fach (4.5 miles). On left.

	Charles & Edmund Inkin
tel	01874 620111
fax	01874 620120
email	enquiries@eatdrinksleep.ltd.uk
web	www.eatdrinksleep.ltd.uk

Inn

Map 2 Entry 298

Gliffaes Hotel

Crickhowell, Powys NP8 1RH

Gliffaes is matchless: grandly comfortable but as casual and warm as home. It's a house for all seasons — not even driving rain could mask its beauty. Wander the 33 acres of stunning gardens and woodland; bask in the sun on the buttressed terrace as the river Usk cuts through the valley 150 feet below. Tea is a feast of scones and cakes laid out on a long table at one end of a sitting room of polished floors and panelled walls, served by a winter fire; dinner is an Italian-influenced feast. Membership of the Slow Food movement means local and seasonal food is used as much as possible, and the fish and meat in this area are outstanding. With the Suter clan at the helm — they've been welcoming guests for nearly 60 years — improvements are always underway. The free-standing roll top bath with a view is gathering a fan club, a mix of fresh, bold and elegant fabrics have spruced up the rooms, furniture is chosen to suit and original Welsh paintings are becoming a feature. Fisherfolk can cast to their hearts' content on a prime 2.5-mile stretch overlooked, perhaps, by red kite and buzzards.

rooms	22: 3 doubles, 13 twins/doubles, 6 singles.
price	£85–£200. Singles from £75.
meals	Light lunch from £3.50. Dinner £30.75.
closed	First 3 weeks in January.
directions	From Crickhowell, A40 west for 2.5 miles. Entrance on left, signed. Hotel 1 mile up windy hill.

James & Susie Suter
tel   01874 730371
fax   01874 730463
email calls@gliffaeshotel.com
web   www.gliffaeshotel.com

Hotel

Map 2 Entry 299

Fairyhill Hotel

Reynoldston, Gower, Swansea SA3 1BS

The Gower has legions of fans who come for its glorious heathland, its rugged coastline and some of the best beaches in the country. Fairyhill is bang in the middle of it all, but just to ensure absolute silence, it is wrapped in 24 acres of its own. Follow your nose and discover a stream-fed lake, an ancient orchard, a walled garden with asparagus beds and, somewhere, a family of Muscovy ducks. Inside, an informal house-party feel comes courtesy of Andrew and Paul, who've been here since 1992. Most bedrooms are big and fancy, a couple are smaller and simpler. The plush ones have painted beams, striking stripes, bold colours, immaculate bathrooms. Mattresses are Vi-sprung, but if that's not enough you'll find a treatment room, so book a massage. There's croquet on the lawn in summer and seriously good food all year round. Lamb, poultry, beef and cheese come from the Gower, so tuck into duck eggs with white asparagus mousse, grilled lemon sole with beurre noisette, twice-glazed lemon tart with sour-apple ice cream. Fabulous walking, too. *Minimum stay two nights at weekends.*

rooms	11: 6 doubles, 5 twins/doubles.
price	£150–£250. Singles from £130. Half-board from £100 p.p.
meals	Lunch from £15.95. Dinner £29.50–£37.50.
closed	1st three weeks in January.
directions	M4 junc. 47; A483 south; A484 west to Gowerton; B4295 to Llanrhidian; through Oldwalls and 1 mile up on left.

	Andrew Hetherington & Paul Davies
tel	01792 390139
fax	01792 391358
email	andrew@fairyhill.net
web	www.fairyhill.net

Hotel

Map 2 Entry 300

Our offices

Beautiful as they were, our old offices leaked heat, used electricity to heat water and rooms, flooded whole rooms with light to illuminate one person, and were not ours to alter. We failed our eco-audit in spite of using recycled cooking oil in one car and gas in another, recycling everything we could and gently promoting 'greenery' in our travel books. (Our Fragile Earth series takes a harder line.)

After two eco-audits we leaped at the chance to buy some old barns closer to Bristol, to create our own eco-offices and start again. Our accountants thought we were mad and there was no time for proper budgeting. The back of every envelope bore the signs of frenzied calculations, and then I shook hands and went off on holiday.
Two years later we moved in.

As I write, swallows are nesting in our wood-pellet store, the fountain plays in the pond, the grasses bend

Photos above Quentin Craven

before a gentle breeze and the solar panels heat water too hot to touch. We have, to our delight, created an inspiring and serene place.

The roof was lifted to allow us to fix thick insulation panels beneath the tiles. More panels were fitted between the rafters and as a separate wall inside the old ones, and laid under the under-floor heating pipes. We are insulated for the Arctic, and almost totally air-tight. Ventilation is natural, and we open windows. An Austrian boiler sucks wood-pellets in from an outside store and slowly consumes them, cleanly and - of course - without using any fossil fuels. Rain-water is channelled to a 6,000-litre underground tank and then, filtered, flushes loos and fills basins. Sun-pipes funnel the daylight into dark corners and double-glazed Velux windows, most facing north, pour it into every office.

We built a small green-oak barn between two old barns, and this has become the heart of the offices, warm, light and beautiful. Wood plays a major role: our simple oak desks were made by a local carpenter, my office floor is of oak, and there is oak panelling. Even the carpet tiles tell a story; they are made from the wool of Herdwick sheep from the Lake District.

Our electricity consumption is extraordinarily low. We set out not to flood the buildings with light, but to provide attractive, low background lighting and individual 'task' lights to be used only as needed. Materials, too, have been a focus: we used non-toxic paints and finishes.

Events blew our budgets apart, but we have a building of which we are proud and which has helped us win two national awards this year. Architects and designers are fascinated and we are all working with a renewed commitment. But, best of all, we are now in a better

position to encourage our 'owners' and readers to take 'sustainability' more seriously.

I end by answering an obvious question: our office carbon emissions will be reduced by about 75%. We await our bills, but they will be low and, as time goes by, relatively lower – and lower. It has been worth every penny and every ounce of effort.

Alastair Sawday

Photo above www.paulgroom.com
Photo below Tom Germain

If everyone in the world consumed the planet's natural resources at the same rate as people in the UK, we would need THREE planets to support us

The Solution? **One Planet Living**

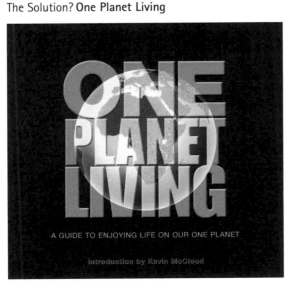

One Planet Living   Edition 1, £4.99
A practical guide providing us with easy, affordable and attractive alternatives for achieving a higher quality of life while using our fair share of the planet's capacity. Two environmental organisations, BioRegional and WWF, have come together to promote a simple set of principles to make sustainable living achievable.

The Little Food Book   Edition 1, £6.99
By Craig Sams, Chairman of the Soil Association
An explosive account of the food we eat today. Never have we been at such risk – from our food. This book will help clarify what's at stake.

The Little Money Book   Edition 1, £6.99
By David Boyle, associate of the New Economics Foundation
This pithy, wry little guide will tell you where money comes from, what it means, what it's doing to the planet and what we might be able to do about it.

www.fragile-earth.com

Where on the web?

The World Wide Web is big – very big. So big, in fact, that it can be a fruitless search if you don't know where to find reliable, trustworthy, up-to-date information about fantastic places to stay in Europe, India, Morocco and beyond...

Fortunately, there's www.specialplacestostay.com, where you can dip into all of our guides, find special offers from owners, catch up on news about the series and tell us about the special places you've been to.

www.specialplacestostay.com

Discover your perfect self-catering escape in Britain... With the same punch and attitude as all our printed guides, Special Escapes celebrates only those places we have visited and genuinely like.

www.special-escapes.co.uk

Order form

All these books are available in major bookshops or you may order them direct.
Post and packaging are FREE within the UK.

Bed & Breakfast for Garden Lovers	£14.99
British Hotels, Inns & Other Places	£14.99
British Bed & Breakfast	£14.99
French Bed & Breakfast	£15.99
French Hotels, Châteaux & Other Places	£14.99
French Holiday Homes	£12.99
Green Places to Stay	**£13.99**
Greece	£11.99
India	£11.99
Ireland	£12.99
Italy	£14.99
London	£9.99
Morocco	£11.99
Mountains of Europe	£9.99
Paris Hotels	£9.99
Portugal	£10.99
Pubs & Inns of England & Wales	£13.99
Spain	£14.99
Turkey	£11.99
The Little Food Book	£6.99
The Little Money Book	£6.99
Six Days	£12.99

Please make cheques payable to Alastair Sawday Publishing   Total £ _____

Please send cheques to: Alastair Sawday Publishing, The Old Farmyard, Yanley
Lane, Long Ashton, Bristol BS41 9LR. For credit card orders call 01275 395431
or order directly from our web site www.specialplacestostay.com

Title   First name   Surname
_____

Address
_____

_____

Postcode   Tel
_____

If you do not wish to receive mail from other like-minded companies, please tick here ☐
If you would prefer not to receive information about special offers on our books, please tick here ☐

Report form

If you have any comments on entries in this guide, please let us have them.
If you have a favourite house, hotel, inn or other new discovery, please let us
know about it. You can return this form, email info@sawdays.co.uk, or visit
www.specialplacestostay.com and click on 'contact'.

Existing entry
Property name:_____

Entry number: _____ Date of visit: ___ / ___ / ___

New recommendation
Property name:_____

Address: _____

_____

Tel: _____

Your comments
What did you like (or dislike) about this place? Were the people friendly?
What was the location like? What sort of food did they serve?

_____

_____

_____

_____

_____

_____

_____

_____

Your details
Name: _____

Address: _____

Postcode: _____ Tel: _____

BH8

Quick reference indices

Quick reference indices

Pool
Want to swim? You can here.

Gardens
These are the places for lazing on the lawn or gasping at the greenery.

Peace and quiet

These places are particularly
peaceful.

Quick reference indices

Weddings
Want to tie the knot?
You can here.

Sound systems

Disco divas will find hi-fis in bedrooms, so bring your CDs.

Quick reference indices

Photo Russell Wilkinson

① Dorset

The Priory Hotel
Church Green, Wareham, Dorset BH20 4ND

② Come for a slice of old England. The lawns of this 16th-century priory run down to the river Frome. Behind, a church rises, beyond, a neat Georgian square; in short, a little bit of time travel. A stone-flagged courtyard leads up to the hotel, where comfortable country-house interiors include a first-floor drawing room with views of the garden and a stone-vaulted dining room in the old cellar. Best of all is the terrace; 200 yards of dreamy English gardens front the river, so sit in the sun and watch yacht masts flutter. Bedrooms in the main house come in different sizes, some cosy under beams, others grandly adorned in reds and golds. Also: mahogany dressers, padded window seats, bowls of fruit, the odd sofa. Bathrooms - some new, some old - come with white robes. Eight have river views, others look onto the garden or church. Rooms in the boathouse, a 16th-century clay barn, are opulent, with oak panelling, stone walls, the odd chest and sublime views. Four acres of idyllic gardens have climbing roses, a duck pond and banks of daffs. Wonderful. *Minimum two nights at weekends in summer.*

rooms	18: 14 twins/doubles. Boat House: 1 double, 3 suites.	**③**
price	£210-£280. Suites from £340. Half-board (obligatory at weekends) from £130 p.p.	**④**
meals	Lunch from £20. Dinner from £35.	**⑤**
closed	Never.	**⑥**
directions	West from Poole on A35, then A351 for Wareham and B3075 into town. Through lights, 1st left, right out of square, then keep left and entrance on left beyond church.	**⑦**

	Jeremy Merchant
tel	01929 551666
fax	01929 554519
email	reservations@theprioryhotel.co.uk
web	theprioryhotel.co.uk

⑧ Hotel

⑨ Map 3 Entry 91

⑩